The Archaeologist's Fieldwork Companion

THE ARCHAEOLOGIST'S
FIELDWORK COMPANION

Barbara Ann Kipfer

Blackwell
Publishing

BLACKWELL PUBLISHING
350 Main Street, Malden, MA 02148-5020, USA
9600 Garsington Road, Oxford OX4 2DQ, UK
550 Swanston Street, Carlton, Victoria 3053, Australia

First published 2007 by Blackwell Publishing Ltd

3   2009

Library of Congress Cataloging-in-Publication Data

Kipfer, Barbara Ann.
The archaeologist's fieldwork companion / Barbara Ann Kipfer.
p. cm.
Includes bibliographical references.
ISBN 978-1-4051-1885-9 (hardcover : alk. paper)
ISBN 978-1-4051-1886-6 (pbk. : alk. paper)
1. Archaeology–Field work. I. Title.

CC76.K57 2007
930.1028–dc22
2005031879

A catalogue record for this title is available from the British Library.

Set in 10/12pt Sabon
by Graphicraft Limited, Hong Kong

The publisher's policy is to use permanent paper from mills that operate a
sustainable forestry policy, and which has been manufactured from pulp processed
using acid-free and elementary chlorine-free practices. Furthermore, the publisher
ensures that the text paper and cover board used have met acceptable
environmental accreditation standards.

For further information on
Blackwell Publishing, visit our website:
www.blackwellpublishing.com

Contents

2 Forms and Records

3 Lists and Checklists

4 Mapping, Drawing, and Photographing   243

xiii

Acknowledgments

The following forms are reprinted from *The Crow Canyon Archaeological Center Field Manual* (Crow Canyon Archaeological Center, 2001a): provenience designation catalog, provenience designation form, study unit catalog, study unit form, feature catalog, feature form, point location catalog, masonry form, stratigraphic description form, human remains occurrence form, photographic record form, field inventory form, total station datum form, total station field notes form. Copyright © 2001 by Crow Canyon Archaeological Center. Reprinted by permission.

The following figures are reprinted from *The Crow Canyon Archaeological Center Field Manual* (Crow Canyon Archaeological Center, 2001a): Table 1.1 "Table 1: Characteristics of major sediment textural classes"; Figure 1.10 "Figure 1: Flow diagram for determining sediment texture on the basis of ribboning and grittiness (after Thien 1979)"; Figure 3.9c "Figure 3: Masonry wall attributes"; Figure 3.9d "Figure 4: Wall cross-section types"; Figure 3.9e "Figure 6: Mortar forms: (a) concave; (b) extruded; (c) flush." Copyright © 2001 by Crow Canyon Archaeological Center. Reprinted by permission.

The following are reprinted from *The Castle Rock Pueblo Database* (Crow Canyon Archaeological Center, 2001b): Figure 4.2: "Site 5MT1825, Structure 110, Surface 2"; Figure 4.8d: "Site 5MT1825, Structure 104, Stratigraphic profile." Copyright © 2001 by Crow Canyon Archaeological Center. Reprinted by permission.

Introduction

The Archaeologist's Fieldwork Companion offers concrete, practical information for fieldwork to the archaeologist, teachers of archaeology, students of archaeology, archaeology volunteers, and archaeology enthusiasts.

The book includes: lists and checklists; planning help; recording and measurement charts and tables; analysis and classification guides; information on drawing, mapping, and photography; abbreviations; sample forms and records; and resources, including an extensive bibliography. It contains the information archaeologists need in the field but often do not have with them unless they carry a large box of books. Instead of going back to the laboratory, office, or home to make a copy of something or find the book to bring back out to the field, there is this book. *The Archaeologist's Fieldwork Companion* presents information in a nuts-and-bolts, practical, down-to-earth way that will make the volume indispensable to a wide range of people, from the student and volunteer to the professor in the field. Professional archaeologists will also find many of the sections to be helpful in the field. In many cases, the information is a springboard for the practitioner to use or develop specifically for a project. There are example forms, classification systems, abbreviation lists, etc. In other cases, lists and checklists and instructional sections can be used as refreshers or reminders for fieldwork tasks.

The chapters in the book, which are ordered alphabetically, are:

1 Classification and Typology
2 Forms and Records
3 Lists and Checklists
4 Mapping, Drawing, and Photographing

CLASSIFICATION AND TYPOLOGY

Classification schemes may be useful to archaeologists in the field. Archaeologists can use taxonomic classification to organize artifacts around a dimension and may also break a dimension into more specific units.

FORMS AND RECORDS

These sample forms and records are supplied as templates for the archaeologist to design his or her own versions.

LISTS AND CHECKLISTS

Various lists and checklists can be useful to anyone involved in archaeological fieldwork. Simply having a daily what-to-take-along list can assist with efficiency and prevent having to do without something or having to borrow items. Other lists and checklists here are reminders or refreshers on important field topics.

MAPPING, DRAWING, AND PHOTOGRAPHING

This chapter touches on three different areas that help the archaeologist describe the physical setting, features, and artifacts. There are instructional and refresher topics, lists of terms and symbols, and checklists for supplies, among other topics.

2

——— **MEASUREMENT AND CONVERSION** ———

This chapter aids in calculations and measurements. Charts and instructions are offered for conversions. Much information is offered about setting up and using measuring equipment.

——————— **PLANNING HELP** ———————

This chapter offers some guidelines for planning and designing archaeological fieldwork projects and for organizing administrative matters.

——————— **RESOURCES** ———————

This chapter provides useful resources, particularly for reading within the field of archaeology. It offers some guidelines for ethics that have been drawn up by various organizations. The chapter also describes some current legislation covering archaeological fieldwork as well as links to websites which offer more about international legislation. There are website links to US state and federal offices overseeing archaeological projects and links to websites about volunteer opportunities. There is also a complete bibliography for the information provided in this book.

——— **APPENDIX: ABBREVIATIONS AND CODES** ———

The lists of abbreviations in this chapter are examples/samples of coding that may be used for various topics, especially on forms and records. These may be adapted by the archaeologist for use in a specific project.

1

Classification and Typology

Classifications are central to archaeology. Classification schemes may be useful to archaeologists in the field. Archaeologists can use taxonomic classification to organize artifacts around a dimension and may also break a dimension into more specific units. There are various ways in which field archaeologists set about making and using classifications to meet a variety of practical needs. Though much classification takes place in the laboratory and office, there are some classification needs in the field and this chapter provides basic typologies that may be useful during excavations.

CONTENTS

CLASSIFICATION AND TYPOLOGY

CLASSIFICATION AND TYPOLOGY

———————————— APPLIQUÉ TYPES ————————————

(representative)

band
band with thumb impressions and ridge
banded finger impressions and wavy grooves
button
double nipple
earlike
fillet
flange
nipple
other attachment
parallel raised bands with finger impressions
pellet
perpendicular raised bands
pie-rim
raised angular band
raised band
raised band with concave groove
raised band with finger impressions
raised band with incisions
smooth raised band
snakelike
spike
zoomorphic

——— ATTRIBUTES, BASIC CATEGORIES OF ———

■ Form/shape attributes, such as length, width, thickness, shape.
■ Stylistic/surface attributes, such as color, decoration, texture.
■ Technological attributes, constituent attributes, such as the raw
  materials used; manufacturing attributes, such as the way it was
  made.

6

■ Coiled: foundation of horizontal elements with rigid materials interwoven vertically; about 100 different types of coiled basketry exist.

■ Plaited: weave is basically the same in both directions; simple plaiting has one element passing over another and twill plaiting has more than one element passing over more than one element.

■ Twined: vertical warp foundation and horizontal weft stitching; S-twined (weft angled to maker's right) or Z-twined (weft angled to maker's left).

CLASSIFICATION AND TYPOLOGY

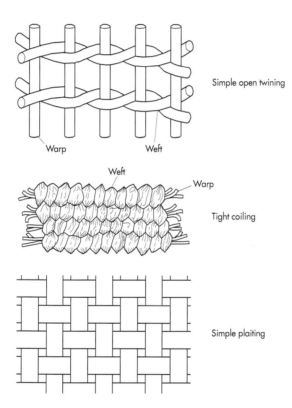

Simple open twining

Warp   Weft

Weft   Warp

Tight coiling

Simple plaiting

Figure 1.1 Basketry types. (Mark Q. Sutton and Brooke S. Arkush, Figure 68: The three basic techniques of basketry manufacture (no scale), p. 151 from *Archaeological Laboratory Methods: An Introduction*, third edition. Dubuque, IA: Kendall/Hunt Publishing, 2002. Copyright © 2002 by Kendall/Hunt Publishing Company. Reprinted by permission of the publisher)

BINFORD PIPESTEM CHRONOLOGY

Diameter (in/)	Dates
9/64	1590–1620
8/64	1620–50
7/64	1650–80
6/64	1680–1720
5/64	1720–50
4/64	1750–1800

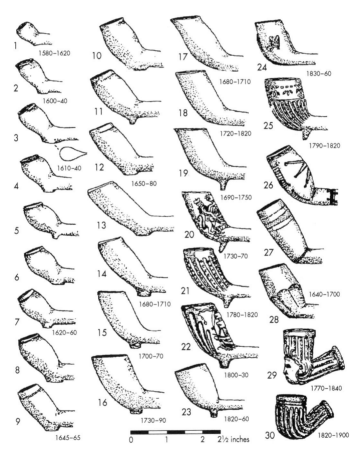

Figure 1.2 Pipestems. (Ivor Noël Hume, Binford pipe stem, from *A Guide to Artifacts of Colonial America*. New York: Knopf, 1970. Copyright © 1969 by Ivor Noël Hume. Reprinted by permission of Alfred A. Knopf, a division of Random House, Inc.)

— BONE CLASSIFICATION AND DESCRIPTION —

Categories of bones

flat bones (cranial, innominates, scapula)
irregular bones
long tubular bones (e.g. limbs)
short/small tubular bones (e.g. metacarpals, metatarsals, phalanges)
unknown

Position of skeleton

lying on left side
lying on right side
prone
supine

Limb position

crouched
extended
flexed
indeterminate

Condition of bone

complete
disturbed
incomplete
intact

BOTTLE MOLD TYPES/BOTTLE MANUFACTURING TYPES

Non-shoulder molds

dip mold
hinged shoulder-height mold
pattern mold

Full-height molds

automatic bottle machine
blow-back mold

| Dip mold | Hinged shoulder-height mold | Bottom-hinged mold | Three-part dip mold |
| Three-part leaf mold | Post-bottom mold | Cup-bottom mold | Automatic bottle machine |

Figure 1.3 Types of bottle mold. (Mark Q. Sutton and Brooke S. Arkush, Figure 80: Major bottle mold types, p. 185 from *Archaeological Laboratory Methods: An Introduction*, third edition. Dubuque, IA: Kendall/Hunt Publishing, 2002. Copyright © 2002 by Kendall/Hunt Publishing Company. Reprinted by permission of the publisher)

bottom-hinged mold
cup-bottom mold
post-bottom mold
three-part leaf mold
three-part mold with dip mold body

BOTTLE PARTS

- Base/basal surface: the bottom, which can be convex "round bottom," slightly concave "push-up," or deeply concave "kick-up."
- Body: main and widest part of bottle.
- Bore: the opening of the bottle.
- Finish: top section attached to neck and which has a closure; the part to which a cap would be attached is the "sealing surface," the diameter of the opening is the "bore," and the ring of glass around the neck to secure the closure is a "collar."

10

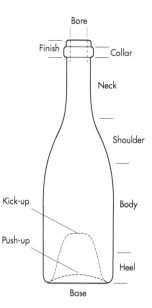

Figure 1.4 Bottle parts. (Mark Q. Sutton and Brooke S. Arkush, Figure 79: Bottle nomenclature and corresponding areas, p. 180 from *Archaeological Laboratory Methods: An Introduction*, third edition. Dubuque, IA: Kendall/Hunt Publishing, 2002. Copyright © 2002 by Kendall/Hunt Publishing Company. Reprinted by permission of the publisher)

- Insweep/heel: lower section of the body which attaches to the base.
- Lip: the edge of the opening of the bottle.
- Neck: an extension of the finish connecting it to the shoulder; the point at which it connects is "root of the neck."
- Resting point/surface: part of bottle actually touching a surface.
- Shoulder: an extension of the neck to the body.
- String rim: thick band of glass on upper neck of bottle around which strap was secured.

BOUNDARY TYPES

- Archaeological boundary: evaluation of spatial relationships such as size, structure, and manmade modifications by describing and mapping these features and site activities/uses.
- Legal boundary: before undertaking a survey, this should be determined through the city or county engineering department.

■ Natural site boundary: found by studying the interrelationships between a site and its surroundings and a topographic map that covers all aspects of the site and its natural boundaries.

BURIAL TYPES AND DESCRIPTIONS

Burial types

barrow or tumulus
bundle
chamber tomb
collective burial
cremation
mass burial/ossuary
monumental tomb
pithos or jar burial
rock-shelter or cave tomb
sarcophagus
secondary burial
shaft or chamber tomb
simple burial
tholos

Burial positions

fully extended
left arm crossed over chest
left arm crossed over pelvis
left arm extended at side
left arm raised toward head
right arm crossed over chest
right arm crossed over pelvis
right arm extended at side
right arm raised toward head
semi-extended
semi-flexed
tightly flexed

Burial deposition

kneeling
lying on left side

12

lying on back
lying on face
lying on right side
sitting
standing

Bone preservation

fair
good
poor

BUTTON ATTRIBUTES

Buttons are made from a wide variety of materials: agate, aluminum, Bakelite, bone, brass, celluloid, glass, horn, ivory, japanning, pewter, plastic, porcelain, rubber, shell, etc.

Button size is expressed in lines/linges, with 40 lines equal to one inch. Some equivalencies are 12 lines = $1/4$ inch, 14 lines = $5/16$ inch, 16 lines = $3/8$ inch, 18 lines = $7/16$ inch, 20 lines = $1/2$ inch, 22 lines = $9/16$ inch, and 24 lines = $5/8$ inch.

Buttons may have a 1) back mark (stamping on back denoting quality, manufacturer, uniform makers' names, stars, dots, or eagles); 2) quality mark (on back); or 3) registry marks (on back of British-made, is diamond-shaped with letters or numbers at points of diamond).

CEMETERY TYPES

church cemetery
customary/neighborhood cemetery
ethnic cemetery
family cemetery

lodge cemetery
mass grave
private cemetery
public cemetery

CERAMICS ATTRIBUTES

(Can use Panetone Color Chart available on the Internet for identifying color)

General

decoration (technique by which a pattern is applied to the ceramic
   surface)
decorative pattern name (name used to list a particular pattern)
glaze (glassy vitreous coating on outside of ceramic)
maker's mark (printed or impressed mark on base of ceramic)
paste (clay fabric which forms the ceramic object)

Specific (used to create a type-series)

part of vessel (rim, handle, etc.)
function (pot, bowl, etc.)
shape
ware-fabric and manufacture (plain wheel, coarse hand, etc.)
color (using Munsell)
hardness (using Mohs)
inclusion type (pebble, granule, etc.)
inclusion size (using Wentworth) and density
core color (even, uneven, etc.)
sherd size
paint placement
slip/wash/glaze placement
liquid decoration type (slip, wash, glaze, etc.)
decoration color
decoration condition (flaky, mottled, etc.)
painted decoration trait (monochrome, bichrome, etc.)
bichrome paint colors
polychrome paint colors
painted motifs (arc, basket, lattice, etc.)
burnish and luster
burnish direction (oblique, vertical, etc.)
burnish application in relation to liquid direction (before or after
   slip, etc.)
excision and traits (combing, zigzag, etc.)
incision and traits (herringbone, pinpricks, etc.)
appliqué and traits (raised band, etc.)
impression and traits (finger-running bands, etc.)
perforation and traits (circular, oblong, etc.)
plastic decoration placement

concave base
disk base
flat base
knob base
loop base

pod base
pointed base
ring base
stump base
trumpet or ogee base

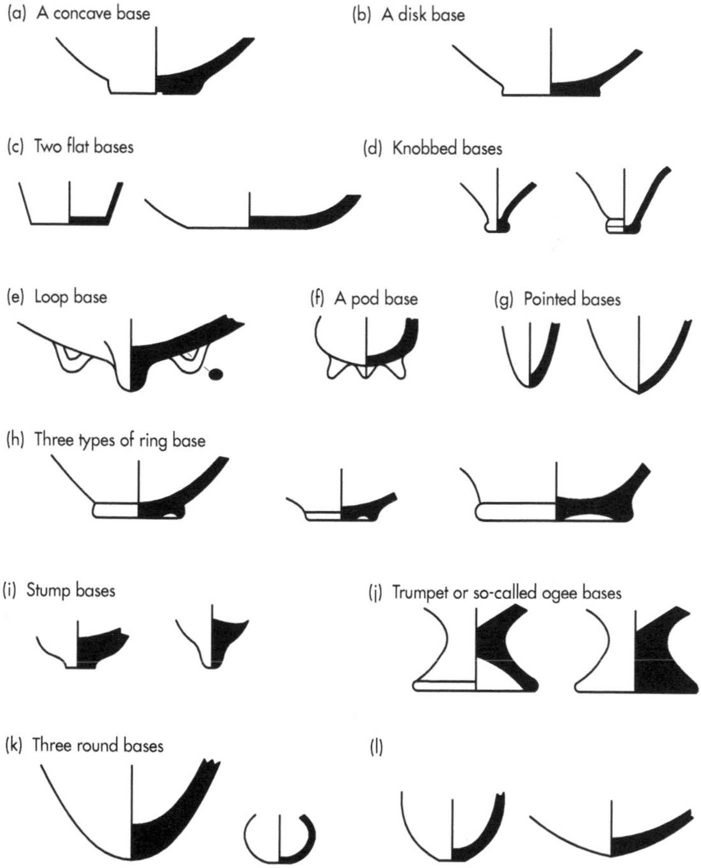

(a) A concave base

(b) A disk base

(c) Two flat bases

(d) Knobbed bases

(e) Loop base

(f) A pod base

(g) Pointed bases

(h) Three types of ring base

(i) Stump bases

(j) Trumpet or so-called ogee bases

(k) Three round bases

(l)

Figure 1.5 Types of ceramics base. (Martha Joukowsky, Figures 14.10–14.21: Ceramics bases, pp. 343–5 from *A Complete Manual of Field Archaeology*. Englewood Cliffs, NJ: Prentice Hall, 1980. Copyright © 1980 by Martha Joukowsky. Reprinted by permission of Simon & Schuster Adult Publishing Group)

CERAMICS BASIC BODY SHAPES

biconical (two cones back to back)
conical
cylindrical

ovoid
pyriform/pear-shaped
spherical

CERAMICS CLASSIFICATION BY ATTRIBUTES

Form attributes of vessel

form components: rim/lip, body, base, supports and appendages
overall shape: jar, bowl, other

Stylistic attributes of base surface and color

slipped: polished/unpolished; decorated/undecorated; incised, punctated, impressed, painted, modeled, etc.
unslipped: polished/unpolished; decorated/undecorated; incised, punctated, impressed, painted, modeled, etc.

Technological attributes of vessel

paste: tempered/untempered; color; composition; hardness
surface: slipped/unslipped; color; composition; hardness
other: fingermarks, wheelmarks, coil junctures, etc.

CERAMICS DECORATION TYPES

- Annual/banded design: rings around rim and base of vessel applied with brush while on wheel.
- Burnishing: made by polishing the leather-hard surface to give it sheen.
- Combing: made by a tool with multiple teeth or prongs.
- Decal: multiple color decoration placed over glaze.
- Finger-tipping
- Fretwork: made by piercing wall of vessel.
- Grooving
- Hand-painting

Stylistic attributes

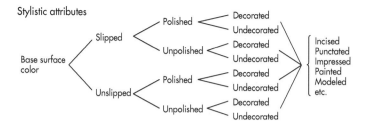

Form attributes

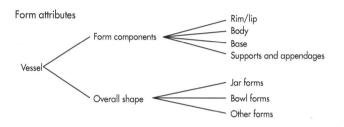

Technological attributes

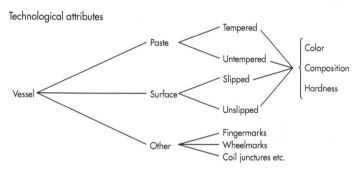

Figure 1.6 Classification of pottery: representative of kinds of attributes used to define stylistic, form, and technological types. (Wendy Ashmore and Robert J. Sharer, Figure 8.7: Classification of pottery: examples of kinds of attributes used to define stylistic, form, and technological types, p. 300 from *Discovering Our Past: A Brief Introduction to Archaeology*, third edition. New York: McGraw-Hill, 1999. Copyright © 1999 by Wendy Ashmore and Robert J. Sharer. Reprinted by permission of The McGraw-Hill Companies)

- Impressing
- Incision
- Knife-trimming
- Molded relief: raised decoration integral to the mold or form.
- Paddle-stamp

- Roller-stamping: made with cylinder-shaped roller with an incised pattern.
- Rouletting: made with metal strip or blade held against the pot as it is turned on wheel.
- Spatter or sponge decoration
- Sprigging: relief design in the form of small flowers or leaves.
- Transfer printing: paper impressions taken off inked engravings, under glaze.

CERAMICS FLUID/LIQUID DECORATION TYPES

- Glaze: glossy layer on surface of ware-fabric, before or after firing.
- Lustrous slip: natural luster from fusion of its elements, applied before firing.

Other liquid decoration

- Paint: generally has additional metal oxides, applied at various stages.
- Secondary slip: applied for special surface effects, applied before second firing.
- Self-same slip: suspension made from body clay, though lighter and freer from inclusions, applied before firing.
- Slip: liquid composed of fine clay suspended in water, applied before firing.
- Slip-wash: qualities of slip and wash, applied before firing.
- Wash: thin creamy suspension, applied after firing.

CERAMICS FRAGMENT SIZE CLASSIFICATION

smaller than 2.5 cm
2.5 cm–7 cm
7 cm–12 cm
12 cm–20 cm
20 cm and larger

CERAMICS IDENTIFICATION CHART

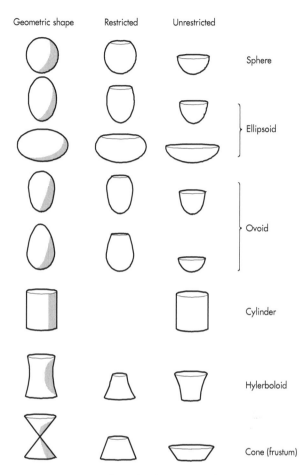

Figure 1.7 Geometric or volume classifications. (Prudence M. Rice, Figure 7.6: Geometric solids and surfaces for references for vessel shape description, p. 219 from *Pottery Analysis: A Sourcebook*. Chicago: University of Chicago Press, 1987. Copyright © 1987 by Prudence M. Rice. Reprinted by permission of The University of Chicago Press)

CERAMICS RIM CLASSES

General rim types

plain rim (vertical or sloping)
articulated rim (inverted or everted)

Rim thickening

external thickening
internal thickening
symmetrical thickening

Rim stances

everted rim
flared rim
horizontal rim
incurving rim
inverted rim
pendant rim
T-shaped rim
vertical rim

Rim edge treatments

flattened edge treatment (horizontal, vertical and horizontal, angular)
pushed, squeezed, or pinched treatment

CERAMICS TYPE-FUNCTION CLASSIFICATION

baking tray
base
bead
body sherd
bowl
carinated body sherd
ceramic disk
clay ball, fired
clay ball, unfired

cooking pot
crescentic ceramic
cup and saucer
handle
idol
jar, jug
lid
loom weight
no function can be ascertained

20

perforated fragment
plaque
spindle whorl
spout

stamp seal
urn
weight
work pot

CERAMICS VESSEL PARTS

appliqué
base
decoration
disk
foot

handle
motif
neck
rim
spout

CERAMICS WARE-FABRIC CLASSIFICATION

color (e.g. Fine Orange ware)
decoration (e.g. black-figured ware)
firing technology (e.g. earthenware)
form (e.g. beaker ware)
function (e.g. kitchenware)
geographical location (e.g. Glastonbury wares)
paste composition or texture (e.g. coarseware)
surface treatment or color (e.g. glazed ware, creamware)
time period (e.g. Iron Age wares)

CERAMICS WARE-FABRIC CLASSIFICATION, HISTORICAL

glaze
maker's mark
paste
porosity, hardness, and translucence
surface treatment
vessel form and function
ware identification (common pottery as terracotta and unrefined
    earthenware, refined earthenware, stoneware, porcelain)

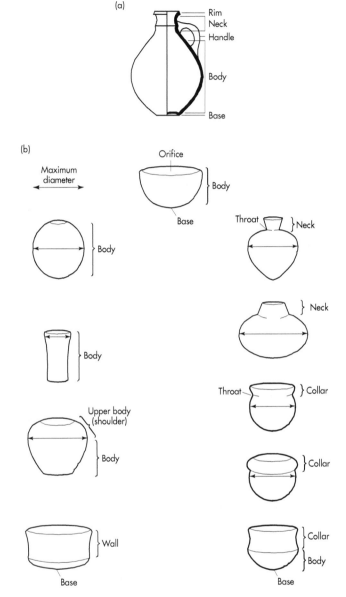

CLASSIFICATION AND TYPOLOGY

(a)

Rim
Neck
Handle

Body

Base

(b)

Orifice

Maximum
diameter

Body

Base

Body

Throat }Neck

Neck

Body

Throat }Collar

Upper body
(shoulder)

Body

Collar

Wall

Collar

Body

Base

Base

Figure 1.8a and b Ceramics vessel parts. (1.8a: Martha Joukowsky, Figure 14.4: Vessel parts, p. 338 from *A Complete Manual of Field Archaeology*. Englewood Cliffs, NJ: Prentice Hall, 1980. Copyright © 1980 by Martha Joukowsky. Reprinted by permission of Simon & Schuster Adult Publishing Group. 1.8b: John P. Staeck, Figures 7.3a–j: The anatomies of different vessel forms, p. 199 from *Back to the Earth: An Introduction to Archaeology*. Mountain View, CA: Mayfield Publishing/McGraw-Hill, 2001. Copyright © 2001 by John Staeck. Reprinted by permission of the author)

CLAY TYPES

Primary (contain only impurities from mother rock)

china clay or kaolin (white, refractory, not very plastic)
fire clay, infusible clay, refractory clay (rich silica with small amounts
  of lime, iron, alkali)

Secondary (have been transported from site of
formation and contain impurities from the process)

ball clay (fine-grained, plastic)
calcareous clay or marl (chalky mixture of carbonates of calcium
  and magnesium, remnants of shell)
fusible clay (capable of being melted or fused, very plastic)
red clay, earthenware clay, or cane (contain iron oxides, very plastic)
sandy clay, siliceous clay (containing high proportion of sand, not
  very plastic)
stoneware clay (usually many impurities, plastic)

COINAGE TYPES

bullion coins
commemorative coins
error coins
foreign currency
native country currency

pattern coins/patterns
proof coins
regular issue currency
tokens or medals

CONTEXT TYPES

- Use-related primary context: result of abandonment during acquisition, manufacture, or use activities.
- Transposed primary context: result of depositional activities, as midden creation.
- Use-related secondary context: result of human activity disturbance after original deposition of material.
- Natural secondary context: result of natural disturbance, as animal/plant activity, weather.

DATA TYPES, HISTORICAL

- Artifacts: glass (window, bottle), ceramics, pipes, metal (nails, tin cans, wire), wood, bone, buttons, etc.
- Documents: family records such as diaries, inventories; public records such as legal records; institutional records such as newspapers; and maps, photographs, drawings, etc.
- Ecofacts: plant and animal remains.
- Features: buildings, wall foundations, graves, gravestones, roads, wells, etc.

DEBITAGE TYPES (LITHIC)

For each of these three flake types – Primary (all cortex), Secondary (some cortex), and Interior (no cortex) – the following classification may be used. This is only one of many classification schemes for debitage analysis.

bipolar
complete, early-stage biface thinning
complete, late-stage biface thinning
complete, middle-stage biface thinning
complete, pressure
fragment, early-stage biface thinning
fragment, late-stage biface thinning
fragment, middle-stage biface thinning
fragment, pressure
nonbiface reduction
other
shatter

EFFIGY CLASSIFICATION

(These can also be classified by type of material, usually lithic or ceramic.)

- Effigy figure: animal, bird, person, other figure.
- Effigy vessel: bowl, canteen, censer, jar, ladle, pipe, pitcher, scoop, other vessel.

FIGURINE DESCRIPTION

color of ware (according to Munsell)
decoration (appliquéd, incised, incised and inlaid, liquid, other)
design (clothing, jewelry, other)
method of manufacture (pinches, coil-formed, molded, other)
position of figure (standing, sitting, reclining, kneeling, other)

GLASS CLASSIFICATION

Appearance

aventurine (containing opaque sparkling particles)
clear
opaque
semi-opaque

Use

bangle
bead
cane or tubing
glass cameo
glassware/vessel
window glass

Decoration

acid etching
applied and fusing
cut
engraved
inclusion of nonvitreous material
inlaid
layering
mosaic

GLAZE CLASSIFICATION

(by visual effect produced)

aventurine glaze (color-flecked)
crackle glaze (crazing)
crystalline glaze (crystals form during cooling)
luster (pearly)
matt glaze (dull)

GROUND-STONE USES

anvil
atlatl weight, bannerstone
ax
ball
bead, charm, ornament
bola
bowl, mortar
bracelet
celt
chisel
cooking slab
cylinder seal
disk
figurine
gorget
hammer
hoe

mano, handstone
maul
metate, milling stone
mill
other tool
palette
pestle
pipe
plummet, plumb
ring
shaft straightener
spindle whorl, loom weight, fishing
weight, net weight
tabular knife
unidentified ground stone
utensil

INVERTEBRATE CLASSIFICATION

Phylums

Acanthocephala (spiny-headed worms)
Aschelminthes (sac worms)
Brachiopoda (lamp shells)
Bryozoa (tube-dwelling aquatic animals)
Coelenterata/Cnidaria (coelenterates, jellyfish, sea anemones)

Ctenophora (comb jellies)
Ectoprocta (ectoprocts, microscopic colonizers)
Entoprocta (entoprocts, tube-dwelling aquatic animals)
Mesozoa (tiny parasites)
Mollusca (clams)
    Amphineura (chitons)
    Cepalopoda (octopuses and squids)
    Gastropoda (univalves)
    Pelecypoda (bivalves)
    Scaphoda (tooth shells)
Nematoda (roundworms)
Nemertina (ribbon worms)
Phoronida (tube-dwelling wormlike animals)
Platyhelminthes (flatworms, flukes, tapeworms)
Porifera (sponges)
Protozoa (amoebas and other protozoa)

True invertebrates

Annelida (segmented; earthworms)
Arthropoda (crustaceans, spiders, ticks, centipedes, insects)
Chaetognatha (arrowworms)
Chordata (sea squirts, amphioxus, tunicates, acorn worms)
Echinodermata (spiny-skinned animals, starfish, sea urchins)
Echiuroidea (spoon worms)
Enterocoelomates (coeloms)
Oncopoda (segmented, claw-footed worms)
Pogonophora (beard worms)
Sipunculoidea (peanut worms, marine worms)

LITHICS ATTRIBUTES

- Cortex: the amount of original exterior surface of the raw material visible on the flake – either as primary (cortex covering virtually all of exterior), secondary (some cortex), and tertiary (little or no cortex).
- Blank form: the basic shape of the flake, which can indicate certain types of technology – e.g. flake blade, blade, point, normal.
- Number of retouched edges: number of edges (distal, proximal, two lateral edges) that show retouch.

- Retouch intensity: light (shallow, sometimes discontinuous retouch with little change of the flake edge), medium (continuous and somewhat invasive into tool edge), heavy (very steep and invasive), and stepped (heavy with tiered or stacked scars).

MATERIALS, BASIC CATEGORIES OF

Artifacts (ceramic, chipped-stone/flaked/knapped, ground-stone, historical, perishable, etc.)
Ecofacts (animal/faunal, plant/floral)
Human remains
Other

METAL ARTIFACT CATEGORIES

hardware and construction (nail, cartridge case)
household and kitchen items (tin can, utensil)
ornaments (apparel accessory)
machinery
coinage
personal items (toy, pocket watch)
transportation items (horseshoe, wagon part)

MOHS SCALE OF HARDNESS

1. Talc (can be crushed or very easily scratched by a fingernail)
2. Gypsum (can be scratched by a fingernail)
3. Calcite (can be scratched by iron nail, easily scratched by knife, barely scratched by penny)
4. Fluorite (can be scratched by glass or knife)
5. Apatite (can be scratched by knife with difficulty)
6. Orthoclase feldspar (can be scratched by quartz; scratches glass with difficulty)
7. Quartz (can be scratched by a steel nail; scratches glass easily)
8. Topaz, beryl (can be scratched by an emerald; scratches glass very easily)
9. Corundum (can be scratched only by diamond; cuts glass)
10. Diamond

1. Talc 2. Gypsum	Scratched by finger nail
3. Calcite 4. Fluorite 5. Apatite	Scratched by steel knife
6. Moonstone 7. Quartz 8. Topaz 9. Corundum 10. Diamond	Will scratch glass – gemstones

NAIL CLASSIFICATION

Types

machine-cut with handmade head
machine-cut
hand-wrought or hand-forged (taper on all four sides toward the
  point; vary in thickness throughout shank)
  rose head
  T head
modern wire
  common
  finish
  flooring
  roofing

Sizes

2d 1″	10d 3″
3d 1¼″	12d 3¼″
4d 1½″	16d 3½″
5d 1¾″	20d 4″
6d 2″	30d 4½″
7d 2¼″	40d 5″
8d 2½″	50d 5½″
9d 2¾″	60d 6″

Uses

annular ring nail	finishing nail
barbed dowel pin	roofing nail
casing nail	sealing roofing nail
common brad	spiral nail
common nail	square-shank concrete nail
corrugated fastener	staple
cut flooring nail	tack
duplex head nail	upholstery nail

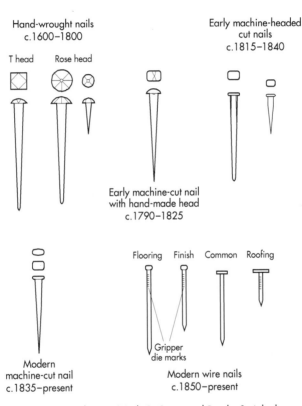

Figure 1.9 Major nail types. (Mark Q. Sutton and Brooke S. Arkush, Figure 76: Major nail types, p. 162 from *Archaeological Laboratory Methods: An Introduction*, Third Edition. Dubuque, IA: Kendall/Hunt Publishing, 2002. Copyright © 2002 by Kendall/Hunt Publishing Company. Reprinted by permission of the publisher)

Sedimentary units

boulder > 256 mm
cobble 64–256 mm
pebble 4–64 mm
granule 2–4 mm
very coarse sand 1–2 mm
coarse sand $^1/_2$–1 mm
medium sand $^1/_4$–$^1/_2$ mm
fine sand $^1/_8$–$^1/_4$ mm
very fine sand $^1/_{16}$–$^1/_8$ mm
silt $^1/_{256}$–$^1/_{16}$ mm
clay < $^1/_{256}$ mm

Volcanic/pyroclastic units

bomb or block > 32 mm
lapilli 4–32 mm
coarse ash $^1/_4$–4 mm
fine ash < $^1/_4$ mm

Igneous units

pegmatitic > 30 mm
coarse grained 5–30 mm
medium grained 1–5 mm
fine grained < 1 mm

PERFORATION TYPES

circular	oval
incomplete	rhomboid
oblong	semi-lunar
other	triangular

PLANT REMAINS CATEGORIES

Macroplant remains

charcoal
fibers
leaves
seeds
tubers

Microplant remains

phytoliths
pollen

Chemical remains

protein residue

PROJECTILE POINT ATTRIBUTES

Shankless

articulate (bow-sided)
    lanceolate (concave base, flat base)
    ovate (pointed base, round base)
    trianguloid
rectilinear (straight-edged)
    pentagonal (concave base, flat base)
    triangular (equilateral, isosceles or spirate)

Shanked

stemmed
    full-stemmed (contracting, flare, pinched, shoulderless, square)
    semi-stemmed
notched blade
    basal notched (double-notched, single-notched or bifurcate)
    corner or bias (notching above corner, notching at corner)
    neck-and-yoke (notched, stemmed)
    side-notched (base as wide or wider than shoulders, base narrower
      than shoulders)

base width
distal end (point, tip, working end)
maximum length
maximum thickness
maximum width
neck width (if present)
proximal end (butt, handle)

CLASSIFICATION AND TYPOLOGY

SHELL CLASSIFICATION

Bivalves

Arctic hard-shelled clams (Arcticidae)
ark shells (Arcidae, Noetiidae)
astartes (Astartidae)
basket clams (Corbulidae)
bean clams (Donacidae)
bittersweet shells (Glycymerididae)
carditas (Carditidae)
cleft clams (Thyasiridae)
cockles (Cardiidae)
coral-boring clams (Trapeziidae)
crassatellas (Crassatellidae)
diplodons (Ungulinidae)
dipper clams (Cuspidariidae)
dipper clams (Poromyidae)
false mussels (Dreissenidae)
file shells (Limidae)
gaping clams (Gastrochaenidae)
gari shells (Psammobiidae)
hard-shelled clams (Veneridae)
jewel boxes (Chamidae)
jingle shells (Anomiidae)
kitten paws (Plicatulidae)
limopsis (Limopsidae)
lucines (Lucinidae)
marsh clams (Corbiculiidae)
marsh clams (Cyrenoididae)
mussels (Mytilidae)

nut shells (Nuculidae)
nut shells and yoldias (Nuculanidae)
oysters (Ostreidae)
pandoras (Pandoridae)
paper shells (Lyonsiidae)
pearl oysters (Pteriidae)
pen shells (Pinnidae)
piddocks (Pholadidae)
purse shells (Isognomonidae)
razor clams (Solenidae)
rock borers (Hiatellidae)
rock dwellers (Petricolidae)
scallops (Pectinidae)
semeles (Semelidae)
shipworms (Teredinidae)
soft-shelled clams (Myidae)
spiny oysters (Spondylidae)
spoon shells (Periplomatidae)
surf clams (Mactridae)
tellins (Tellinidae)
thracias (Thraciidae)
veiled clams (Solemyidae)
verticords (Verticordiidae)
wedge clams (Mesodesmatidae)

Gastropods

abalones (Haliotidae)
atlantas (Atlantidae)
atom snails (Omalogyridae)
auger shells (Terebridae)
barrel bubble shells (Retusidae)
barrel shells (Cylichnidae)
bivalved snails (Juliidae)
blind limpets (Lepetidae)
caecum (Caecidae)
canoe shells (Scaphandridae)
cap shells (Capulidae)
carinarias (Carinariidae)
carrier-shells (Xenophoridae)
chank shells (Turbinellidae)
chink shell (Lacunidae)
clione sea butterflies (Clionidae)

cone shells (Conidae)
coral snails (Coralliophilidae)
cowries (Cypraeidae)
crown conchs (Melongenidae)
cup-and-saucer and slipper shells (Crepidulidae)
dog whelks (Nassariidae)
doris nudibranch (Chromodorididae, Cadlinidae)
dove shells (Columbellidae)
duckfoot shells (Aporrhaidae)
elysias (Elysiidae)
eolid nudibranch (Aeolididae, Dendronotidae)
facelina nudibranch (Facelinidae, Favorinidae)
false limpets (Siphonariidae)
fig shells (Ficidae)
flat snails (Skeneopsidae)
fossarus (Fossaridae)
frog shells (Bursidae)
glassy bubble shells (Atyidae)
hairy-keeled snails (Trichotropidae)
harp shells (Harpidae)
helmet shells (Cassidae)
hoof shells (Hipponicidae)
horn shells (Cerithiidae)
horn shells (Potamididae)
keyhole limpets (Fissurellidae)
left-handed snails (Triphoridae)
limpets (Acmaeidae)
marginellas (Marginellidae)
melanella shells (Melanellidae)
miter shells (Mitridae)
modulus (Modulidae)
moon shells (Naticidae)
nerites (Neritidae)
nutmegs (Cancellariidae)
olive shells (Olividae)
paper bubble shells (Hydatinidae)
pearly top shells (Trochidae)
periwinkles (Littorinidae)
pheasant shells (Phasianellidae)
planaxis (Planaxidae)
polycera nudibranch (Polyceratidae, Phyllidiidae, Tritoniidae,
    Dotoidae)
pyramid shells (Pyramidellidae)

rissos (Rissoidae)
rock or dye shells (Muricidae)
rock shells or dogwinkles (Thaididae)
salt-marsh snails (Ellobiidae)
sea butterflies (Cavolinidae)
sea buttons (Eratoidae)
sea hares (Aplysidae)
simnias (Ovulidae)
slit worm shells (Siliquariidae)
slit-shells (Pleurotomariidae)
small bubble shells (Acteonidae)
spindle shells (Fusininae)
strombs (Strombidae)
sundials (Architectonicidae)
swamp snails (Hydrobiidae)
tritons (Ranellidae)
true bubble shells (Bullidae)
tulip shells (Fasciolariidae)
tun shells (Tonnidae)
turbans (Turbinidae)
turret-shells (Turritellidae)
turrids (Turridae)
umbrella shells (Umbraculidae)
vase shells (Vasidae)
violet snails (Janthinidae)
vitreous snails (Vitrinellidae)
volutes (Volutidae)
wentletraps (Epitoniidae)
whelks (Buccinidae)
wide-mouthed bubble shells (Philinidae)
wide-mouthed snails (Lamellariidae)
worm shells (Vermetidae)

Amphineurans or Chitons

chitons (Chitonidae)
chitons (Ischnochitonidae)
glass-haired chitons (Acanthochitonidae)
red chitons (Lepidochitonidae)

Scaphopods

swollen tusk shells (Siphonodentaliidae)
tusk shells (Dentaliidae)

Cephalopods

octopods (Octopodidae)
paper argonauts (Argonautidae)
spirulas (Spirulidae)
squids (Gonatidae, Loliginidae, Ommastrephidae)

--- **SITE BY FUNCTION** ---

art sites
burial sites
ceremonial and ritual sites
commerce sites
fishing stations
flint collection sites
habitation and industry sites
habitation sites
habitation, industry, and ritual sites

hunting sites
industry sites
kill sites
quarry sites
shell middens
trading sites
water collection sites
way stations for migrations
wild food collection sites

--- **SITE BY TYPE** ---

camps
caves
cemeteries
flintknapping stations
gathering stations
hunting stations
monumental cities
mounds
plains
quarries
raised beaches

riverside terraces
rock carvings
sacred areas
shell middens
specialized camps
tells or tumuli
towns
underwater sites
villages
waterholes

--- **SOIL CLASSIFICATION, GENERAL** ---

#1

■ Azonal soil: recently deposited soil in river deltas, mountain
regions, sand dunes, often with no profile.

- Intrazonal soil: e.g. swamps and marshes, having poorly defined profiles.
- Zonal soil: which has two distinct zones or horizons, topsoil and subsoil.

#2

Seventh Approximation Soil Classification, US Dept of Agriculture
- Alfisols: soil with more clay in B horizon than in A, high base status.
- Andisols: formed from volcanic parent materials.
- Aridsols: dry soil with salic, calcic, and gypsic horizon
- Entisols: young soils lacking horizons.
- Histosols: wet soils made of decaying plants.
- Inceptisols: young soils with poor horizons, e.g. rice paddies.
- Mollisols: fertile soil that is base rich.
- Oxisols: mature, well-leached soils with distinct oxic horizon.
- Spodsols: podosol with illuvial accumulation of humus with iron and/or aluminum.
- Ultisols: red soil, less leached, with clay argillic horizon.
- Vertisols: dark soil with deep vertical cracks.

--- **SOIL HORIZONS AND SUBDIVISIONS** ---

O horizon: fresh or decomposed organic material, dark in color.

O1: fresh organic material, still identifiable
O2: decomposed organic material, not identifiable

A horizon: mainly inorganic or mineral, dark in color; also called topsoil.

A1: mineral with dark colors
A2: lower portion of A horizon where leaching is intense
A3: transitional, more like A than underlying B; also called A/B

E horizon: mineral with intense leaching or removal of well-decomposed organic matter, clay, iron, or aluminum; gray or grayish brown, lighter than A or B; also called subsurface layer.

B horizon: mineral, zone of illuviation or accumulation of clay, iron, aluminum, carbonates, gypsum, silica, illuviated organic matter; yellowish brown to reddish brown compared to overlying and underlying horizons; also called subsoil.

B1: transitional, more like B than A; also called B/A
B2: zone of accumulation for clay, iron, aluminum, illuviated organic matter; strong development of blocky, subangular blocky, prismatic, columnar structure
B3: transitional, more like B than C; also called B/C

C horizon: unweathered and unconsolidated material; also called parent material; also called substratum.

R horizon: bedrock or consolidated rock underlying soil.

──────────── **SOIL LAYERS** ────────────

humus (O horizon, decaying plant material and leaves)
topsoil (A horizon, top layer where moisture seeps down, dissolving chemical elements; minerals in the moisture enter bodies of water)
subsoil (B horizon, middle layer including iron oxides, clay, other insoluble substances, touched by deep-rooted plants, as trees)
parent rock (C horizon, bottom layer which is combination of decomposed rock and shale-like materials)
rock zone (D horizon, underlying bedroom, layer of crumbled rock)

──────────── **SOIL PARTICLE SHAPE** ────────────

(for sand- and gravel-sized particles)

angular (all edges are sharp)
rounded (all edges are smooth)
subangular (one-third of edges are smooth)
subrounded (two-thirds of edges are smooth)
very angular (all edges very sharp)
well-rounded (all edges smooth and very round)

SOIL STRUCTURE TYPES

#1

Blocky: blocks with sharp faces that fit adjoining ped faces; can break into smaller blocky peds.
Columnar: particles aggregate and create columnlike peds with rounded caps.
Crumb: relatively porous, small and spheroidally shaped peds; not fitted to adjoining aggregates.
Granular: relatively nonporous, small and spheroidally shaped peds; not fitted to adjoining aggregates.
Platy: platelike aggregates that often overlap.
Prismatic: particles aggregate and create columnlike peds without rounded caps.
Subangular blocky: blocks with rounded faces that accommodate adjoining peds.

#2

Blocky
very fine < 5 mm
fine 5–10 mm
medium 10–20 mm
coarse 20–50 mm
very coarse > 50 mm

Granular
very fine < 1 mm
fine 1–2 mm
medium 2–5 mm
coarse 5–10 mm
very coarse > 10 mm

Platy
very fine/very thin < 1 mm
fine/thin 1–2 mm
medium 2–5 mm
coarse 5–10 mm
very coarse > 10 mm

CLASSIFICATION AND TYPOLOGY

40

Prismatic
very fine < 10 mm
fine 10–20 mm
medium 20–50 mm
coarse 50–100 mm
very coarse > 100 mm

SOIL TAXONOMY

Epipedons

- Anthropic: similar to a mollic, but man-made with a large amount of phosphate accumulated by continuous farming.
- Histic: peaty surface horizon, saturated with water part or all of the year, having a large amount of organic carbon.
- Mellanic: black, thick epipedon occurring in soils developed in volcanic ash.
- Mollic: dark-colored, thick surface horizon, heavy base.
- Ochric: light in color, low in organic carbon, thin.
- Plaggen: man-made epipedon more than 50 cm thick raised above the original soil surface with properties that depend on the original soil.
- Umbric: similar to mollic, except that the base saturation is less than 50%.

Diagnostic subsurface horizons

- Agric: compact horizon formed immediately below the plow layer by cultivation, and contains significant amounts of illuvial silt, clay, and humus.
- Albic: bleached, light colored horizon from which the clay and free iron oxides have been removed.
- Argillic: illuvial horizon enriched with clay.
- Calcic: enriched with calcium carbonate or calcium and magnesium carbonate in the form of powdery lime or secondary concretions, more than 15 cm thick.
- Cambic: altered horizon in which the parent material has been changed into soil by formation, of soil structure, liberation of iron oxides, clay formation, and obliteration of the original rock structure.
- Gypsic: enriched with calcium sulphate, more than 15 cm thick.

- Kandic: kaolinitic clay minerals with abrupt change of texture between the surface and lower horizons.
- Natric: clay-enriched illuvial horizon, with the cation exchange complex dominated by a high sodium content.
- Oxic: very low content of weatherable minerals, clay composed largely of kaolinite, contains accessory highly insoluble minerals such as quartz sand, low exchange capacity, and clays are poorly dispersed.
- Placic: thin, black or reddish-brown brittle pan, cemented with iron, iron and manganese, or an iron-organic complex; forms a barrier to roots.
- Salic: enriched with salts more soluble than gypsum, more than 15 cm thick.
- Sombric: freely drained, dark subsurface horizon containing illuvial humus with low base saturation.
- Spodic: illuvial enriched with organic matter, iron, and aluminum.
- Sulfuric: mineral or organic horizon more than 15 cm thick which has a pH of 3.5 or less and contains the mineral jarosite or more than 0.05% water-soluble sulphate.

Other diagnostic horizons

- Andic: composed of volcanic glass.
- Duripan: subsurface horizon cemented by silica or aluminum silicate.
- Fragipan: compact slowly permeable loamy subsurface horizon with a high bulk density, brittle when moist, but hard when dry.
- Glossic: more than 5 cm thick in which an upper E horizon penetrates (tongues) down into a lower argillic, natric, or kandic horizon.
- Permafrost: horizon where temperature is constantly below 0°C, with permanent ice.
- Petrocalcic: cemented calcic horizon.
- Petrogypsic: cemented gypsic horizon.
- Plinthite: found in tropical regions, arising due to laterization soil formation processes; hardens into iron crust.

SOIL TEXTURAL CLASSES

- Sand: very gritty, does not form stable ball, does not ribbon out, does not soil hands, no plastic properties, not sticky, loose moist consistency, loose dry consistency.

Table 1.1 Characteristics of major sediment textural classes (adapted from Foss et al. 1975). [Table 1: Characteristics of major sediment textural classes, p. 41 from *The Crow Canyon Archaeological Center Field Manual* [HTML Title]. Crow Canyon Archaeological Center, 2001a. Copyright © 2001 by Crow Canyon Archaeological Center. Reprinted by permission]

| TEXTURAL CLASSES | CONSISTENCE | | | | FORMS STABLE | | Properties when moist |
| | Dry | Moist | Wet | | Molded ball | Ribboning | |
			Stickiness	Plasticity			
Sand	Loose	Loose	Nonsticky	Nonplastic	None	None	Very gritty
Loamy sand	Loose to soft	Loose	Nonsticky	Nonplastic	Very weak	None	Very gritty
Sandy loam	Soft to slightly hard	Very friable	Nonsticky to slightly sticky	Nonplastic to slightly plastic	Very weak to fragile	None	Gritty
Loam	Slightly hard to soft	Friable	Slightly sticky to nonsticky	Slightly plastic to nonplastic	Strong to fragile	Slight to none	Gritty
Silt loam	Slightly hard to soft	Friable	Slightly sticky to nonsticky	Slightly plastic to nonplastic	Strong	Slight	Velvety
Silt	Soft to slightly hard	Friable to firm	Nonsticky	Nonplastic		Slight	Velvety
Silty clay loam	Slightly hard to hard	Friable to firm	Sticky	Plastic	Strong	Medium	Velvety
Clay loam	Slightly hard to hard	Firm	Sticky	Plastic	Strong	Medium	Gritty
Sandy clay loam	Slightly hard to hard	Friable to firm	Sticky	Plastic	Strong	Medium	Very gritty
Silty clay	Hard to very hard	Firm to extremely firm	Very sticky	Very plastic	Very strong	High	Very smooth
Clay	Hard to extremely hard	Firm to extremely firm	Very sticky	Very plastic	Very strong	High	Smooth
Sandy clay	Hard to very hard	Firm to extremely firm	Very sticky	Very plastic	Very strong	High	Gritty

43

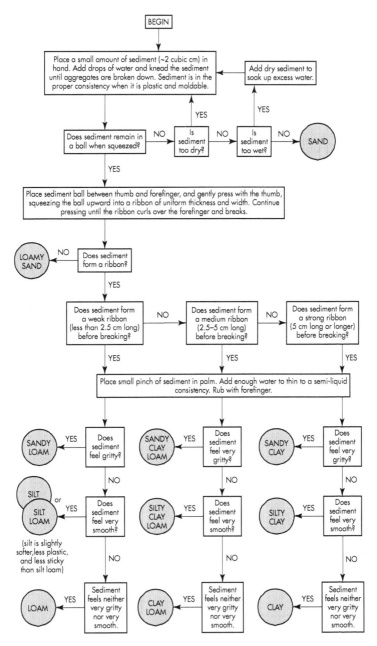

Figure 1.10 Flow diagram for determining sediment texture (after Thien 1979). (Figure 1, p. 42 from *The Crow Canyon Archaeological Center Field Manual [HTML Title]*. Crow Canyon Archaeological Center, 2001a. Copyright © 2001 by Crow Canyon Archaeological Center. Reprinted by permission)

- Loamy sand: very gritty, does not form stable ball, does not ribbon out, slightly soils hands, no plastic properties, not sticky, loose moist consistency, loose dry consistency.
- Sandy loam: gritty, forms stable ball that is easily deformed, ribbons out but poorly formed with dull surface, soils hands, no plastic properties, not sticky, very friable moist consistency, soft dry consistency.
- Loam: gritty, forms stable ball, ribbons out but poorly formed with dull surface, soils hands, slight plastic properties, slightly sticky, friable moist consistency, soft dry consistency.
- Silt loam: velvety, forms stable ball, ribbons out but poorly formed with dull surface, soils hands, slight to moderate plastic properties, friable moist consistency, soft dry consistency.
- Silty clay loam: velvety and sticky, forms very stable ball, ribbons out well with shiny surface, soils hands, moderate plastic properties, sticky, friable to firm moist consistency, slightly hard dry consistency.
- Clay loam: gritty and sticky, forms very stable ball, ribbons out well with shiny surface, soils hands, moderate plastic properties, sticky, firm moist consistency, slightly hard to hard dry consistency.
- Sandy clay loam: very gritty and sticky, forms very stable ball, ribbons out well with shiny surface, soils hands, moderate plastic properties, sticky, friable to firm moist consistency, slightly hard to hard dry consistency.
- Silty clay: extremely sticky and very smooth, forms ball that is very resistant to molding, ribbons out well with very shiny surface, soils hands, strong plastic properties, very sticky, firm to extremely firm moist consistency, hard to very hard dry consistency.
- Clay: extremely sticky, forms ball that is resistant to molding, ribbons out well with very shiny surface, soils hands, strong plastic properties, very sticky, firm to extremely firm moist consistency, hard to very hard dry consistency.

STONE TOOL CLASSIFICATION, FLAKED OR CHIPPED

#1

- Blade: parallel-sided flake tool struck from prepared core.
- Core: the mass from which flakes are removed.
- Flake: tool that has been chipped or knapped from a core.

#2

- Biface: flaked alternately on two sides or surfaces, producing a series of platforms along a margin/tool's edge; includes projectile points.

  early-stage bifaces (sinuous margins and limited number of flake scars)
  late-stage bifaces (straight margins and numerous patterned flake scars)

- Uniface: worked only on one side.

— STONE TOOL CLASSIFICATION, GROUND —

Ground in manufacture

atlatl weight/ bannerstone	hoe
ax	loom weight/fishing weight/
ball	net weight
bead	maul
bola	ornament
bowl	other
bracelet	palette
celt	pipe
charm	plummet/plumb
chisel	ring
cooking slab	ritual object
cylinder seal	spindle whorl
disk	stone bead or ornament
figurine	tabular knife
gorget	utensil
hammer	

Ground in use

handstone/mano
mill
milling stone/metate
mortar/bowl
other
pestle

STRATIGRAPHICAL CONTEXT AND RELATIONSHIP TYPES

Context

artificial layer
cut
horizontal interface

no context
stratigraphical layer
vertical interface

Relationship

above/below
abuts/abutted by
cut/cut by

equals
fills/is filled by
no relationship

SURVEY CLASSES

Plane survey

land survey
   pedestrian or foot survey
   subsurface survey
ongoing excavation survey
topographic survey

Other types of plane survey

forest survey (forest resources)
geologic survey (geological deposits)
hydrographic survey (measure of water resources)
mine survey (mine shafts, tunnels, deposits)
photogrammetric survey (aerial photography of ground checks)

Geophysical/geodetic survey

SURVEY METHODS OF INSPECTION

aerial photography with ground checks, also SAT images
geophysical survey

auguring
bosing
chemical survey
dowsing
electromagnetic survey (for sump features/pits/houses/trenches/
metal objects, moderate cost, limited by environmental interference)
ground-penetrating radar (for voids/grave shafts/tombs/coffins/
foundations/cellars/cisterns, high cost, limited by wet matrix/
clay/saline soils)
magnetometer survey (for subsurface anomalies/pits/houses/
trenches, foundations/wells, moderate cost, limited by magnetic
storms, diurnal variation, random intrusions)
metal detector survey (for metal objects, relatively low cost, limited
to shallow depths)
probing
seismic survey
soil resistivity survey (for features near surface/rocks features/
hearths/pits/houses/mounds, low-to-moderate cost, limited
when there is thick brush)
sonar or acoustic survey
thermal survey
pedestrian surface survey
subsurface survey by test pits, divoting, coring, or augering
underwater survey

TIN CAN TYPES

hole-and-cap (filler hole at one end, closed by a cap)
hole-in-cap (filler hole at one end, sealed with a tin plate cap that
has a pinhole vent in its center)
vent hole (stamped ends and single pinhole or "matchstick" filler
hole no larger than $1/8$ inch in center of one end)
sanitary (also called open-top; ends attached to body by crimping
edges together and made airtight)

TOOTH TYPES

canine   molar
incisor   premolar

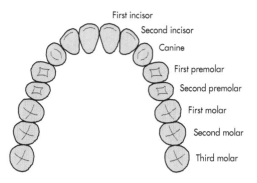

First incisor
Second incisor
Canine
First premolar
Second premolar
First molar
Second molar
Third molar

Figure 1.11 Permanent human teeth

TYLER SCALE/GRADES OF CLASTIC SEDIMENTS

Dimensions	Fragment/ particle	Unconsolidated aggregate	Consolidated rock
> 256 mm	boulder	boulder gravel	boulder conglomerate
64–256 mm	cobble	cobble gravel	cobble conglomerate
4–64 mm	pebble	pebble gravel	pebble conglomerate
2–4 mm	granule	granule gravel	granulate conglomerate
1–2 mm	very coarse sand grain	very coarse sand	very coarse sandstone
$^1/_2$–1 mm	coarse sand grain	coarse sand	coarse sandstone
$^1/_4$–$^1/_2$ mm	medium sand grain	medium sand	medium sandstone
$^1/_8$–$^1/_4$ mm	fine sand grain	fine sand	fine sandstone
$^1/_{16}$–$^1/_8$ mm	very fine sand grain	very fine sand	very fine sandstone
$^1/_{256}$–$^1/_{16}$ mm	silt particle	silt	siltstone
< $^1/_{256}$ mm	clay particle	clay	claystone

UNITS AND SPATIAL DIVISIONS

Basic units

■ Phase: defined by artifacts and cultural traits identified precisely in time and space and which distinguish it from other units.
■ Component: the manifestation of a given archaeological phase at a site.

Spatial divisions

(Some archaeologists see the four spatial divisions as being Artifact, Structure, Site, and Region.)

■ Site: any location that demonstrates past human activity, especially community activity, evidenced by the presence of artifacts, ecofacts, features, structures, or other material remains.
■ Locality: a large site composed of two or more clusters of material remains.
■ Region: geographically defined area containing a series of interrelated human communities sharing a single cultural-ecological system; sometimes referred to as a settlement pattern.
■ Area: broad tracts of land which roughly correspond to ethnographically-defined cultural areas recognized by early anthropological work.

VERTEBRATE CLASSIFICATION

Cyclostomata (jawless fishes)
Chondrichthyes (cartilaginous fishes)
Osteichthyes (bony fishes)
Reptilia: reptiles
    Chelonia (turtles, tortoises)
    Squamata (lizards, snakes)
    Crocodilia (crocodiles, alligators)
    Tuatara (lizard-like New Zealand creatures)
Amphibians
    Caecilians (limbless, worm-like)
    Caudata (tailed amphibians)
    Anura (tailless amphibians, i.e. frogs, toads)

Birds
Struthioniformes (ostriches)
Rheiformes (rheas)
Casuariiformes (emus, cassowaries)
Apterygiformes (kiwis)
Tinamiformes (tinamous)
Gaviiformes (divers)
Podicipediformes (grebes)
Sphenisciformes (penguins)
Procellariiformes (albatrosses, petrels)
Pelecaniformes (pelicans, cormorants, gannets)
Ciconiiformes (herons, storks)
Phoenicopteriformes (flamingos)
Anseriformes (ducks, geese)
Falconiformes (falcons, eagles, hawks, vultures)
Galliformes (pheasant, turkey, game birds)
Gruiformes (cranes, rails)
Charadriiformes (gulls, waders, terns, plovers)
Columbiformes (doves, pigeons)
Psittaciformes (parakeets, parrots, cockatoos)
Cuculiformes (cuckoos)
Strigiformes (owls)
Caprimulgiformes (goatsuckers, nightjars)
Apodiformes (hummingbirds, swifts)
Coliiformes (colies, mousebirds)
Trogoniformes (trogons)
Coraciiformes (kingfishers, hornbills, toucans)
Piciformes (woodpeckers)
Passeriformes (perching birds, thrushes, sparrows)
Mammals
Monotremata (monotremes, as duck-billed platypus)
Marsupiala (pouched animals, koalas)
Eutheria (placental animals)
Insectivora (insectivores, moles, shrews)
Tupaioidea (tree shrews)
Dermoptera (colugos, flying lemurs)
Chiroptera (bats)
Primates (monkeys, humans, apes)
Edentata (anteaters, armadillos)
Pholidota (pangolins)
Lagomorpha (rabbits, hares)
Rodentia (mice, squirrels, rats)
Cetacea (whales, dolphins)

Carnivora (bears, cats, wolves)
Pinnipedia (sea lions)
Tubulidentata (aardvarks)
Proboscidea (elephants)
Hyracoidea (hyrax)
Sirenia (sea cows)
Perissodactyla (horses, rhinos)
Artiodactyla (camels, giraffes, pigs, cattle)

WENTWORTH GRAIN SIZE CLASSIFICATION

(for sediments)

boulder 256–4,096 mm
cobble 64–256 mm
pebble 4–64 mm
granule 2–4 mm
very coarse sand 1–2 mm
coarse sand 0.5–1 mm
medium sand 0.25–0.50 mm
fine sand 0.125–0.25 mm
very fine sand 0.0625–0.125 mm
coarse silt 0.0312–0.0625 mm
medium silt 0.0156–0.0312 mm
fine silt 0.0078–0.0156 mm
very fine silt 0.0039–0.0078 mm
clay < 0.0039 mm

2

Forms and Records

The sample forms and records in this chapter are supplied as templates for the archaeologist to design his or her own versions. Some may be photocopied as is and used in the field. In archaeology textbooks that cover fieldwork, you may also find sample forms. Local, state, and federal agencies will also provide their forms to interested parties and those may be used as templates for creating forms and recordkeeping documents.

―――――――――――― **CONTENTS** ――――――――――――

FORMS AND RECORDS

54

AGREEMENT BETWEEN LANDLORD/
PROPERTY OWNER AND SURVEY PARTY

(to be filled out by landlord/property owner and director of survey)

This agreement is made and entered into between _____(name of organization) and _____(landlord/property owner) effective this _____ day of _____, _____. In advance of a formal survey by _____(name of organization), this agreement is to summarize our understanding concerning the proposed survey.

1. Title of survey: _____
2. Property to be surveyed: _____
3. Period of survey: _____
4. Schedule: _____
5. Type of survey: _____
6. Plan of survey fieldwork: _____
7. Ownership of surface finds, maps, survey results: _____
8. Documents to be provided by landlord/property owner: _____
9. Compensation to landlord/property owner ____, to be paid as follows ____.

This survey is subject to the approval of the undersigned parties. Should the survey be canceled or its intent changed, _____(landlord/property owner) will be notified immediately and in writing.

Landlord/property owner _____
Address _____
Telephone _____ Fax _____ Email _____

Survey Organization _____
Address _____
Telephone _____ Fax _____ Email _____

FORMS AND RECORDS

ARTIFACT/FIELD SPECIMEN INVENTORY
OR CATALOG (1)

Site name _____ Site # _____ Year _____ Recorded by _____

Catalog accession #	Unit	Level	Feature #	Find #	Description	Excavation date

56

ARTIFACT/FIELD SPECIMEN INVENTORY OR CATALOG (2)

Site name .... Operation # .... Recorded by ....
Excavation unit .... MCU .... Date(s) collected ....
Level .... Lot .... Feature ....

Materials and characteristics	Comments (type, etc.)	# of Pieces	Weight
Ceramic			
brick			
dish			
glazed pipe			
globular			
other			
pottery, uniden. frag.			
smoking pipe			
Glass			
curved (container)			
flat (window)			
fragments			
Metal			
fragments			
lead			
nail, round x-section			
nail, square x-section			
nail, wire			
other			
pipe L M S (cm)			
tack			
tube L M S (cm)			
Stone			
chipped/flaked			
fragments			
ground			
other			
polished			
slate			
Miscellaneous			
animal bone			
cement			
charcoal			
coal			
leather			
mortar			
shell			
wood			

FORMS AND RECORDS

ARTIFACT (PROVENIENCE) LABEL/TAG (1)

Site # _____ Catalog # _____ Bag # _____

Unit _____ Level _____ Provenience _____

Feature _____

Artifact # on map _____ Description _____

Excavator _____ Date _____

ARTIFACT (PROVENIENCE) LABEL/TAG (2)

Site name _____ Operation _____ Unit _____ MCU _____

Level _____ Lot _____

Material/description: _____

Excavator _____ Date _____

BASKETRY RECORD

Site name _____ Site # _____ Catalog # _____

Complete/fragment _____

Element _____

Height _____ Diameter _____ Volume _____

Length _____ Width _____

Shape/form _____

Construction technique _____

Materials used _____

Weave elements _____

Weave twist _____

Weave variations _____

Wear/repair/splicing _____ (location, severity)

Resins, sealants, mastics, seeds, residues _____

— BUILDING/STRUCTURE INVENTORY FORM —

Site identifier ____
Site # ____
Recorder ____ Organization ____ Address ____ Phone ____ Date ____
Quad name ____
Survey ____
National Register category ____

○ **Identification**
Building name ____
Street ____
County ____ Township ____ City ____
Cross streets ____
Subdivision name ____ Block ____ Lot # ____
Ownership ____
Use, original ____ Use, present ____
Name of public tract ____
Accessibility ____
○ Surroundings ____
Relationship of building to surroundings ____
Notable features of building and site ____
Date of initial construction ____
Architect ____
Builder ____
Earliest map of building ____
Historical and architectural importance ____
Original uses ____
Intermediate uses ____
○ Present uses ____
Ownership history ____
Moves ____
Alterations ____
Additions ____
Photo(s) ____
Map(s) ____ USGS 7.5 map name ____
Other mapping ____
Bibliographic references ____

Description

Building material _____

Structural system _____

Style _____

Exterior plan _____

No. of stories _____

Foundation _____

Construction _____

Exterior materials _____

Roof type _____ Roof materials _____

Chimney _____

Windows _____

Main entrance _____

Porches _____

Exterior ornament _____

Interior plan _____

Condition _____

Integrity _____

Threats to building _____

Related outbuildings and property _____

Nature of site _____

Archaeological remains _____

Narrative description of site _____

Discussion of significance _____

History and bibliography of past work at site _____

Surveyor's evaluation

Eligibility for local designation _____

Eligibility for National Register _____

Eligibility as contributor to National Register District _____

Historical associations _____

Evaluation _____

Research methods _____

Recorder _____

BULK SAMPLE LOG

Site name _____

Operation	Excavation unit	Date	Level	Lot	Feature	Number	Material	MCU

BULK SOIL SAMPLE LABEL/TAG

Site name _____ Operation _____ Unit _____ Level _____

Lot _____ Feature _____ MCU _____

Material/description _____

_____

_____

Excavator _____ Date _____

BURIAL RECORD

Site name _____ Site # _____ Date _____

Burial # _____

Unit _____ Level _____

Cemetery _____

Depth from datum _____

⃝ Depth from surface _____

Depth from floor _____

Soil sample # _____

Soil description _____

Stratification _____

Munsell _____

Wentworth _____

Type of burial _____ Grave size _____ Grave type _____

⃝ Number of individuals _____

Position of skeleton _____

Position of head _____

Orientation _____

Position of limbs _____

Condition of bones _____ Bones present _____

Sex _____ Age estimate _____ Pathology _____

Preservation of bone _____

Completeness: skull _____ vertebrae _____ clavicle _____ sternum _____

⃝ sacrum _____ innominates _____ scapula _____ ribs _____ humerus _____

radius _____ ulna _____ carpus _____ metacarpals _____ phalanges _____

femur _____ tibia _____ patella _____ tarsus _____ metatarsals _____

phalanges _____

Bones absent _____

Measurements of specific bones _____

Peculiarities _____

Taphonomic features _____

Comments: _____

Associated tissue or hair: _____

Associated features: _____

Associated artifacts: _____

Catalog # _____ Find # _____ Provenience _____ Description _____

Measurements _____

Coffin description: _____

Photo roll _____ Photo # _____

Drawings (this form must be accompanied by field diagram) _____

Other samples _____

Conservation method _____ Packing method _____

Notebook cross-reference _____

Conclusions and interpretive information: _____

Excavator _____

CATALOG CARD

Site name _____ Site # _____

Unit/level _____ Provenience _____ Bag # _____

Catalog # _____ Date collected _____ Date catalogued _____

Excavator _____

Find # _____

Object's function (if known): _____

Material: _____

Condition: _____

Description: _____

Measurements: _____

Context/associations: _____

Drawing # _____ Photo # _____

Storage location _____

Notes: _____

CATALOG FORM/SITE CATALOG
FORM/FIELD CATALOG/CATALOG LOG

Site name _____ Site # _____ Catalogued by _____ Catalog date _____
Unit/level _____ Excavator _____

Catalog #	Description	Material	Quantity	Measurements	Conservation	Drawing	Photograph	Storage	Notes

68

CERAMIC RECORDING FORM

Site name _____ Site # _____
Unit/level _____ Excavator _____ Date excavated _____
Photo roll # _____ Photo frame # _____ Drawing _____
Function _____
Ware _____
Condition, state of preservation _____
Form/shape
  base _____
  body _____
  neck _____
  rim and rim edge treatment _____
  handle(s) _____
  spout(s) _____
Size
  length _____
  width _____
  thickness _____
Context/fabric
  Mohs hardness _____
  other qualities _____
  resistance to scraping and abrasion _____
  strength _____
  fracture _____
  clay _____
Manufacture
  shaping _____
  proof of manufacture _____
  finishing methods and tool _____
  clay at time of finishing _____
  drying _____
Firing _____
Surface treatment and condition _____
Color _____
Temper and texture
  Wentworth _____
  shape _____
Feel of ceramic _____
Inclusions
  frequency _____
  size _____
  sorting _____
  rounding _____
Decoration
  plastic _____
  liquid _____
Notes _____
External dating _____
Associated types _____

COIN CATALOG CARD

Site name _____ Site # _____

Unit/level _____ Provenience _____ Date excavated _____ Excavator _____

Bag # _____

Metal _____ Condition _____

Measurements _____ Quantity _____

Obverse legend _____

Reverse legend _____

Diameter _____ Weight in gms _____

Mint mark _____ Date minted _____ Country/city, etc. _____

Notes _____

Catalog # _____ Date catalogued _____ Catalogued by _____

Drawing # _____ Photograph # _____

Storage _____

CREW ATTENDANCE SHEET

	MO	TU	WE	TH	FR	SA	SU
(hours on each day)							
Field director							
Principal investigator							
Administrative assistant							
Site supervisor(s)							
Foreman or crew chief							
Field technicians							
Unit supervisors							
Staff members							
Volunteers							
Architect							
Artifact analyst							
Cataloger							
Computer specialist							
Conservator							
Dating specialist							
Draftsperson/cartographer							
Ethnobotanist/palynologist							
Geologist/geoarchaeologist							
Laboratory staff							
Laboratory supervisor							
Other specialists							
Photographer							
Small-finds specialist							
Support crew (cook, etc.)							
Surveyor							
Zooarchaeologist							

CRM FEDERAL BID FORM REQUIREMENTS

Form SF-33
services and price/cost schedule
checklists for bidder to certify and represent certain aspects of the CRM firm
Form SF-254
Form SF-255

CRM PHASE I FIELD NOTES AND RECORDS

General project information

    logistics
    project maps and figures
    records of interviews and communications
    right-of-entry materials
    scope of work

General field notes kept by supervisor

    Environmental description, including tree distribution and growth characteristics; understory vegetation and ground cover; fence lines, non-random trees or herbaceous vegetation; other built environment; soils and soil changes; exposed rocks, nature of stream beds; gullies, steepness of gully sides, lineality of gullies.
    Overall narrative with date, location, weather conditions, crew present, who dug/collected where, number of transects or areas done.
    Positive transects and nature of each.

Specific shovel-test field notes kept by crew and supervisor

    feature inventory
    individual shovel-test records, arranged by transect
    photographic records

Field specimen sheets/bag inventory

CRM PHASE I SHOVEL TEST BAG LABEL

Project or site name _____ Site # _____ Transect number _____

Shovel test number _____ Soil horizon _____

Upper bounds of depth of level below surface ____

Lower bounds of depth of level below surface _____

Date _____ Crew member _____

CRM PHASE II FIELD NOTES AND RECORDS

General project information

    logistics (budget and hour allocations for tasks)
    parts of Phase I report
    project maps and figures
    records of communications
    right-of-entry materials
    scope of work

General field notes kept by supervisor

    Overall narrative with date, location, weather conditions, crew present, who dug/collected where, number of transects or areas done.
    Summary details on test units or on the controlled surface collection.

Specific unit and unit/level notes
Feature records
Other records, inventories, logs, such as mapping and land-survey notes, photo logs, bag inventory, soil or flotation sample inventory.

CRM PHASE II ARTIFACT BAG LABEL

Project or site name _____ Site # _____

Unit/level _____ Provenience _____

Depth below surface _____ Soil horizon (if known) _____

Specimen # _____

Date _____ Crew member _____

CRM PHASE III FIELD NOTES AND RECORDS

Section 1 General project information

scope of work and accompanying correspondence
summation of the data recovery plan and project schedule
logistics, including budget/hour allocations for tasks
parts of Phase I and Phase II reports having a bearing on excavation questions
project maps and figures
permits, clearances, and right-of-entry materials
records of communications

Section 2 General field notes

Overall narrative of project, including environment and day-to-day bookkeeping
summary details on buildings, rooms, units, features, etc. in excavation.

Section 3 Specific excavation records
Section 4 Feature records
Section 5 Mapping and land-survey notes
Section 6 Photo log
Section 7 Bag inventory
Section 8 Soil, matrix, and flotation sample inventory

FORMS AND RECORDS

DAILY FIELD REPORT

Site name _____ Site # _____ Excavator _____ Date _____

Units worked _____

Level: from _____ to _____ depth

Levels worked _____

Features worked _____

Burials worked _____

Summary of artifacts _____

Additional field observations (stratigraphy, associations, evidence of
disturbance) _____

Inference and interpretation (e.g. ecology, technology, social features, other
cultural information) _____

Other work – mapping, photography, survey, catalog _____

Sketch of excavation unit:

DAILY VEHICLE LOG

Odometer start _____ Odometer end _____ Miles traveled _____

Time in _____ Time out _____ Stops _____ Layover time _____

Starting point _____ Destination _____ Operator _____

Fuel gal./cost _____ Oil qt./cost _____

Repairs and parts _____

Vehicle inspection report _____

DATABLE SAMPLE FORM

Site name _____ Site # _____ Site address _____

Material _____

Measurements or weight _____

Type of test(s) to run _____

Unit/level _____ Depth of sample _____

Excavated by _____ Date excavated _____

Removal procedure _____

Field condition and microenvironment _____

Moisture content for thermoluminescence _____

Condition of specimen when packed _____

Packing method and materials _____

Notes _____

Date sent to lab _____

Laboratory name and address _____

Results to be sent to _____

Signed _____ (title)

DEBITAGE FORM (LITHIC)

Site name _____ Site # _____ Unit _____ Level _____
Material _____ Catalog # _____

Classification

Flake Type	Primary	Secondary	Interior	Total	Weight (g)	Notes
complete, early-stage biface thinning						
fragment, early-stage biface thinning						
complete, middle-stage biface thinning						
fragment, middle-stage biface thinning						
complete, late-stage biface thinning						
fragment, late-stage biface thinning						
complete, pressure						
fragment, pressure						
shatter						
nonbiface reduction						
bipolar						
other						

FORMS AND RECORDS

81

DIET EVIDENCE CHART ———

Plant species	Weight of 1 unit of food (g)	x Total items recovered	= Total weight	Rank order	Protein	Fat	Carbohydrate	Fiber

Subtotal: ——

Fish	Weight of 1 unit of food (g)	x 2	= Total weight	Rank order	Protein	Fat	Carbohydrate	Fiber

Meat	Weight of 1 unit of food (g)	x 1	= Total weight	Rank order	Protein	Fat	Carbohydrate	Fiber

Comments: ————————

DRAWINGS CATALOG

Site name _____ Site # _____

Drawing #	Section or Plan #	Unit	Level	Notes

ECOLOGICAL INFORMATION FORM

Site name _____ Site # _____ Recorded by _____ Date _____

Vegetation _____

Fauna _____

Soil _____

Soil type and sample # _____

Physiographic zone _____

Ecological Features _____

Habitats _____

Nearest water _____

Ponds, streams _____

Quarries _____

Wetlands _____

Woodlands _____

Other features _____

Notes _____

EXCAVATION LEVEL FORM

Site name _____ Site # _____ Unit _____ Level _____ Recorder _____ Date _____

Dimensions _____ Provenience _____ Quadrant or other subdivision _____

Elevation datum location _____

Field catalog # _____

Date opened _____ Date closed _____

○ Opening elevations of level:

NW _____ NE _____ SW _____ SE _____ Center _____

Closing elevations of level:

NW _____ NE _____ SW _____ SE _____ Center _____

Excavation method _____ Screening method _____

Soil sample bag numbers _____

Matrix color (Munsell) _____ Matrix texture _____ Matrix structure _____

Wentworth _____

○ Samples collected (type, location) _____

Features (location, description) _____

Disturbance description _____

Volume of matrix/sediment removed _____ pH of matrix/sediment _____

Plan view _____ Profile _____ Drawings _____

Photographs, digital _____ Photographs, other _____

Artifact bag numbers _____

○ Artifacts recovered (type/class, quantity) _____

Artifacts provenienced _____

Artifacts discarded or sampled _____

Level notes (debris other than artifacts, stratigraphy, disturbances, features, etc.)

_____

EXCAVATION RECORD

Operation _____ Unit _____ Level _____
Date _____ / _____ Excavator _____

Horizontal location for first level,
SW corner, N _____ E _____
Unit size _____

Elevation (m below datum)
SW opening _____   SW closing _____
SE opening _____   SE closing _____
NW opening _____   NW closing _____
NE opening _____   NE closing _____

Matrix D/M/W _____
Munsell chart _____ Color name _____
Description _____
_____
_____
_____

Location notes _____
Level above _____   Correlated with _____
Level below _____   Intrusive into _____

# of bags _____
Notable artifacts _____
Features _____
Interpretation _____

Sections _____   Slides _____
Plans _____   B&W _____
Polaroids _____   Digital _____

Scale _____

Notes _____

_____

_____

_____

_____

_____

_____

_____

_____

_____

EXCAVATION SUMMARY
FORM/UNIT SUMMARY FORM

Site name _____ Site # _____ Unit _____ Recorder _____ Date _____
Dimensions (length, width, etc.) _____ Provenience _____ GPS location _____
Elevation datum location _____ Elevation _____ Benchmark tie-in _____
Depth of excavation _____ Number of strata excavated _____
Number of levels excavated _____
Number of plan views _____ Number of profiles _____
Photographs _____
Feature types and numbers assigned _____
Dates opened _____ Dates closed _____
Field catalog numbers _____
Excavators _____ Field supervisor _____

Stratum	Level	Artifact frequency	Diagnostic artifacts	Diagnostic ecofacts	Feature numbers

Samples for dating (type and provenience) _____
Recovery method _____
Stratification _____
Notes on methodology, disturbances, interpretations, recommendations _____
Field notes cross-references _____

1. Draw a plan map of your excavation unit on the grid provided (be sure to include a scale and a north arrow). Put in beginning elevation and ending elevation for each corner. (See Participant Note Form in this chapter.)
2. What research question(s) were you trying to answer by excavating this unit?
3. Did you excavate in natural strata or arbitrary levels and why? What tools did you use and why?
4. Describe the fill/matrix in your excavation unit. Color _____ Texture _____ Inclusions _____
5. What types of artifacts and samples did you collect? Were they naturally or culturally deposited?
6. On the basis of the information recorded above, what activities do you think took place in your unit?

FAUNAL ATTRIBUTE RECORD

Site name _____ Site # _____ Storage container _____ Recorder _____ Date _____

Lot	Quantity	Taxon	Element	Portion of element	Side	Age criteria	Age breakage	Burning	Gnawing	Cut	Notes

FEATURE CATALOG

 THE CROW CANYON ARCHAEOLOGICAL CENTER

FEATURE CATALOG

Site Number _____ Study Unit _____

Site Name _____ *Revised 2/2001*

NO.	FEATURE TYPE / DESCRIPTION	PD	EXCAVATED	MAPPED	RECORDED	PHOTOS

FEATURE FORM

FEATURE FORM

Site Number _____   Site Name _____ Revised 2/2001

Initials_____   Date _____

Study Unit Type & Number _____   Feature Type _____   Feature No _____

Study Unit Horizontal _____   Study Unit Vertical_____

PD TABLE

PD	FEATURE HORIZONTAL	FEATURE VERTICAL

	DIMENSIONS (ACTUAL)	COMPLETE?	DIMENSIONS (INFERRED)	COMMENTS
LENGTH				
WIDTH				
HEIGHT				
DEPTH				

Excavation/Sampling Strategy Description
Excavation Procedure:

Portion excavated:

Feature Description
General description:

Degree of preservation: Excellent ☐   Good ☐   Poor ☐
Cause and amount of deterioration:

Actual shape in plan view _____   Actual shape in cross section_____

Inferred shape in plan view _____   Inferred shape in cross section_____

FORMS AND RECORDS

91

FEATURE FORM

Site Number _____   Study Unit Type & Number _____

Feature Type _____   Feature Number _____

Horizontal Location:

Vertical Location:

Description of How Feature Was Constructed:

Thermal Alteration: Yes ☐   No ☐ _____

Sooting: Yes ☐   No ☐ _____

Description of Modification/Remodeling: Yes ☐   No ☐ _____

_____

_____

Sealed?   Yes ☐   No ☐ _____

FILL TABLE

STRAT. #	COLOR	TEXTURE	INCLUSIONS	DISTURBANCE	INTERPRETATION

Artifacts and Samples Recovered:

Interpretations
  Use history:

  Associated features:

FEATURE LEVEL FORM

Site name _____ Site # _____ Feature # _____ Recorder _____ Date _____
Unit _____ Level _____ Other provenience _____ Excavator _____
Type of feature _____ Percent of feature exposed _____
Shape of feature _____ Top of feature encountered in (stratum, level) _____
Feature dimensions, length _____ width _____ diameter _____
Elevation datum location _____ Elevation of top of feature _____
Converted? _____
Feature level designation _____ Type of level (entire feature, arbitrary, natural) _____
Field catalog # _____

Date opened _____ Date closed _____
Opening elevations of level:
NW _____ NE _____ SW _____ SE _____ Center _____
Closing elevations of level:
NW _____ NE _____ SW _____ SE _____ Center _____
Converted? _____
Cross-section (yes/no, axis, description) _____
Bi-section (yes/no, axis, description) _____
Quarter-section (yes/no, axis, description) _____

Excavation method _____ Screening method _____

Soil sample bag numbers _____
Matrix color (Munsell) _____ Matrix texture _____ Matrix structure _____
Wentworth _____

Samples collected (type, location) _____

Plan view _____ Profile _____ Drawings _____
Photographs, digital _____ Photographs, other _____

Artifact bag numbers _____
Artifacts recovered (type/class, quantity) _____
Artifacts provenienced _____
Artifacts discarded or sampled _____

Notes _____

FEATURE RECORD LOG

Site name _____

Operation	Excavation unit	Feature designation	MCU	Level	Lot	Feature record completed?	Excavator	Date	

FEATURE SUMMARY
FORM/FEATURE RECORD (1)

Site name _____ Site # _____ Feature # _____ Recorder _____ Date _____
Unit _____ Level _____ Provenience of feature _____
Location from the _____ corner of excavation unit _____ to the _____ of the
feature, the distances are _____.
Type of feature _____ Percent of feature exposed _____
Shape of feature _____
Top of feature encountered in (stratum, level) _____
Base of feature in (stratum, level) _____
Number of levels excavated _____ Type of levels (entire feature, arbitrary,
natural) _____
Strata, levels, and other features cut by feature _____
Elevation datum location _____
Vertical (below datum to top of feature) _____ Converted? _____
Vertical (below datum to bottom of feature) _____ Converted? _____
Horizontal (distance of center point of feature from N and W walls) _____
Depth from surface _____
Feature dimensions, length _____ width _____ diameter _____ depth _____
Feature orientation _____
Feature shape horizontal _____ Feature shape vertical _____
Field catalog numbers _____
Dates opened _____ Dates closed _____
Excavators _____ Field supervisor _____

Plan views _____ Cross-sections _____ Profiles _____
Photograph numbers _____

Description of feature (matrix – color, texture, variations; contents; disturbances;
stratification) _____
Artifacts recovered within feature _____
Ecofacts recovered macroscopically _____
Associated debris _____
Description of artifact/feature associations (any and all clusterings of artifacts
and/or features, giving dimensions, distances, spatial relationships, types of
artifacts and/or features) _____

Samples for dating (type and provenience) _____
Other samples collected _____
Field notes cross-references _____
Interpretations, inferences, and comments _____

FEATURE SUMMARY
FORM/FEATURE RECORD (2)

_____   _____

Site name _____   Feature # _____

Excavator _____   Date _____ MCU _____

Excavation unit _____   Level _____ Lot _____

Feature type: hearth _____   Earth even _____

              pit _____   roasting platform _____

              postmold _____   burial _____

              cache _____   workshop _____

              other _____

_____

_____

_____

Depth feature first recognized   _____ cm below datum

                                        _____ cm below surface

Depth of feature bottom   _____ cm below datum

                                        _____ cm below surface

Artifacts recovered within feature _____

_____

_____

Ecofacts recovered macroscopically _____

_____

_____

Briefly describe the feature _____

_____

_____

_____

_____

(Over)

Feature plan drawing: Draw a detailed, accurate and complete plan of your square and the feature located.

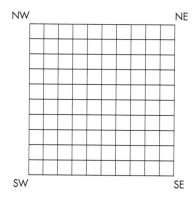

NW

NE

SW

SE

Draw a detailed and accurate cross section of the feature.

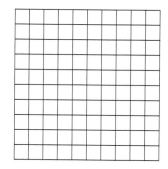

Photo # _____

FIELD LABORATORY LOG

Site name _____ Site # _____ Recorder _____ Date _____

Artifact _____ Material _____ Catalog # _____

Unit/level _____ Provenience _____

Dimensions of artifact _____

○ Field condition before treatment _____ Treatment in situ _____

Date excavated _____ Excavator _____

Drawings _____

Photographs _____

Field notebook cross-references _____

Natural processes affecting artifact (accident, air, algae, biological growth, dampness, dirt, dust, fog, frost, fungi, heat, insects, mildew, other, sunlight, vegetation, water, wind) _____

○ Human process affecting artifact (neglect, other, vandalism) _____

Micro-environment description _____

Weather conditions _____

Excavation method _____ Cleaning method _____ Field conservation method _____

Restoration method _____

Cleaning agents _____ Chemicals _____

○ Adhesives _____ Sealants _____

Packing method _____

Disposal _____

FIELD INVENTORY FORM

 THE CROW CANYON ARCHAEOLOGICAL CENTER

FIELD INVENTORY FORM

Site Number _____   Site Name _____   *Revised 2/2001*

Inventory Date _____   Prepared by _____ Page ____ of ____

Check-in Date _____   Checked in by _____

REC'D	PD	BAG DATE	CONTENTS

FORMS AND RECORDS

FIELD NOTEBOOK SYSTEM

The notebooks for the project should have a standard cover with:

site name, site number
plot or area excavation
units
year
excavator's name

All field notebooks should have page numbers so they can be used as cross-references to other records.

A separate page should be used for each day. A separate page should be used for each new level.

Measurements should be recorded as soon as they are taken.

Each day, record: date, location, weather, field conditions, people you are working with, unit and beginning level, activities performed and methods used, results of activities, interpretation of results and relevance to research design, notes on further/recommended action, bag numbers, and time you were in the field. The basic set of forms is: site report, daily field report, feature level form, feature summary form, stratigraphy record, photography log, drawings log, burial record, excavation level form, excavation summary form, and artifact bag inventory.

All field forms and field notebooks should be filled out in the field!

FIGURINE RECORD

Site name _____ Site # _____ Unit _____ Level _____ Date excavated _____

Other provenience _____ Depth _____

Type of figurine _____ Material _____ Position _____

Description _____

Munsell color (exterior, interior, core) _____

Decoration _____ Placement of design _____

Design traits _____ Munsell color of decoration _____

Measurements

Profile part   Front   Back

Front view part   Vertical

Front view part   Horizontal

Profile drawings _____ Plan drawings _____

Photographs _____

Disposal _____

Notes _____

GARBAGE PROJECT FORM

Item type	Item code	Number of items	Brand name	Package composition	Code	Weight (g)

FORMS AND RECORDS

GIFT FORM

I (donor) _____, of (address) _____ do hereby give to (name of excavation) _____, the sum of (dollars) _____ to be used solely and entirely in the furtherance of the scholarly research being conducted by (project name/organization) _____ under the direction of (director) _____.

Signature of donor _____

Date _____

All donations are tax-deductible and should be sent to _____ and a copy confirming the donation will be sent to _____.

Site name _____ Site # _____

GRAIN SIZE ANALYSIS FORM

Site name _____ Operation _____

Unit _____ Level _____ Lot _____ MCU _____ Feature _____

Material/description _____

Excavator _____ Date excavated _____

Processed by _____ Date processed _____

Scale: Ohaus/Sartorius/Other   Beginning sediment weight (g) _____

Sieve #	Mesh (mm)	Grain size (mm)	Empty pan & sieve (g)	Mass (g)	Net mass (g)
6	3.0	> 3.0			
20	1.0	1.0–3.0			
40	0.5	0.5–1.0			
100	0.25	0.25–0.5			
Pan	–	< 0.25			

HISTORICAL RESOURCES INVENTORY

HISTORIC RESOURCES INVENTORY
HISTORIC ARCHAEOLOGICAL SITES
HIST-5 NEW 9/77

STATE OF CONNECTICUT
CONNECTICUT HISTORICAL COMMISSION
59 SOUTH PROSPECT STREET, HARTFORD, CONNECTICUT, 06106

FOR OFFICE USE ONLY	
Town No. :	Site No. :

UTM

QUAD:

NR: ☐ ACT ☐ ELIG. ☐ NO   DISTRICT ☐ Yes

SR: ☐ ACT ☐ ELIG. ☐ NO   ☐ No

STATE SITE NO.   CAS. NO.

IDENTIFICATION

1. SITE NAME

2. TOWN/CITY   VILLAGE   COUNTY

3. STREET AND NUMBER (and/or location)

4. OWNER(S)
☐ Public   ☐ Private

5. ATTITUDE TOWARD EXCAVATION

6. USE (Present)   (Historic)

DESCRIPTION

7A. PERIOD
☐ Contact ☐ 17th C. ☐ 18th C. ☐ 19th C. ☐ 20th C. ☐ Unknown ☐ Other (Specify)
7B. ESTIMATED OCCUPATION RANGE

8. DATING METHOD | DOCUMENTS | COMPARATIVE MATERIALS | OTHER

9. SITE TYPE
☐ Contact   ☐ Commercial   ☐ Rural   ☐ Other (Specify)
☐ Agrarian   ☐ Industrial   ☐ Urban   ☐ Unknown
10. APPROXIMATE SIZE AND BOUNDARIES

11. STRATIGRAPHY
☐ No Visible evidence ☐ Standing ruins ☐ Stratified ☐ Not stratified ☐ Other (Specify)
☐ Surface finds ☐ Cellar hole ☐ Plowed ☐ Major Disturbance

ENVIRONMENT

12. SOIL | USDA SOIL SERIES | CONTOUR ELEVATION | SLOPE %
☐ 0-5 ☐ 5-15 ☐ 15-25 ☐ over 25
TEXTURE | OTHER (Specify) | ACIDITY
☐ sand ☐ clay ☐ Silt | ☐ less than 4.5 ☐ 4.5-5.5 ☐ 5.6-6.5 ☐ 6.6-7.3 ☐ 7.4-8.4
13. WATER | NEAREST WATER SOURCE | SIZE AND SPEED | DISTANCE FROM SITE | SEASONABLE AVAILABILITY
14. VEGETATION | PRESENT | PAST

CONDITION

15. SITE INTEGRITY
☐ Undisturbed   ☐ Good   ☐ Fair   ☐ Destroyed
16. THREATS TO SITE
☐ None known   ☐ Highways ☐ Vandalism   ☐ Developers ☐ Other (Specify)
☐ Renewal   ☐ Private   ☐ Deterioration ☐ Zoning   ☐ Unknown
17. SURROUNDING ENVIRONMENT
☐ Open Land   ☐ Woodland   ☐ Residential ☐ Scattered Buildings visible from site.
☐ Commercial   ☐ Industrial ☐ Rural   ☐ High building density
☐ Coastal   ☐ Isolated
18. ACCESSIBILITY TO PUBLIC-VISIBLE FROM PUBLIC ROAD
☐ Yes   ☐ No

(OVER)

RESEARCH POTENTIAL

19. PREVIOUS EXCAVATIONS	BY WHOM/AFFILIATION	DATE
☐ Surface Collected		
☐ "Pot hunted"	BY WHOM/AFFILIATION	DATE
☐ Tested	BY WHOM/AFFILIATION	DATE
☐ Excavation	BY WHOM/AFFILIATION	DATE

20. PRESENT LOCATION OF MATERIALS

21. PUBLISHED REFERENCES

22. RECOVERED DATA (Identify IN DETAIL, including structures, related outbuildings, landscape features, etc.)

SIGNIFICANCE

23. ARCHAEOLOGICAL OR HISTORICAL IMPORTANCE

PHOTOGRAPH

PHOTOGRAPHER

DATE

VIEW

NEGATIVE ON FILE

Place
35mm contact print
here

ADD'L INFORMATION

REPORTED BY:

NAME	ADDRESS	
ORGANIZATION		DATE

FOR OFFICE USE ONLY

FIELD EVALUATION

COMMENTS

106

HISTORIC RESOURCES INVENTORY
PREHISTORIC ARCHAEOLOGICAL SITES
HIST-7 NEW 9/77

STATE OF CONNECTICUT
CONNECTICUT HISTORICAL COMMISSION
59 SOUTH PROSPECT STREET, HARTFORD, CONNECTICUT, 06106

FOR OFFICE USE ONLY	
Town No. :	Site No. :

UTM : | | | | | | | | | | | |
QUAD:

NR: ☐ ACT ☐ ELIG. ☐ NO ☐ Yes (DISTRICT)
SR: ☐ ACT ☐ ELIG. ☐ NO ☐ No

STATE SITE NO.   CAS. NO.

IDENTIFICATION

1. SITE NAME

2. TOWN/CITY   VILLAGE   COUNTY

3. STREET AND NUMBER (and/or location)

4. OWNER(S)
☐ Public   ☐ Private

5. ATTITUDE TOWARD EXCAVATION

6. USE (Present)   (Historic)

DESCRIPTION

7. PERIOD
☐ Paleo   ☐ Early Archaic   ☐ Early Woodland   ☐ Contact
☐ Middle Archaic   ☐ Middle Woodland   ☐ Unknown
☐ Late Archaic   ☐ Late Woodland   ☐ Other (Specify)

8. DATING METHOD
C-14
COMPARATIVE MATERIALS
☐ Intuition   ☐ Other (Specify)

9. SITE TYPE
☐ Quarry   ☐ Camp   ☐ Rockshelter   ☐ Shell Midden   ☐ Cemetery   ☐ Village   ☐ OTHER (Specify)

10. APPROXIMATE SIZE AND BOUNDARIES

ENVIRONMENT

11. STRATIGRAPHY
☐ Surface finds   ☐ Plowed   ☐ Not stratified   ☐ Stratified   ☐ Major Disturbance   ☐ OTHER (Specify)

12. SOIL
USDA SOIL SERIES   CONTOUR ELEVATION   SLOPE %
☐ 0–5   ☐ 5–15   ☐ 15–25   ☐ over 25
TEXTURE   OTHER (Specify)   ACIDITY
☐ sand   ☐ clay   ☐ Silt   ☐ less than 4.5   ☐ 4.5-5.5   ☐ 5.6-6.5   ☐ 6.6-7.3   ☐ 7.4-8.4

13. WATER
NEAREST WATER SOURCE   SIZE AND SPEED   DISTANCE FROM SITE | SEASONABLE AVAILABILITY

14. VEGETATION
PRESENT   PAST

CONDITION

15. SITE INTEGRITY
☐ Undisturbed   ☐ Good   ☐ Fair   ☐ Destroyed

16. THREATS TO SITE
☐ None known   ☐ Highways   ☐ Vandalism   ☐ Developers   ☐ Other (Specify)
☐ Renewal   ☐ Private   ☐ Deterioration   ☐ Zoning   ☐ Unknown

17. SURROUNDING ENVIRONMENT
☐ Open Land   ☐ Woodland   ☐ Residential   ☐ Scattered Buildings visible from site.
☐ Commercial   ☐ Industrial   ☐ Rural   ☐ High building density
☐ Coastal   ☐ Isolated

18. ACCESSIBILITY TO PUBLIC-VISIBLE FROM PUBLIC ROAD
☐ Yes   ☐ No

(OVER)

RESEARCH POTENTIAL

19. PREVIOUS EXCAVATIONS	BY WHOM/AFFILIATION	DATE
☐ Surface Collected		
☐ "Pot hunted"	BY WHOM/AFFILIATION	DATE
☐ Tested	BY WHOM/AFFILIATION	DATE
☐ Excavation	BY WHOM/AFFILIATION	DATE

20. PRESENT LOCATION OF MATERIALS

21. PUBLISHED REFERENCES

22. RECOVERED DATA (Identify in DETAIL, incl. features, burials, faunal material, etc.)

SIGNIFICANCE

23. ARCHAEOLOGICAL OR HISTORICAL IMPORTANCE

PHOTOGRAPH

PHOTOGRAPHER

DATE

VIEW

NEGATIVE ON FILE

Place
35mm contact print
here

ADD'L INFORMATION

REPORTED BY:

NAME	ADDRESS	
ORGANIZATION		DATE

FOR OFFICE USE ONLY

FIELD EVALUATION

COMMENTS

Historic Resources Inventory
Submerged Archaeological Sites

State of Connecticut
Connecticut Historical Commission
59 South Prospect Street, Hartford, CT 06106

Identification

1. Site Name   Vessel Name (if different from Site Name)   Date of Loss

2. Body of Water Site Is In   Town/City (site is in or nearest to)   Closest Landmark

3. Coordinates (G.P.S. position, Compass Bearings, or other information sufficient to relocate site)

4. Owners (if not the State of CT)

☐ Public   ☐ Private

5. Attitude Toward Excavation

Description

6. Site Type
☐ Shipwreck   ☐ Airplane   ☐ Other(specify)

7. Dating Method
☐ Documentation   ☐ Other (specify)
☐ Comparative Materials (artifacts)

8. Vessel Description   Type_____   Length____   Beam____   Where Built_____

Date Built_____   Builder_____   Origin_____   Destination_____

Net Tonnage_____   Gross Tonnage_____   Port of Registry_____

Construction Method_____

9. Approximate Size of Site

10. Visibility of Site
☐ Fully Exposed   ☐ Sand Cover   ☐ Partially Embedded   ☐ Fully Embedded   ☐ Other(specify)

Environment

11. Type of Submerged Land
☐ Reef   ☐ Clay   ☐ Silt   ☐ Sand   ☐ Other Surface (specify)

12. Water Conditions   Depth of Site   Currents

Condition

13. Site Integrity
☐ Undisturbed   ☐ Good   ☐ Fair   ☐ Major Disturbance

14. Threats to Site
☐ None Known   ☐ Deterioration   ☐ Vandalism   ☐ Commercial Salvage

☐ Recreational Salvage   ☐ Fishing   ☐ Shipping   ☐ Development

☐ Other (specify)

FORMS AND RECORDS

15. Previous Excavations	By Whom/Affiliation	Date
☐ Surface Collected		
☐ "Pot Hunted"		
☐ Tested		
☐ Controlled Excavation		

Research Potential

20. Present Location of Materials

21. Published References

Significance

22. Recovered Data (Identify in DETAIL)

23. Archaeological or Historical Importance

Photograph

Photographer	Date	Place
View		35mm contact print
Negative on File		here

Reported By

Name	Address	
Organization		Date Site was Located

Other people associated with discovery

Safety Concerns for Divers (Condition of Site, Depth, Currents, etc.)

Comments   **For Office Use Only**

HUMAN REMAINS OCCURRENCE FORM

THE CROW CANYON ARCHAEOLOGICAL CENTER

HUMAN REMAINS OCCURRENCE FORM

Site Number _____ Site Name _____ *Revised 2/2001*
Page 1 of 2
Initials_____ Date _____

Study Unit Type and Number _____

Feature Number _____ HRO Number _____ PD(s) _____

General description _____
_____

Location _____

HRO type: formal burial ☐   body articulated but not formally interred ☐

   concentration of disarticulated remains ☐   scattered remains ☐   other ☐

Condition of feature _____

Preservation of bone _____

Type: extended ☐   semiflexed ☐   flexed ☐   other ☐   N/A ☐

Position of body: on back ☐   on stomach ☐   on side ☐   other ☐   N/A ☐

Body oriented _____ head to _____ facing_____ other _____

Position of arms and legs: right arm _____ left arm _____

                 right leg _____ left leg _____

Description and interpretation of sediment that remains are in _____
_____

Are remains within a pit? Yes ☐ No ☐ If yes, feature number of pit _____ PD number of pit _____

Describe process or method of interment _____
_____

Describe all observed stones, burned material, or other agents that could have damaged or affected bones
_____

Evidence of animal burrows? Yes ☐ No ☐ What areas of body? _____

Associated funerary artifacts/samples:

DESCRIPTION	LOCATION	PD	PL	COLLECTED? Y/N

In-field analysis ☐   or   **Remains taken to lab** ☐

Map complete? Yes ☐ No ☐   **Photos taken?** Yes ☐ No ☐   **PL catalog complete?** Yes ☐ No ☐

FORMS AND RECORDS

HUMAN REMAINS OCCURRENCE FORM

Site Number _____ Site Name _____

Feature Number _____ HRO Number _____

Comments/Discussion:

_____
_____
_____
_____
_____
_____
_____
_____
_____
_____
_____
_____
_____
_____
_____
_____
_____
_____
_____
_____
_____
_____
_____
_____
_____
_____
_____
_____
_____
_____

FORMS AND RECORDS

LEVEL BAG INVENTORY

Site name _____ Site # _____ Recorder _____ Date _____

Bag #	Unit	Level	Description	Excavator	Date

FORMS AND RECORDS

─────────── **LEVEL LABEL/TAG** ───────────

Site name _____ Site # _____

Catalog # _____ Bag # _____ (of #)

Unit _____ Level _____ Provenience _____

Datum _____ Depth _____

Features, associations _____

Description of level _____

Excavator _____ Date _____

LEVEL LOG/MASTER UNIT LOG

Site name _____

Operation	Excavation unit	Other designation	Excavator	Level	Date	SW x/y/z	SE x/y/z	NW x/y/z	NE x/y/z

MASONRY FORM

THE CROW CANYON ARCHAEOLOGICAL CENTER

MASONRY FORM

Revised 2/2001
Page 1 of 2

Site Number _____   Site Name _____

Initials _____   Date _____

Study Unit Type and Number _____

Feature Type _____   Feature Number _____

Wall Type (check one): room ☐   kiva bench face ☐   kiva upper lining wall ☐   kiva cell wall ☐

tower ☐   extramural wall (describe) _____

coursed masonry deflector ☐   other wall (describe) _____

Cardinal direction of wall (circle one):   N   S   E   W   NW   NE   SE   SW   N/A

Comments _____

For the above-listed structure, this is an interior ☐ exterior ☐   **face (check one)**

Features in this wall _____

Length of wall exposed (top) _____   Length of wall exposed (bottom) _____

Height (max.) _____   Height (min.) _____   Thickness (top) _____

Number of vertical courses (max.) _____   Number of vertical courses (min.) _____

Complete? (Y/N) _____   If "no," inferred original height _____

Comments _____

Corner abutment:

This wall is **abutted to** the   N   S   E   W   NW   NE   SE   SW   wall.

This wall is **abutted by** the   N   S   E   W   NW   NE   SE   SW   wall.

This wall is **tied to** the   N   S   E   W   NW   NE   SE   SW   wall.

Cannot assess ☐   Comments _____

Shaping: pecked: 0 ☐   < 30% ☐   30–75% ☐   > 75% ☐

ground: 0 ☐   < 30% ☐   30–75% ☐   > 75% ☐

flaked: 0 ☐   < 30% ☐   30–75% ☐   > 75% ☐

unshaped: 0 ☐   < 30% ☐   30–75% ☐   > 75% ☐

other (describe) _____

Comments _____

Shapes: block: 0 ☐   < 30% ☐   30–75% ☐   > 75% ☐

tabular: 0 ☐   < 30% ☐   30–75% ☐   > 75% ☐

irregular: 0 ☐   < 30% ☐   30–75% ☐   > 75% ☐

other (describe) _____

Comments _____

Site Number _____   Site Name _____

Study Unit Type and Number _____

Feature Type_____   Feature Number _____

Basal stones: blocks ☐   other (describe) _____   not visible ☐

Footings: rubble ☐   other (describe) _____   not visible ☐

Foundation: bedrock ☐   fill ☐   undisturbed natural ☐   other ☐   not visible ☐

Chinking: tabular ☐   chunk ☐   spall ☐   other _____

Mortar: size of horizontal beds   _____ cm thick maximum

           size of vertical beds   _____ cm wide maximum

           form: flush ☐   extruded ☐   concave ☐

           texture: fine ☐   medium ☐   coarse ☐

           color _____

           inclusions _____

           Comments _____

Plaster (% of face) _____   Description _____

_____

Wall construction materials: sandstone ☐   other _____

Coursing: uncoursed ☐   semicoursed ☐   fully coursed ☐   patterned ☐

           vertical slab ☐   other _____

Comments _____

Cross section: single stone ☐   double stone ☐   compound ☐   double/core ☐

           compound/core ☐   double bonded ☐   other _____

           cannot assess (explain below) ☐

Comments _____

_____

_____

FORMS AND RECORDS

MINIMUM COLLECTION UNIT (MCU) LOG

MCU	Operation	Unit	Level	Lot	Feature	Date	Description

FORMS AND RECORDS

ORAL HISTORY FORM

I hereby give and grant permission for the described versions of my storytelling materials to be used by _____ for such scholarly and educational purposes as shall be determined under the discretion of the Director of the aforementioned Program. As such, full literary rights to these materials are granted to the program for scholarly pursuits.

Project Title

_____

Description of Materials

_____
_____
_____
_____

Title(s) (if any) _____

Medium

___ Transcript ___ Sound Recording

___ Video Recording ___ Illustration

___ Other (Describe _____)

Signed _____

Date _____

Permanent Address and Phone of Signer

_____
_____
_____
_____
_____

PARTICIPANT NOTE FORM

THE CROW CANYON ARCHAEOLOGICAL CENTER

PARTICIPANT NOTE FORM

Revised 4/2005

Site Number _____   Site Name _____

Study Unit _____   PD Number _____

Horizontal Sub. _____   Vertical Sub. _____

Date _____ Supervisor _____   Excavator _____

Excavator _____   Excavator _____

1. Draw a plan map of your excavation unit on the back of this page (be sure to include a scale and a north arrow).

2. What reserach question(s) were you trying to answer by excavating this unit?

3. Did you excavate in natural strata or arbitrary levels, and why? What tools did you use (shovel, trowel, pick, brush, dental pick, etc.), and why?

4. Describe the fill (dirt) in your excavation unit.

    Color:

    Texture (silt, clay, sand, or some combination):

    Inclusions (rocks, charcoal, roots, etc.):

5. What types of artifacts and samples did you collect? Were they naturally or culturally deposited?

6. On the basis of the information recorded above, what activities do you think took place in the area you are working in?

FORMS AND RECORDS

PARTICIPANT NOTE FORM

Draw a plan map (looking down) of your excavation unit.
Be sure to include the coordinates, a key, and a scale.

Beginning elevation _____   Beginning elevation _____
Ending elevation _____   Ending elevation _____

Beginning elevation _____   Beginning elevation _____
Ending elevation _____   Ending elevation _____

FORMS AND RECORDS

PERISHABLES RECORD

Site name _____ Site # _____

Perishable item _____

Measurements (length, width, thickness, diameter, capacity) _____

Decoration (size, shape, color, etc.) _____

Residues or adhering materials _____

PHOTOGRAPHIC LOG

Site name _____ Site # _____
Camera type _____ Film type _____ ASA/ISO _____ Roll designation _____

Photo #	Negative #	Camera	Photographer	Date	Unit	Level	Feature	Subject	Direction facing	Notes

(could also include or note: lens or filter used, shutter speed, f stop, time picture was taken)

PHOTOGRAPHIC LOG, DIGITAL

Site name ____

Operation	Date	Photo #	Digital frame #	Facing	Unit	Description

PHOTOGRAPHIC LOG, POLAROID

Site name ____

Operation	Date	Print #	Facing	Unit	Description

FORMS AND RECORDS

PHOTOGRAPHIC RECORD FORM

THE CROW CANYON ARCHAEOLOGICAL CENTER

PHOTOGRAPHIC RECORD FORM   Roll No. _____

Camera No. _____ Film Type _____ ASA _____ Project _____ Page _____ of _____ *Revised 2/2001*

EXPOSURE # / DATE / INITIALS	SITE NUMBER	DESCRIPTION
		SU: SU Horiz: SU Vert: Feat. Type: Feat. No: View: Direction: Comments: People? K A
		SU: SU Horiz: SU Vert: Feat. Type: Feat. No: View: Direction: Comments: People? K A
		SU: SU Horiz: SU Vert: Feat. Type: Feat. No: View: Direction: Comments: People? K A
		SU: SU Horiz: SU Vert: Feat. Type: Feat. No: View: Direction: Comments: People? K A
		SU: SU Horiz: SU Vert: Feat. Type: Feat. No: View: Direction: Comments: People? K A
		SU: SU Horiz: SU Vert: Feat. Type: Feat. No: View: Direction: Comments: People? K A

View choices:

Plan view
Plan view, before excavation
Plan view, excavation in progress
Plan view, feature
Plan view, feature before excavation

Plan view, PLs
Plan view, structure floor with assemblage
Plan view, final excavation photo
Face view, architecture
Profile view, feature

Profile view, stratigraphy
Field crew photo
Scenic photo
Other
K=kids; A=adults

FORMS AND RECORDS

POINT LOCATION CATALOG

 THE CROW CANYON ARCHAEOLOGICAL CENTER

POINT LOCATION CATALOG

Site Number _____ Site Name _____ *Revised 2/2001*

Study Unit _____ Vertical _____

PL	PD	DESCRIPTION	ELEVATION	COMMENTS	DATE

FORMS AND RECORDS

FORMS AND RECORDS

POLLEN COUNT RECORD

Site name _____ Site # _____ Recorder _____ Date _____

Grain type	Total grains	Conversion value	×	Number of grains	Conversion grains	% of total

Total grains _____ Total _____
Interpretation of pollen findings _____

Pollen Conversion Index
elm, spruce = multiply by 1.75
oak = multiply by 0.44
alder, birch, pine = multiply by 0.55
ash, beech, fir = multiply by 1.00
basswood/lime, maple, willow = multiply by 2.00

PROVENIENCE DESIGNATION CATALOG

THE CROW CANYON ARCHAEOLOGICAL CENTER

PROVENIENCE DESIGNATION CATALOG

Site Number _____ Site Name _____ *Revised 2/2001*

PD	DESCRIPTION	FORM	NAME/DATE
○	SU Hor.　　　　　Vert. Feat. #　　　　Type Hor.　　　　　Vert.		
	SU Hor.　　　　　Vert. Feat. #　　　　Type Hor.　　　　　Vert.		
	SU Hor.　　　　　Vert. Feat. #　　　　Type Hor.　　　　　Vert.		
	SU Hor.　　　　　Vert. Feat. #　　　　Type Hor.　　　　　Vert.		
○	SU Hor.　　　　　Vert. Feat. #　　　　Type Hor.　　　　　Vert.		
	SU Hor.　　　　　Vert. Feat. #　　　　Type Hor.　　　　　Vert.		
	SU Hor.　　　　　Vert. Feat. #　　　　Type Hor.　　　　　Vert.		
	SU Hor.　　　　　Vert. Feat. #　　　　Type Hor.　　　　　Vert.		
	SU Hor.　　　　　Vert. Feat. #　　　　Type Hor.　　　　　Vert.		
○	SU Hor.　　　　　Vert. Feat. #　　　　Type Hor.　　　　　Vert.		

PROVENIENCE DESIGNATION FORM

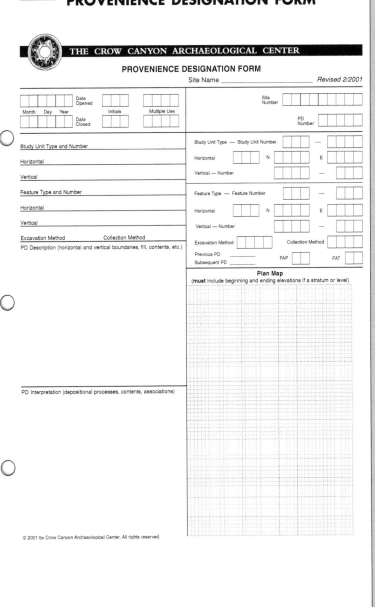

THE CROW CANYON ARCHAEOLOGICAL CENTER

PROVENIENCE DESIGNATION FORM

Site Name _____ *Revised 2/2001*

Date Opened

Month   Day   Year   Initials   Multiple Use

Date Closed

Site Number

PD Number

Study Unit Type and Number

Horizontal

Vertical

Feature Type and Number

Horizontal

Vertical

Excavation Method   Collection Method

PD Description (horizontal and vertical boundaries, fill, contents, etc.)

Study Unit Type — Study Unit Number —

Horizontal   N   E

Vertical — Number —

Feature Type — Feature Number —

Horizontal   N   E

Vertical — Number —

Excavation Method   Collection Method

Previous PD _____ FAP

Subsequent PD _____ FAT

Plan Map
(**must** include beginning and ending elevations if a stratum or level)

PD Interpretation (depositional processes, contents, associations)

FORMS AND RECORDS

ROCK ART RECORD

Site name _____ Site # _____ Recorder _____ Date _____
Location/coordinates _____
Location type (cave, rock shelter, open-air rock, boulder, other) _____
Site description _____
Elevation _____ Total size of decorated area _____
Number of decorated faces _____
Archaeological remains _____ Associated cultural remains _____

Prevailing site exposure (N, S, E, W) _____
Slope (horizontal, oblique, steep, vertical) _____
Prevailing topography (mountainous, hilly, flat, other) _____
Landform at site (hilltop, valley, ridge, saddle, other) _____
Prevailing rock (igneous, sedimentary, metamorphic) _____
Type of rock (sandstone, limestone, schist, granite, conglomerate, etc) _____
Surface type (smooth, smooth with local fractures, rough, very rough, etc) _____

Production technique/art type (petroglyphs, pictographs, high/low reliefs, other) _____
Prevailing technique _____
Color (monochrome, bichrome, polychrome) _____
Prevailing color (Munsell) _____
Number of figures at site (counted, estimated) _____
Description of rock art _____
Estimated date (absolute, relative) _____ Methods used to date _____

Typology (also note clear figures or traces)
Anthropomorphic _____ Zoomorphic _____
Structures/enclosures/topographic _____
Tools/weapons/objects _____ Geometric motifs/symbols _____
Writing/other signs _____ Undefined _____
Total _____

Preservation _____ Condition _____ Agents of deterioration _____
Geophysical effects _____ Physio-chemical effects _____
Physio-biochemical effects _____ Human effects _____ Animal effects _____
Conservation actions taken and to be taken _____

Classification suggested (local/regional/national/World Heritage) _____
Cultural promotion actions taken and to be taken _____
Tourism access _____
Existing facilities _____
Recommendations _____
Documentation (maps, drawings, photos, etc) _____
Bibliography _____
Notes _____

SAMPLE BAG LABEL/TAG

Site name _____ Site # _____ Date _____

Unit _____ Level _____ Provenience _____

Sample # _____ Excavator _____

SITE RECORD/SITE REPORT/SITE INVENTORY/SITE SURVEY REPORT

Site name _____ Site # _____ Survey # _____ Recorder _____ Date _____
Site identifier(s) _____ Site address _____
Survey parcel legal description _____
Present owner _____ Address of owner _____ Phone _____
Occupant or tenant _____ Phone _____ Present use of site _____
Instructions for reaching site _____ Attitude toward excavation _____
Date constructed or occupation period _____
Previous owners, if known _____ Previous use of site _____
Modifications, if known _____
Dimensions of site _____ Visibility from public road _____ Accessible? _____
Map references: USGS _____ UTM _____ Natl Grid Ref _____ Other _____
Historic map references _____
Existing photographs _____
Published references to site _____
Persons with memory of site _____
Previous excavations _____ Present location of collections _____

Ecological zone _____ Climate _____ Vegetation _____
Altitude above mean sea level _____
Geology (soil, etc) _____ Geomorphology (erosion, etc) _____
Period of site _____ Dating method _____ Comparative materials _____

Site description	
Location/grounds	**Site integrity**
flood plain	destroyed
never cultivated	major disturbance
pastureland	minor disturbance
previously cultivated	redeposited
sustaining erosion	undisturbed
under cultivation	vandalism
upland	
wetland	
woodland	

Site type	
(check all appropriate categories) burial buried evidence camp/temporary stop cave/rock shelter cemetery cremation dump/refuse exposed features farmstead fort habitat/homestead intact occupation floor material below plow zone material in plow zone mound multi-component other quarry road segment rock art/pictograph/petroglyph shell midden shipwreck simple-component stratified stray find subsurface features	surface evidence village well workshop Slope % _____ Contour elevation _____ Site elevation _____ flat gentle moderate steep Nearest water source _____ Size and speed _____ Distance from site _____ Seasonal availability _____ Vegetation present _____ Vegetation past _____ Soil Description _____ USDA Soil series _____ Texture _____ Acidity _____ **Soil Drainage** excellent fair good poor
Stratigraphy	**Structure**
major disturbance minor disturbance not stratified other plowed redeposited stratified surface finds	foundation above ground level foundation below ground level foundation not evident road(s) on site superstructure collapsed superstructure complete superstructure not evident superstructure partial structural subdivisions apparent _____ surface traces only _____ buried traces detected _____ construction materials _____

Surrounding environment	Threats to site
coastal	deterioration
commercial	developers
high building density	highways
industrial	none known
isolated	other
open land	private
residential	renewal
rural	unknown
scattered buildings visible from site	vandalism
woodland	zoning

Site examination

Determination of site boundaries _____ Extent of site _____

Literature search _____ Informant report _____ Remote sensing _____

Surface Date _____ Site map _____ Collection method _____

Subsurface Date _____ Shovel test _____ Coring _____ Other _____

Unit size _____ # of units _____ Site plan _____

Excavation Date _____ Unit size _____ # of units _____ Site plan _____

Depth/stratigraphy of cultural deposit _____

Artifact categories _____ Artifact bag numbers _____

Artifacts broken down by type _____

Feature categories _____

Features broken down by type _____

Total number of artifacts _____

Report _____ Investigator _____

Photographs _____ Drawings _____ Site maps _____

Repository for materials _____ Owner of materials _____

Components (cultural affiliation, dates) _____

Recovered data/material remains _____

Historic materials _____

Prehistoric materials _____

Archaeological or historical importance _____

Eligibility for designation _____

Recommendations _____

SITE SURVEY RECORD

Site name _____ Site # _____ Surveyor _____ Dates of survey _____
Organization _____ Field director _____ Survey team _____
Requesting organization _____ Type of survey _____
Survey location _____ Map reference _____
Measurements of survey area _____ Control point/datum _____
Description of location _____
Conditions _____
Weather _____
Equipment/instruments used _____
Methods used _____

Owner and address _____ Previous owners _____ Tenant _____
Attitude toward excavation _____ Previous name of site _____ Informants _____
Owner of material _____

Control station	Point	Deflection	Description

Stratigraphy information
Character of soil:
0–10 cm _____ 10–20 cm _____ 20–30 cm _____ 30–40 cm _____
40–50 cm _____ 50–60 cm _____ 60–70 cm _____ 70–80 cm _____
80–90 cm _____ 90–100 cm _____

Nearest water source _____
Environment and surroundings _____
Present condition _____
Previous excavations _____

Collection method _____ Artifact bag numbers _____
Surface artifacts _____
Surface artifacts collected _____
Ecofacts _____
Samples _____ Sample bag numbers _____
Photographs _____ Drawings _____ Maps _____
Observations _____
Recommendations _____

SKIN AND HIDE RECORD

Site name _____ Site # _____ Excavator _____ Date _____

Unit/level _____ Provenience _____ Stratigraphic information _____

Associations _____

Measurements (length, width, thickness, weight) _____

Species of animal _____

Surface preparation _____ Tool marks _____

Decoration _____

Sewing details _____

Condition (including repairs) _____

Samples _____

SPECIAL FINDS FORM

Site name _____ Site # _____ Find # _____ Excavator _____ Date _____

Unit _____ Level _____ Provenience _____

Catalog # _____ Type of find _____ Description _____

Photo # _____ Drawing # _____

STORAGE LOG, ON-SITE

Site name _____ Site # _____ Excavator _____ Date _____

Catalog # _____ Unit _____ Level _____

Treatment _____ Storage container _____

Disposal area _____

STRATIGRAPHIC DESCRIPTION FORM

THE CROW CANYON ARCHAEOLOGICAL CENTER

STRATIGRAPHIC DESCRIPTION FORM

Site Number _____   Site Name _____   *Revised 2/2001*

Study Unit _____   Horizontal _____   Profile of _____ face

Stratum Letter _____   Corresponds with Map Number_____

Initials _____   Date _____

COLOR: (Dry) Munsell # _____   Description _____

TEXTURE TESTS

Consistence (dry):	Loose □	Soft □	Slightly hard □	Hard □	Very hard □	Extremely hard □
Consistence (moist):	Loose □	Very friable □	Friable □	Firm □	Very firm □	Extremely firm □

Stickiness (wet):   Nonsticky □   Slightly sticky □   Moderately sticky □   Very sticky □

Plasticity (wet):   Nonplastic □   Slightly plastic □   Moderately plastic □   Very plastic □

Molded Ball (wet):   None □   Very weak □   Fragile □   Strong □   Very strong □

Ribbon (wet):   None □   Slight □   Medium □   High □

Smoothness/Grittiness: Gritty □   Smooth □   Neither gritty nor smooth □

TEXTURE _____

INCLUSIONS:

Rock Type	Size	Shape	Frequency	Eroded?	Worked?	Oriented to Bedding Plane?	Comments

	Size	Frequency	Size	Frequency		Size	Frequency	Size	Frequency
Charcoal	___	___	___	___	**Unburned adobe** ___	___	___	___
CaCO$_3$	___	___	___	___	**Burned adobe** ___	___	___	___
Ash:	mixed with sediment	___		in lenses or pockets	___			

Visible artifacts _____

Other inclusions _____

DISTURBANCES: Frequency   **BOUNDARIES:**

Roots _____   From statum _____   to stratum _____

Animals/insects _____   Distinctness: Abrupt □   Clear □   Gradual □   Diffuse □

Looting _____   Topography: Smooth □   Wavy □   Irregular □   Broken □

INTERPRETATIONS:

How deposited?   Naturally □   Culturally □   Mixed □   Indeterminate □

When deposited?   Pre-occupational □   Occupational □   Postoccupational □   Mixed □   Indeterminate □

Interpretive Comments:

*Note: Description sheets and profile drawing **must** be turned in to the lab together.*

FORMS AND RECORDS

STRATIGRAPHY RECORD

Site name _____ Site # _____ Recorder _____ Date _____
Unit _____ Number of layers excavated _____

Stratified layers	Depth	Color	Texture	Amt & nature of disturbance	Features	Artifacts
0–10 cm						
10–20 cm						
20–30 cm						
30–40 cm						
40–50 cm						
50–60 cm						
60–70 cm						
70–80 cm						
80–90 cm						
90–100 cm						

Shovel test _____ Core _____ Auger boring _____ Probe _____

Strata cut _____ Machine cut _____

Dimensions _____

Excavation method _____

Screened (method, mesh size) _____

Soil samples _____ Soil sample bag numbers _____

Photographs _____ Profile drawings _____

Notes _____

STUDY UNIT CATALOG

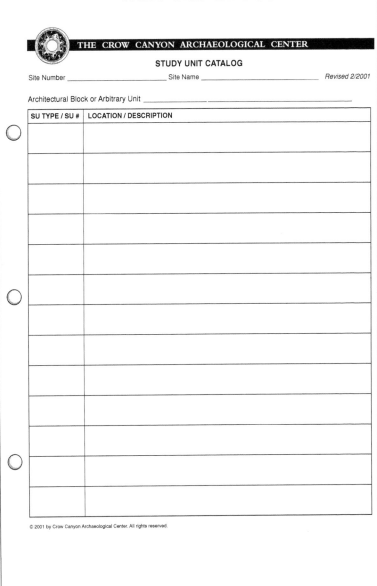

THE CROW CANYON ARCHAEOLOGICAL CENTER

STUDY UNIT CATALOG

Site Number _____ Site Name _____ *Revised 2/2001*

Architectural Block or Arbitrary Unit _____

SU TYPE / SU #	LOCATION / DESCRIPTION

FORMS AND RECORDS

STUDY UNIT FORM

THE CROW CANYON ARCHAEOLOGICAL CENTER

STUDY UNIT FORM

Site Number _____ Site Name _____ *Revised 2/2001*

Initials _____

Date _____

Study Unit Type, Name, and Explanation _____

Whole Study Unit Dimensions (m):

	ACTUAL	INFERRED	BASIS FOR INFERENCE
DIAMETER			
LENGTH			
WIDTH			
HEIGHT			
DEPTH			

Excavation/Sampling Strategy:

Description:

Interpretation:

TEXTILE RECORD

Site name _____ Site # _____ Excavator _____ Date _____

Unit/level _____ Provenience _____ Stratigraphic information _____

Associations _____

Measurements (length, width, thickness, weight) _____

Material _____ Decoration _____ Attached materials _____

Evidence of wear _____

Cordage ply _____ Cordage twist _____

Samples _____

TOTAL STATION DATUM TABLE

 THE CROW CANYON ARCHAEOLOGICAL CENTER

TOTAL STATION DATUM TABLE

Site Number _____   Site Name _____   *Revised 2/2001*

DATUM NO.	PT. NO.	COORDINATES	ELEVATION (m)	LOCATION	NEAREST BACKSIGHT	NOTES

TOTAL STATION FIELD NOTES FORM

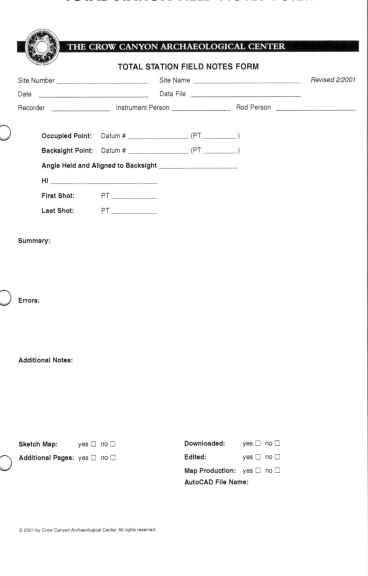

THE CROW CANYON ARCHAEOLOGICAL CENTER

TOTAL STATION FIELD NOTES FORM

Site Number _____ Site Name _____ *Revised 2/2001*

Date _____ Data File _____

Recorder _____ Instrument Person _____ Rod Person _____

    Occupied Point: Datum # _____ (PT _____)

    Backsight Point: Datum # _____ (PT _____)

    Angle Held and Aligned to Backsight _____

    HI _____

    First Shot: PT _____

    Last Shot: PT _____

Summary:

Errors:

Additional Notes:

Sketch Map: yes ☐ no ☐

Additional Pages: yes ☐ no ☐

Downloaded: yes ☐ no ☐

Edited: yes ☐ no ☐

Map Production: yes ☐ no ☐

AutoCAD File Name:

FORMS AND RECORDS

WALL PROFILE/PLAN VIEW FORM

Site name _____ Site # _____ Recorder _____ Date _____

Unit _____ Level _____

Orientation _____ Scale _____

WOOD AND CANE RECORD

Site name _____ Site # _____ Excavator _____ Date _____

Unit/level _____ Provenience _____ Stratigraphic information _____

Associations _____

Measurements (length, width, thickness, weight) _____

Species of plant _____

Modifications _____ Tool marks _____

Decoration _____ Resins _____ Attached materials _____

Evidence of wear _____

Samples _____

3

Lists and Checklists

Various lists and checklists can be useful to anyone involved in archaeological fieldwork. Simply having a daily what-to-take-along list can assist with efficiency and prevent having to do without something or having to borrow items. Other lists and checklists here are reminders or refreshers on important field topics.

——— CONTENTS ———

LISTS AND CHECKLISTS

ANALYSIS-IN-THE-FIELD
EQUIPMENT LIST

10X magnifying glass
brushes
calculator
drafting materials
graph paper
labels
line level
masking tape
Munsell Soil Color Chart
other storage containers
pencils, erasers

pen knife
permanent markers
pH kit
plastic bags
plastic surveyors' tape
plumb bob
rulers, tapes
scissors
stapler and staples
string

ARBITRARY LEVELS, WORKING IN

Arbitrary levels allow one to learn more about the natural strata, which are the primary unit of analysis in initial exploration of a deposit.

■ The base of the first arbitrary level is determined by depth measurements, which are adjusted to the surface elevations of the unit.

■ If a level floor is desired, then excavation must proceed off a single standard elevation – either an average, the highest point, or the lowest point (excavating at an arbitrary depth below the four points would mimic the surface topography).

■ To open a unit with an arbitrary level, excavate control points to the base of the level at the corners of the unit and center point of each wall.

■ Repeatedly check the below datum (BD) reading with a line level and ruler.

■ If you are digging to match the existing surface, then measure down from the surface in each corner with a folding ruler or tape to an arbitrary measure below each of the unique readings for the opening of the level.

■ All artifacts from the same level are assigned the provenience for that level.

152

ARTIFACT EXAMINATION METHODS

Rocks and minerals

Mohs scale
microscope examination of powder and thin sections
separation of heavy minerals
chemical spot test (for some minerals)
wet analysis (for some ores)
spectrometry (for some ores)
X-ray diffraction (for crystalline minerals)

Ceramics

Munsell chart
radiography examination of structure
microscope examination of thin sections
refiring of sherds
spectrometry (for homogeneous bodies)
X-ray diffraction (for clay minerals)

Metals

microscope examination of grain structure
spectrometry to establish composition
Brinell hardness test
radiography examination of composite structures
chemical spot test to establish presence of metal
X-ray diffraction to examine crystalline state

Organic material

microscope examination of cellular structures (often with stain)
check solubilities of solvents
chromatography (for non-cellular materials)

LISTS AND CHECKLISTS

ARTIFACT FIELD PROCEDURE

- Plot, photograph, and/or draw.
- Record in field notebook with remarks on association, position, condition.
- Place artifact in container or plastic bag labeled for the find spot.

- Use new container/bag for a) new level, layer, or locus; b) change in soil color or in artifacts; c) at end of day's work; d) when container/bag is full.
- Transport artifacts to analysis area.
- Note: As a general rule, assume that every artifact is fragile. Keep large stone objects separate from more fragile artifacts. Bone artifacts should be arranged so that there is no strain on them.

ARTIFACT HANDLING AND LIFTING

Artifact handling

- Assume every artifact is extremely fragile.
- Pick up artifacts lightly but firmly.
- Pick up artifacts at the thickest strongest part.
- Hold artifacts over a soft surface or table, keeping distance between artifact and table to a minimum.
- Avoid bending flexible materials.
- When you put an artifact down, make sure it is secure before removing your hands.

Artifact lifting

- Never extract an artifact until it is completely exposed, and after associations have been noted.
- Carefully remove dirt surrounding the object so that it is on a pedestal of dirt.
- Use small brushes, paintbrushes, tongue depressors, etc. to clean around the object.
- Make sure the artifact is freed.
- With even pressure around the object, gently dislodge it – do not pry or flick.
- Pick up the artifact carefully and place it in a bag or container.
- When an object is in pieces, make sure you get them all and keep them together.
- Note: Removing artifacts in a block of dirt may be used to lift extremely fragile and less flat objects. Some sort of support (gauze, wax, plastic wrap, foil, etc.) is given to the object and sometimes the soil is consolidated (synthetic material like plaster of Paris is added to make the soil rigid). Another method is to surround the block of dirt with a wooden frame or wrap the block with strips of plaster bandage.

ARTIFACT INDUSTRIES

(representative)

ceramic: beads, figurines, musical instruments, pottery
lithic: chipped/flaked stone, ground stone
metal: bronze, copper, gold, iron, silver, tin
organic: basketry, bone, hide, horn, ivory, shell, textiles, wood

ARTIFACT PACKING

General packing

- Only inert materials, e.g. acid-free tissue or polyethylene, should be used.
- Zip-lock or self-sealing polyethylene or heavy plastic bags are ideal.
- Separate the different materials, whether or not they are inventoried.
- Photographic film containers, plastic food containers, and cardboard boxes may also be used to pack some materials.
- Samples for radiocarbon dating should not be packed in paper or other organic substances.
- Make sure that every container and bag has a label.

Packing for shipment

- Use strong containers, like wood.
- Artifacts should be made secure with cotton balls or pads, styrofoam, bubble-wrap, foam rubber, acid-free tissue, or other inert acid-free materials.
- Small objects should be carefully wrapped and put in small containers.
- The heaviest artifacts should be in the bottom of the strong containers and the bottom layer should be lined with padded material.
- Ample space should be put between objects and the spaces filled with packing material.
- Create an inventory of each box and keep copies.

- There should be an established policy before entering the field about how to handle and/or sample lithic, ceramic, or any other artifacts that might possess organic or other types of residues.
- Excavated artifacts should remain complete and "pure" (self-contained, clean).
- The judicious handling of artifacts in general can prevent damage and support analysis.
- In general, do not clean artifacts that are organic or contain organic matter.
- Handle these as little as possible and bag them separately.
- The matrix inside of any type of container should be collected along with the artifact.
- Wear latex gloves when handling these types of artifacts to prevent accidental contamination.
- Artifacts that are damp when collected (bone, organics) should be placed in breathable containers so they can dry slowly and so that mold/fungi will not develop. If plastic bags are used, puncture the bags in a couple of places.
- Do not place metals in a plastic bag or any container that will sweat moisture since this will promote corrosion.
- Samples for radiocarbon dating should be collected using a clean trowel and wrapped in clean aluminum foil or placed inside clean plastic or glass containers. Floral or faunal remains that might be submitted for radiocarbon dating should first be identified by species.
- Collect pollen, phytolith, and starch grain samples using clean implements and store them in containers that are dry and sterile (e.g. plastic bags).

──────────────── **BASKET PARTS** ────────────────

(not all baskets have all parts)

wall
rim/selvage
start (at bottom, where weaving starts)
shoulder (if body narrows toward opening)

handle(s)
lid (which will also have a wall, rim, start)
warp (fairly rigid foundation)
weft (fairly flexible stitching)

BASKETRY/BARK/WOOD FIELD CONSERVATION

Generally, the rules for conservation of organic remains also apply to basketry, barks, and wood.

- For wet to waterlogged material: if left in situ for recording or photographs, cover it with damp newspaper and keep it wet, possibly spraying with fungicide solution. Once removed, wrap in polyethylene or watertight container surrounded by wet crumpled paper, cloth, etc. If wood was found in water, send to the lab in water with a 10% solution of ethanol added. Polyethylene glycol may be applied to wet wood as a preservative.
- For dry or drier material: Keep in similar conditions to that in which found. When found in dry context, only use light brushing and placement in a stable container.
- For insect-infested objects, isolate in polyethylene bags with no-pest strips or paradichlorobenzene (PDB) crystals. Freezing might also work.

BOAT KIT LIST

dry towels or rags	spare prop pins
knife	spare propeller
pliers or vise grip	spare quick-start spray
plug gapper	spare spark plug sets
sandpaper	spare spray lubricant
safety equipment	spare starting cord
screwdriver(s)	spare wire
spare electrician's tape	spark-plug wrench

BONE IDENTIFICATION CHART

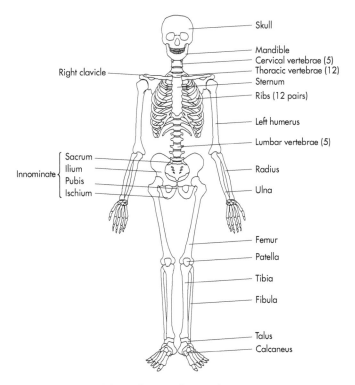

Figure 3.1 Human skeleton: the major bones. (Thomas R. Hester, Harry J. Shafer, and Kenneth L. Feder, Figure 11.7: Articulated human skeleton showing the major bones of the body, p. 265 from *Field Methods in Archaeology*, Seventh Edition. New York: McGraw-Hill, 1997. Copyright © 1997 by Thomas R. Hester, Harry J. Shafer, and Kenneth L. Feder. Reprinted by permission of The McGraw-Hill Companies)

BONE/ANTLER/IVORY/SHELL FIELD CONSERVATION

■ In sediments, bone becomes impregnated with minerals, so that its weight, hardness, and durability generally increase.

■ Generally, bone, antler, ivory, and shell should be protected from the sun. Bone, antler, and ivory should not be washed unless sound. Do not soak. If unsound, clean with a brush or nonmetal tool. Shell should be washed very gently. If the artifact is wet or dry, keep it so respectively. When drying, do so away from direct sources of heat, light, and sunlight.

- Avoid washing worked bone objects; clean by dry-brushing with a soft toothbrush or paintbrush.
- Some badly deteriorated dry specimens may be treated with PVA resin in a 10% solution of ethyl alcohol or acetone. For badly deteriorated wet specimens, you might consider Acryloid B72 or Acrysol WS-24, which can be "reversed" with certain chemicals. The use of a preservative, however, may affect studies of the bone for radiocarbon dating or specialized chemical or DNA analysis. Leave some bone untreated if these types of studies are under consideration.
- For fragile bone artifacts, remove loose dirt and then spray-saturate with a preservative. When dry, coat with PVA. Large fragile bone may need to be encased in plaster bandaging. Alternatively, the specimen may be put in tissue and aluminum foil and placed in a box for the laboratory.
- If a bone is to be used for radiocarbon dating, it must be collected according to the procedure for radiocarbon sampling. It must not be consolidated or chemically treated.
- Any collection of human or animal bones lying together should be kept together. Bones that appear to be articulated should be kept together. All should be drawn or photographed before removal.
- Avoid the use of tube cements, white glues, epoxies, spray acrylics, shellac, beeswax, or paraffin in benzene or gasoline.
- Dry shell may be packed as is; shells from damp soils should be put in containers that preserve their moisture. Sometimes a fragile shell object will need to be consolidated before being lifted from the ground. Delicate or flaking shell can be soaked in a thin PVA solution after cleaning – for example a 3–5% solution of Acryloid B72 in either acetone or toluene. Wet or damp shell can be immersed in a PVA solution diluted 1:4 with water. If sound and unpainted, shell can be washed in water using a soft brush or toothpicks for dislodging dirt. Shell must then dry thoroughly before marking or packing. It can be packed in polyethylene bags as long as it is thoroughly dry. Never pack in foil or hard-edged tissue.
- Identification is made by a specialist or by comparison with a reference collection.

BULK PROVENIENCE PROCEDURE

Bulk proveniences or lots are spatially defined units for recording provenience. The most common lot is the unit level. All artifacts from within the unit and from the same level (stratigraphic or arbitrary) are collected and analyzed together. Lots are given bulk provenience unit and level numbers, tied into the primary site datum via the unit datum. Separately bag different artifact classes from the same provenience.

BURIAL EXCAVATION AND OBSERVATIONS

- Observe the ethics of excavation regarding burials.
- When a burial is discovered, excavation must be halted. Note the level and whether it is sealed by another layer, unit/locus.
- Determine the type of burial (individual, bundle, mass, cremation, etc.).
- Determine if the remains are human or nonhuman.
- Determine if the burial is primary or secondary.
- Determine if it is a complete burial with a) articulated bones, b) disarticulated bones, or c) is isolated bone.
- Determine the burial position, deposition, and orientation.
- Estimate the completeness of the remains.
- Determine the quality of preservation of the burial (good, fair, poor).
- Record the burial's associations – objects or materials on or in a) direct contact, b) in proximity, and/or c) within feature.
- Identify the spatial/lateral extent of burial so that excavation is undertaken as one unit.
- Clear an area of 15 cm beyond the burial on all sides. If there is a container, it must be identified and recorded with measurements and orientation.
- Excavate, leaving the burial isolated in its earth matrix, on a pedestal 20–25 cm higher than floor. Do not use trowels, dental probes, or other metal tools. Try bamboo or cane splits and wooden dowels. As the matrix is removed, it must be screened. Do not use pedestaling if any trace of the burial pit remains (seen in a difference in color and texture between mound soil and subsoil).

160

- Any grave goods should be recorded in situ before removal. Carefully check for and record perishable and nonperishable materials on or around the body.
- Assess bone condition and plan the least destructive removal of bones.
- Clean skeleton with fine tools. Avoid touching bone with any metal object.
- Attempt to expose the bones at relatively the same time on a level plane so that there is no strain on a particular part of the skeleton. Another method is to expose the central area first, then proximal, then distal.
- Take soil samples for the matrix of the burial. This can be used to test for pollen and soil chemistry. Soil samples should be taken from within the body cavity, within the burial pit, and outside the burial area.
- Fully record the burial in writing, drawing, and photographs.
- Do not apply pressure to any of the bones. Do not pry or flick. Limit exposure to the sun.
- Excavate and remove the burial in the same day. If the bones are strong enough, they can be removed individually. Otherwise, they should be removed in total and put in a padded container.
- Wrap separately: long bones, cranium, mandible, the vertebra, fragmentary bones, bones of each hand and foot. The heaviest bones should be packed first in the main container.

BURIAL VARIABLES CHECKLIST

type of burial
human/nonhuman
primary/secondary
surface/sub-surface
cremated/uncremated
articulated/disarticulated/isolated
extended/flexed/semiflexed
lying on back/lying on face/lying on right side/lying on left side
sitting/standing/kneeling
compass alignment of body
compass direction faced by skull
percentage of completeness of remains
good preservation/fair preservation/poor preservation
burial pit/burial container/earth matrix

logs in or covering/slabs in or covering/neither logs nor slabs
ramp/no ramp
ocher/no ocher
hematite/no hematite
perishable materials
nonperishable materials

——————— CATALOGING EQUIPMENT LIST ———————

acetone
ball of string
carbon paper
centimeter rulers
containers, small and large
cotton balls
cotton swabs
dental probes
distilled water
drawing pencils and erasers
graph paper
indelible ink, black and white
indelible pens, felt-tip of various sizes
index or catalog cards
knife and X-Acto knife
labels, permanent self-adhesive

liquid soap
locked storage
log book
magnet
magnifying glass
matches, wooden
nail polish, clear
paper clips
plastic basin
pliers
PVA glue
scissors
small paintbrushes
tags
toothbrushes
zip-lock plastic bags

——————— CATALOGING PROCEDURE ———————

■ Before starting a new level, assign a catalog number for the artifacts and record sheets for the completed level. Every unique context (level or feature) is assigned a unique catalog number.

■ Subnumbers are used when artifacts within the level are given map numbers. The range of subnumbers used should be listed in the catalog.

■ Once a catalog number has been assigned in the field, it should be placed on all relevant artifact tags, bags, record sheets, and maps.

- Handle carefully and take care that tools do not damage the surface of ceramic objects – especially nonglazed, low-fired, relatively soft pottery.
- Complete or restorable pottery vessels require patience and diligent documentation. Pedestal the vessel to free it from the matrix before removal. Do not remove the soil in the vessel as it helps hold the vessel together and it can be used for residue or pollen samples. These should be carefully packed in tissue or bubble-pack for transport to the lab for cleaning, restoration, and cataloging.
- If a vessel is cracked, wrap it with gauze strips to stabilize and support it.
- If sherds or vessels are friable in the field, some consolidation may be done with Acryloid B72 in 3–5% solution or PVA diluted 1:4 with water.
- Sherds impregnated with salts (arid lands, ocean sites) may be treated by soaking in distilled water. Specimens should be tested before any other cleaning procedure is used.
- Once excavated, ceramics should be kept out of the sun. If possible, wash very soon in distilled water and allow to dry in the shade. However, ceramics should be washed only when its strength is known.
- Be careful in screening not to damage the surface decoration, slip, or glaze with the screen or trowel.
- Be careful when removing dirt from a sherd or object.
- Be careful when a sherd has been painted or glazed. Try to test a very small area for cleaning with a brush or water so you can see if it may be cleaned without damaging the paint or glaze.
- Do not wash items if you are planning to examine the residues for dietary data.
- Many sherds and vessels may be bagged in the field without immediate treatment.

Specific procedures:

- Glazed and flaking: let dry, then apply diluted PVA.
- Glazed with chipped-off glaze: brush with diluted PVA on affected areas.
- Glazed with crazing or cracking glaze: apply thin PVA solution to cracked parts.

LISTS AND CHECKLISTS

- Glazed with salts on unglazed parts: soak in distilled water, changing water frequently.
- High-fired with earth crust: wash in fresh water.
- High-fired with flaky surface: brush with diluted PVA, let dry, then brush to clean.
- High-fired with surface salt: gently brush off excess dirt while damp, wash in fresh water, allow to dry naturally, brush salts off.
- Low-fired that is damp and crumbling: gently brush off excess dirt, allow to dry naturally, then put in polyethylene.
- Low-fired that is damp and flaky: allow to dry, then consolidate, dry again, wrap in tissue or polyethylene.
- Sunbaked unfired that is dry and crumbling: gently brush off excess dirt, put in polyethylene.
- Sunbaked unfired that is wet and crumbling: gently brush off excess dirt, allow to dry naturally, then put in polyethylene.

CLOSING OUT A LEVEL

- Make sure the side walls are straight. If the excavation is relatively shallow, position yourself over the taut string that defines the unit's edge and looking straight down, shave the wall until it is plumb. For a deep excavation, you may use a torpedo level to see if the walls are straight.
- Trowel the floor clean, starting at one end and moving to the other end.
- Take closing elevations and record them.

CONTEXT ASSESSMENT

Archaeological context is derived from careful recording of the matrix, provenience, and association of the finds. Context is affected by three factors.

- Manufacture and use of the artifact, feature, or structure by original owners, i.e. can behavior be reconstructed? This can be looked at by examining the four levels of spatial context.
- The way the find was deposited in the ground, i.e. naturally, deliberately, by abandonment? This is the primary context.

- Subsequent history of the find in the ground, i.e. was there disturbance, was there erosion? This is the secondary context.

COORDINATE GRID, SETTING UP

- A coordinate grid is superimposed on a triangulation grid by choosing any point on the triangulation grid and drawing north/south and east/west lines through the chosen point.
- Grid lines are then drawn parallel to the original N/S, E/W lines at set intervals. These are lettered in one direction and numbered in both directions.
- Apexes of the triangulation grid may be used for reference purposes.
- In referring to a grid, you first read the N/S square reference number, then the E/W square reference number.

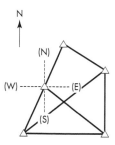 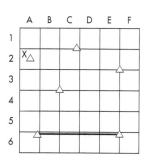

Figure 3.2 Preparing a coordinate grid. (Philip C. Hammond, Coordinate grid, p. 109 from *Archaeological Techniques for Amateurs*. New York: Van Nostrand, 1963. Copyright © 1963 by Philip C. Hammond. Reprinted by permission of the author)

CRM PHASES

- Phase I Survey: An exploratory survey of an area to determine location and boundaries of any historic or archaeological site potentially eligible for the National Register of Historic Places. This means a surface–subsurface field reconnaissance as well as a historic and prehistoric background check to see if any sites or structures are known for the project area, are listed on or nominated for the National Register, etc.

■ Phase II Testing: A thorough investigation of an historic or archaeological site to make recommendations regarding its eligibility for listing on the National Register of Historic Places. This will be needed if the Phase I results found or identified cultural resources but it is not clear if those resources satisfy or fail to satisfy criteria for listing on the National Register.

■ Phase III Data Recovery: An excavation (mitigation or data recovery) of an historic or archaeological site listed or eligible for listing on the National Register of Historic Places prior to its demolition for new construction.

CRM PHASE I SHOVEL TESTING

(also called test pitting)

■ Use a compass and pace the distance to go from one shovel test location to the next.

■ Take a backsight with the compass on the flagging tape marking the previous test, to keep the transects true and parallel.

■ If an Ap horizon (plowed topsoil) is known to have been present, then the first shovel test level should be all of the plowzone material. If unplowed or not definitely plowed, 10 cm arbitrary levels should be used.

■ Remove fill by shovel into screen, looking for cultural material. Bag the recovered material (by shovel test number and level) and record the shovel test, including description of soil horizons.

■ Note the shovel test's location relative to landscape or surveyed features.

■ Backfill. Record the transect number, shovel test number, and compass bearing on a flagging tape. Use a different color tape for positive (containing artifacts) and negative shovel tests. Tie the tape to an overhanging branch, adjacent clump of grass, etc.

CRM PHASE I SHOVEL
TESTING EQUIPMENT

backpack
clipboard
compass
flagging tape, two colors
locking tape measure with metric scale
pencils

permanent ink marker
plastic bags
round-nose shovel
shovel test forms
small screen
trowel

CROSS-SECTIONING A FEATURE

- A cross-section allows feature attributes and variation to be investigated.
- Cross-sections provide a view of the subfloor profile and dimensions of the feature, sediments, and artifacts.
- Cross-sections may be oriented along the length, width, or diameter of a feature as it appears in plan view.
- The possibilities include a longitudinal section, a transverse section, and a quarter section.
- Never create a cross-section larger than the minimal spatial unit being used for control in the excavation.
- Proceeding by quarter sections or even smaller subdivisions enhances control over provenience.
- With small or deep features like postmolds, it may not be possible to excavate a cross-section without also removing some of the surrounding non-feature matrix, but it should be kept to a minimum.
- Cross-sections of partially exposed features should be oriented to complement feature profiles that will be preserved in the side walls of the unit.
- Once the orientation of a cross-section has been chosen, physically create the cross-section line with nails and a taut string.
- With the trowel, make vertical cuts along the string line to initiate the cross-section.
- Work from the section line back to the outer boundaries of the feature.
- Natural or arbitrary levels are moved in a feature cross-section just like any excavation.

LISTS AND CHECKLISTS

167

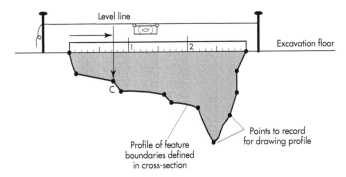

Figure 3.3 Recording the profile of a cross-section through a feature. (R. M. Stewart, Figure 9.36: Recording a profile of the cross-section through a feature, from *Archaeology Basic Field Methods*. Dubuque, IA: Kendall/Hunt, 2002. Copyright © 2002 by Kendall/Hunt Publishing Company. Reprinted by permission of the publisher)

- Only remove the matrix that can be identified as feature fill and stop when you encounter natural undisturbed soil.
- Draw and photograph a profile of the cross-sectioned feature.

─── DATING METHODS BY MATERIAL ───

- Archaeomagnetism: stone, baked clay, iron deposit.
- Astronomical dating: sun's position on structures.
- Cation ratio: rock.
- Cultural affiliation: people, DNA.
- Dendrochronology: trees.
- Electron spin resonance: sedimentary quartz, fossilized teeth, flint, and calcium carbonate in limestone, coral and egg shells.
- Fission track: volcanic material, glass, apatite, mica, fossil bone.
- Fluorine dating: bone, teeth.
- Obsidian hydration: obsidian.
- Optically scanned luminescence: unheated sediments that are no older than 500,000 years.
- Oxidizable carbon ratio: soil, humus, charcoal.
- Patination: glass, metal, etc.
- Pollen analysis: trees with pollen, peat bogs.
- Potassium-argon: rock, meteorite, feldspar, volcanic glass.
- Racemization: organic materials (or fossil materials) such as human and animal bones, teeth, plants, ostrich egg shells,

mollusks, marine sediments, freshwater and marine shells, oyster shells, carbonate shells (foraminifera, snails, clams, ostracods), calcareous sediments and peats.
- Radiocarbon/Carbon-14: plant life, animal life, charcoal, wood, burned bone.
- Rate of accumulation: rock, metal, soil.
- Seriation: ceramics.
- Thermoluminescence: rock, mineral, ceramics.
- Uranium-thorium dating.
- Varve analysis: lake sediment from glacial advance.

DIRECTION FINDING WITH COMPASS

- Hold the base plate compass flat in front of your chest so that the compass needle floats freely and points to magnetic north. (The only thing a compass needle can do is point to magnetic north.)
- Rotate the entire compass housing until the needle sits within the orienting arrow stenciled onto the base of the compass housing. (Usually the orienting arrow is red.)
- The zero degree mark on the compass housing and the north end of the needle should be aligned – they now point to magnetic north.
- Keep the orienting arrow and the compass needle pointing north. Twist the base plate until the direction-of-travel line points exactly at the distant landmark you wish to move toward. Double-check to make sure everything is still properly aligned.
- Note the exact number of degrees marked on the compass dial where the direction-of-travel line intersects the compass dial. That number of degrees is the direction to the distant landmark.

DISTURBANCE/EXPOSURE TYPES TO LOOK FOR

agricultural fields
animal activity areas, e.g. pasture, range
animal burrows
area of little vegetation, e.g. arid, eroded
banks, grades, or vertical sections of waterways, ditches, gullies, roads, railways

bases of large trees
boundary area of bodies of water or beaches
boundary area of slopes
burned-over areas (freed of vegetation by fire)
dirt or undeveloped roads
exposed surfaces
fence and tree lines bordering agricultural fields
freshly sunken or sagging areas
logged areas
new or continuing construction areas
orchards, tree nurseries
scars from earth slides
trails
tree dislocations
utility right-of-ways

ECOLOGICAL SAMPLE COLLECTION

Dating samples

charcoal for radiocarbon dating
shell for radiocarbon dating, especially thick bivalve fragments
pollen for/by palynologist using augur or spot samples from pit walls
soil vials from a continuous vertical profile

Midden samples

small samples by column
large samples
miscellaneous samples from walls or pits

Specimen samples

shell from natural layers, attempting to get whole shells for species
   identification
bone from natural layers, attempting species identification and
   possible chemical analysis
feature specimens of wood, stone, etc. for examination or chemical
   analysis
pocket or lens specimens for identification

Soil samples

sample from natural levels for chemical analysis
sample from nonsite pit to determine natural soil horizons and
history, possible chemical analysis

EMERGENCY/DISASTER STRATEGIES = FIRST AID

Generally:

- carry a complete first aid kit
- carry a cellular telephone

Allergic reaction, severe

- Know in advance what your companions are allergic to and where they keep their inhalers, epinephrine kits, and allergy medications. Consider wearing a medic alert bracelet if you know you are susceptible to anaphylactic shock.
- Learn to identify the signs and symptoms of anaphylaxis: difficulty breathing; wheezing; rash; itching; hives; swelling of the feet, hands, eyes or face; flushed skin; nausea; vomiting; abdominal pain; rapid pulse.
- Remove the person from contact with the allergen, if the allergen is suspected to be something in the air or on the skin.
- Administer injectable epinephrine (adrenaline) immediately if the person is having difficulty talking or breathing. Epinephrine is usually prescribed in an Anakit or Epipen with a preloaded syringe, and injected intramuscularly in the thigh for rapid absorption.
- Monitor airway, breathing, and circulation.
- Treat for shock.
- Inject a second dose of epinephrine within 12 to 15 minutes after the first dose was administered, to prevent a relapse. Most kits contain at least two doses.
- Administer an oral antihistamine once the epinephrine has taken effect and the person is able to take the medication by himself or herself.
- Hydrate well.

■ Evacuate immediately, administering oral antihistamines at regular intervals until the person has reached professional medical care.

Allergies, mild

■ Take an antihistamine such as Benadryl.
■ Avoid scratching as this will further irritate the rash, increase the risk of infection, and cause scarring.
■ Apply cornstarch packs to reduce the itching of hives.
■ Apply a thin layer of steroid cream, such as hydrocortisone, to rashes caused by allergens rubbing against the skin.
■ Apply Calamine lotion to poison oak and insect bites. Steroid cream may also be effective with poison oak.

Bite, animal

■ Move away from the animal and ensure the safety of the scene to prevent additional bites.
■ Put on latex gloves as protection from infectious disease.
■ Clean the wound thoroughly and aggressively with an antiseptic soap or povidone–iodine solution.
■ Keep the wound open – do not attempt to close it with closure strips or butterfly bandages.
■ Dress and bandage the wound.
■ Keep the patient well-hydrated.
■ Monitor carefully for infection.
■ Evacuate immediately to a hospital, regardless of whether you believe the animal was rabid.

Bite, snake

■ Move away from the snake and ensure safety of the scene to prevent additional bites.
■ Calm the patient down and keep him or her still and quiet.
■ Elevate the bite at or below the level of the heart.
■ Remove any jewelry or other articles which may constrict with swelling.
■ Suction immediately with a Sawyer Extractor, ideally within three minutes after the patient has been bitten.
■ If extractor not available: Apply hard direct pressure over bite using a 4 × 4 gauze pad folded in half twice. Tape in place with adhesive tape.

- Soak gauze pad in antiseptic soap or solution if available.
- Strap gauze pad tightly in place with adhesive tape.
- Overwrap dressing above and below bite area with ACE or crepe bandage, but not too tight. Overwrap no tighter than you would use for a sprain. Make sure pulses are present.
- Wrap ACE (elastic) bandage as tight as one would for a sprain, but not too tight.
- Check for pulse above and below elastic wrap; if absent it is too tight. Unpin and loosen.
- Immobilize the extremity and splint if possible.
- Keep the patient well-hydrated.
- Evacuate immediately, preferably without any effort on the part of the patient. An ideal evacuation would involve sending others to arrange for a helicopter evacuation. Get the patient to the hospital immediately.

Burn

- Remove the source of the burn: For flame burns, stop, drop and roll; for wet chemical burns, flush the area with water for 20 minutes; for dry chemical burns, brush off the dry chemicals.
- Remove any clothing and jewelry, since they retain heat and can exacerbate burning.
- Check airway, breathing, and circulation. Treat with rescue breathing and/or CPR as necessary.
- Cool the burn with cold (but warmer than ice-cold) water, or with cloths dampened with cold water.
- Assess the depth and extent of the burn.
- Elevate the burn site above the heart.
- Have the injured person drink as much as possible, unless he or she is unconscious and/or showing signs of shock.
- Clean the burn area gently with disinfected lukewarm water and mild soap. Pat dry, and flush any debris out with an irrigation syringe. Pat dry again.
- Apply a thin layer of antibiotic ointment to the burn site with a cotton swab.
- Cover the burn with dry, sterile gauze.
- Give ibuprofen to reduce pain and swelling.
- Evacuate unless only minor superficial burns are involved.
- Re-dress the burn twice a day on the way out: Remove the dressing (which may require soaking it first), rewash the burn site, reapply antibiotic ointment, and re-dress with gauze.

Bleeding, stopping

- Elevate the injured area above the heart.
- Apply direct pressure to the bleeding area, using sterile cloth or gauze.
- Keep the pressure on for five minutes.
- Check to see if the bleeding has stopped. If it hasn't, apply pressure for 15 minutes.

Cleaning a wound

- Scrub hands thoroughly with soap and disinfected water.
- Put on latex gloves to prevent the spread of infectious disease.
- Prepare a disinfectant solution of 1 oz povidone–iodine and 1 liter disinfected water.
- Set the disinfectant solution aside for about five minutes.

CPR

- Determine if the surrounding scene is safe.
- Tell someone nearby to call 911, if not in a wilderness setting.
- Determine if the injured person is breathing.
- Position the injured person on his or her back, being extremely careful not to move or twist the head, neck, or spine. If several rescuers are present, use their assistance to minimize this danger.
- Maintain an open airway while you pinch the injured person's nose shut.
- Give two long, slow breaths, being sure to maintain a seal between your mouth and his or hers
- Begin CPR if the person is neither breathing nor has a pulse.
- Position the hands: Find the lower tip of the breastbone. Measure two finger widths towards the head, and place the heel of one hand in this location.
- Place your other hand on top of the first hand, interlacing your fingers of both hands.
- Lean forward so that your shoulders are over your hands.
- Push downward on the chest, using the weight of your upper body for strength.
- Compress 15 times in 10 seconds.
- Give two more slow breaths after the 15 compressions.
- Do 15 more compressions followed again by two slow breaths.
- Perform the 15-compression, two-breath cycle a total of four times.
- Re-check pulse and breathing.

- Continue repeating this entire cycle – four sets of chest compressions and breaths followed by re-checking pulse and breathing – until the injured person regains a pulse, until professional medical help arrives, or until you are too exhausted to continue.

Frostbite

- Consider taking a pain reliever such as ibuprofen to brace for the inevitable pain of rewarming.
- Gather the following supplies if possible: a camp stove with fuel, a pot in which to heat water, a receptacle large enough to hold the affected body part without allowing it to touch the sides, and a thermometer to check the water's temperature.
- Heat the right amount of water – enough to cover the affected area once it's in the receptacle – to between 104 and 108 degrees F.
- Pour the heated water into the receptacle.
- Immerse the affected part – stripped of all clothing and covering – in the water, taking care that it doesn't touch the sides of the receptacle.
- Heat more water, again to between 104 and 108 degrees F.
- Replace the water in the receptacle once it has cooled to below 100 degrees F.
- Repeat the heat-and-replace cycle until all discoloration has disappeared and all tissue is once again soft and pliable. This usually takes 30 to 60 minutes.
- Prepare a bath of water mixed with antibacterial soap. Immerse the affected area for 5 minutes to minimize risk of infection.
- Air-dry the injured area and gingerly apply aloe vera ointment.
- Cover the injured area gently with dry sterile gauze and insulating layers.
- Evacuate if you are outdoors, taking extreme care not to let the frostbitten body part refreeze.

Frostbite, severe

- Figure out if it's possible to evacuate without the affected area being used. For instance, can the person be moved without walking on a frostbitten foot?
- Decide if you'll be able to keep the person, including the affected area, warm throughout the eventual evacuation.
- Determine if you have all the supplies for field rewarming: the ability to heat a lot of water for a long time, a receptacle large

LISTS AND CHECKLISTS

175

enough to hold the affected part without allowing it to touch the sides, and a thermometer to check the water's temperature.

- Rewarm in the field only if the above three conditions are met: no necessity to use the affected area before reaching a hospital, ability to keep the person warm during future evacuation, and adequate supplies to rewarm properly. Otherwise evacuate before rewarming.

Heat cramps

- Move the person out of direct sunlight, preferably into a cool, shaded area.
- Stretch the calf and thigh muscles gently through the cramp. This will usually bring immediate relief.
- Hydrate well, preferably with a diluted sports drink or oral rehydration solution. A teaspoon of salt in a liter of water will also do.
- Have the person rest quietly.

Heat exhaustion

- Evaluate for heat exhaustion. If you suspect heat exhaustion, treat with the following steps.
- Move the person out of direct sunlight, preferably into a cool, shaded area.
- Have the person lie flat and elevate his or her feet if the person feels dizzy or has fainted suddenly.
- Have the person rest quietly.
- Hydrate well with lots of water, a diluted sports drink, or oral rehydration solution.
- Remove heat-retaining clothing.
- Wet the person down and fan him or her.
- Place a wet bandanna or thin strip of cotton cloth on the person's forehead, top of the head, or back of the neck.
- Monitor body temperature frequently. If it rises to above 104 degrees, aggressively cool the person.

Heatstroke

- Evaluate for heatstroke. Warning signs vary but may include: high temperature (over 103°F), red hot dry skin with no sweating, rapid strong pulse, throbbing headache, dizziness, nausea, confusion, unconsciousness. If you suspect heatstroke, treat with the following steps.

- Move the patient out of direct sunlight, preferably into a cool, shaded area.
- Have the patient lie flat and elevate his or her feet.
- Remove heat-retaining clothing.
- Wet the patient down and fan him or her, or immerse the patient in cool water.
- Place ice packs on the patient's head, back of the neck, armpits, palms of the hands, soles of the feet, and groin.
- Hydrate well with lots of water, a diluted sports drink, or oral rehydration solution, but only if the patient is conscious enough to hold a cup and drink unassisted.
- Monitor body temperature frequently, keeping careful notes on how long the patient remains at a given temperature. Transfer these notes when you transfer care.
- Evacuate immediately, continually monitoring and writing down the patient's body temperature.

Hypothermia, mild

- Remove the affected person from the cold, wet, and/or windy environment.
- Dry the person off, replacing wet clothing with dry clothing.
- Shelter the person however possible: in a cave, under an overhang, in an improvised shelter such as a tent, or under a rain fly.
- Make sure he or she is wearing a dry hat – a large percentage of body-heat loss occurs through the head.
- Cover the neck with something dry – a lot of heat is also lost through the neck.
- Prepare a warm (not hot) beverage with your camp stove and have the hypothermic person drink it.
- Encourage the person to eat carbohydrate-rich foods.
- Encourage the person to move around, generating heat and helping with rewarming.

Hypothermia, moderate

- Remove the affected person from the cold, wet, and/or windy environment.
- Dry the person off, replacing wet clothing with dry clothing.
- Shelter the person however possible: in a cave, under an overhang, in an improvised shelter such as a tent, or under a rain fly.
- Make sure the person is wearing a dry hat – a large percentage of body-heat loss occurs through the head.

- Cover the neck with something dry – a lot of heat is also lost through the neck.
- Insulate the person from the ground and the surrounding cold by having him or her lie in a sleeping bag on a sleeping pad.
- Prepare a warm (not hot) beverage with your camp stove and have the hypothermic person drink it.
- Encourage the person to eat carbohydrate-rich foods.
- Place hot water bottles (filled with hot water) and/or chemical heat packs inside the sleeping bag and against the clothing of the hypothermic person.
- Build a fire near the person, but take care that it isn't close enough to risk catching anything on fire.
- Monitor closely for changes in level of consciousness – a worsening condition may indicate severe hypothermia.

Hypothermia, severe

- Remove the affected person from the cold, wet, and/or windy environment.
- Dry the person off, replacing wet clothing with dry clothing.
- Shelter the person however possible: in a cave, under an overhang, in an improvised shelter such as a tent, or under a rain fly.
- Make sure the person is wearing a dry hat – a large percentage of body-heat loss occurs through the head.
- Cover the neck with something dry – a lot of heat is also lost through the neck.
- Insulate the person from the ground and the surrounding cold by having him or her lie in a sleeping bag on a sleeping pad.
- Place hot water bottles (filled with hot water) and/or chemical heat packs inside the sleeping bag and against the clothing of the hypothermic person.
- Build a "hypothermia wrap" by placing dry clothing over all exposed parts of the person except his or her mouth and nose, and wrap a vapor barrier – a tent fly, plastic garbage bags, anything that will minimize the escape of heat – around the person.

Muscle pull

- Apply an ice pack for 20 minutes to any area that hurts. Repeat this every hour until the pain subsides.
- Stretch the sore area gently to rid your body of lactic acid, which contributes to the pain.
- Avoid strenuous activity as long as you're in pain.

Poisonous plant

- Immediately wash everything that might have touched the plant. You may be able to take off the offending oil completely or at least reduce the impending rash.
- Soothe itching with cool, wet compresses.
- Apply lotion containing calamine, alcohol, and zinc acetate; these will dry the blisters and help speed healing.
- Leave rash open to air. This will help it heal.
- Remember that toxic oils from poisonous plants need to be washed out of clothes before they are worn again.

Tick removal

- Check your naked body from head to toe for ticks – small black, brown, reddish or tan disklike arachnids (having eight legs), from the size of a pinhead to almost the size of a thumbtack. Pay special attention to the backs of your knees, your groin area, and your torso.
- Ask a friend or family member for help if you find a tick in a hard-to-reach spot. Hold (or have the other person hold) a pair of tweezers in one hand and grasp the tick with the tweezers close to the surface of your skin. Avoid grabbing the body of the tick with your fingers and trying to pull it out. This method may cause you to leave some parts of the tick under your skin and will also expose your hands to any disease the tick is carrying.
- Gently but firmly pull the tick straight out, working for several seconds if necessary until it loosens and comes free. Occasionally, parts of the tick's mouth become separated from the rest of the tick; if they do, pull them out separately.
- Dispose of the tick by throwing it into a fire or by squishing it using a tissue and then flushing it down the toilet. Don't smash it with your foot or your bare hands.
- Clean the bite site thoroughly with soap and water or Betadine, and thoroughly wash your hands.

Wound, bandaging

- Protect yourself. Scrub your hands thoroughly with soap and disinfected water and put on latex gloves to prevent the spread of infectious disease.
- Clean the wound and carefully remove any excess debris.

- Remove any jewelry, such as rings or watches, that might impair circulation.
- Apply antibiotic cream to the inside of the material you are using as the dressing.
- Cover the wound with the dressing. The dressing should extend beyond the wound by about $1/2$ an inch so that it covers the wound completely and allows room to affix the dressing to uninjured skin.
- Cut four strips of athletic tape and affix them to the dressing and skin on all four sides of the dressing. The purpose of the bandage is to help keep the dressing in place, and it shouldn't be too loose (able to move around) or too tight (impairing circulation).
- If there is a risk that the wound will be exposed to water, cover the bandage with waterproof material such as waterproof tape or plastic.
- Look at and feel the area and limb surrounding the wound to make certain the dressing does not impair circulation.
- Ask the injured person if he or she can feel the area you are touching, feels no pain or tingling, and can move the limb fully. The skin should be pink and slightly warm to the touch.

—— EXCAVATION EQUIPMENT LIST/FIELD KIT ——

Most excavations provide all standard equipment, though volunteers and students may want to bring their own small equipment. The following list can be modified to meet the needs of the particular excavation.

15-meter (50 foot) steel measuring tape
20 cm and 10 cm nails
20 cm directional arrow
3-meter steel measuring tape
aluminum foil (for laboratory samples)
auger and/or coring device
auger extensions
backpack or other bag (for supplies)
ball of string
bamboo or wood splits (for cleaning burials, features)
battery generator
boxes, cardboard (for carrying and storage)

bristle brushes (stiff and soft)
broom
buckets (durable)
bulb syringe (for air-dusting)
calculator
clipboards
cloth bags (for soil samples)
compass
conservation materials (cotton, bandages, preservatives, etc.)
containers (for artifacts, esp. for small finds, like vials or photo film canisters)
dental picks (assorted)
disposable dust masks
drawing board
dustpans, scoops, or coal shovels
field notebook
first-aid kit
flagging tape
folding ruler (2 meter engineers')
folding table
forms
GPS receiver
graph paper
hammer and mallet
hardhats
heavy cord
heavy equipment (backhoe, front-end loader)
hoes (short- and long-handled)
hose (for flotation)
indelible felt-tip pens (like Sharpie markers)
insect repellent
kneeling pads (also, possibly wood planks)
knife (Swiss army, palette knife)
labels (various possibilities such as tie-on, gummed, etc.)
ladder (for trenches)
laptop computer
large metal toolbox
latex gloves
line levels
magnifying glass (at least 10X)
major clearing tools (such as scythe, machete, ax, saw, sledge-hammer, crowbar, chainsaw, weed-eater, spading fork, maul, pruning hook)

maps
measuring scales
measuring spoons
miscellaneous collection of screws, nails, tacks (in vials)
Munsell Soil Color Charts
nylon line
paintbrushes (2-inch width)
pencils, erasers, pencil sharpener, ballpoint pens
personal items (e.g. food and beverages, hat, sunscreen, sunglasses,
    water bottle, work boots, work gloves)
pH kit
photo menu board
photographic equipment
pickaxes, short hand-picks, or pick mattocks
plane table and alidade, dumpy level and staff, or theodolite
plastic bags of various sizes (for artifacts)
plastic wrap
pliers
plumb bob
posthole digger, scissors-type
provenience drawing square
rakes
recording forms and notebooks
root clippers (or pruning shears)
screwdrivers
shovels (square/flat-bladed, round-pointed no. 2)
sieve
sifters/screening devices and replacement parts
stakes
surveyor's level and compass
tarpaulins or plastic sheeting (for covering units in progress at end
    of day)
tent or shade cloth
tile probe
toilet paper
toothbrushes
towels
transparent ruler and triangle
trash bags
trowels (mainly pointing Marshalltown #4 or #5, some margin
    trowels)
tweezers
water

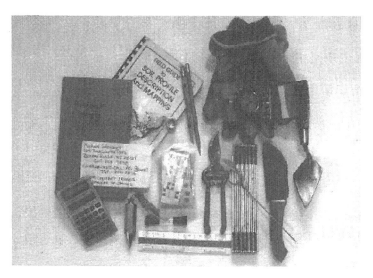

watering can or water sprayer
weed killer
wheelbarrows
whisk broom
work gloves
wrench, pipe

LISTS AND CHECKLISTS

EXCAVATION FLOW CHART

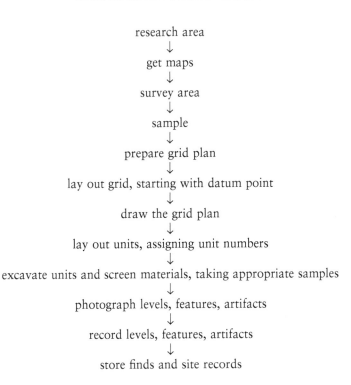

research area
↓
get maps
↓
survey area
↓
sample
↓
prepare grid plan
↓
lay out grid, starting with datum point
↓
draw the grid plan
↓
lay out units, assigning unit numbers
↓
excavate units and screen materials, taking appropriate samples
↓
photograph levels, features, artifacts
↓
record levels, features, artifacts
↓
store finds and site records

For feature:

clean area
↓
identify limits of context, number of units in which feature lies
↓
photograph
↓
draw a plan of feature
↓
take levels
↓
record and describe
↓
excavate and sample

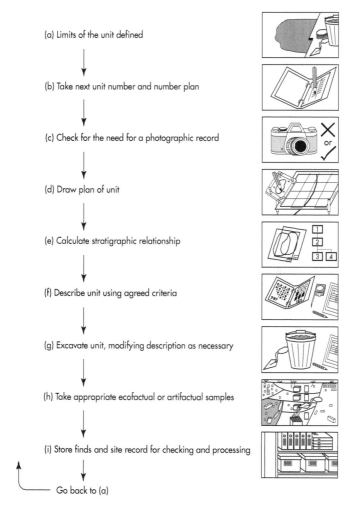

(a) Limits of the unit defined

↓

(b) Take next unit number and number plan

↓

(c) Check for the need for a photographic record

↓

(d) Draw plan of unit

↓

(e) Calculate stratigraphic relationship

↓

(f) Describe unit using agreed criteria

↓

(g) Excavate unit, modifying description as necessary

↓

(h) Take appropriate ecofactual or artifactual samples

↓

(i) Store finds and site record for checking and processing

↓

Go back to (a)

Figure 3.5 Excavation flow chart. (Steve Roskams, Figure 8: A flow diagram for recording a single stratigraphic unit, p. 115 from *Excavation*. New York: Cambridge University Press, 2001. Copyright © 2001 by Cambridge University Press. Redrawn and reprinted with permission of the author and Cambridge University Press)

EXCAVATION GRID, SETTING UP BY TAPING/TRIANGULATION

(also called 3–4–5 method, using Pythagorean theorem; points A and B are known and point C is to be located)

- Use three tapes; they should be taut and level.
- Establish a datum point – it is most desirable to have this in the southwest corner of the site so that all horizontal measurements will be to the north and east.
- Secure tape #1 at the datum point and run it due north 40 meters to point B (using transit, theodolite, siting compass, or another instrument).
- Secure tape #2 at the datum and run it along the baseline to 30 meters.
- Secure tape #3 at point B and run it to meet the end of tape #2.
- Holding tape #3 in your left hand and tape #2 in your right, bring them together as level as possible – the right angle is formed when tape #2 reads 30 m and tape #3 reads 50 m, e.g. the base-line forms a right angle in relation to the meridian.

- **Alternative**: tape #1 is run along the meridian and looped to continue at an angle to tape #2, which is laid along the baseline.
- **Alternative**: from the datum point, map in a straight line due north; points are then measured along this baseline and marked (with wooden stakes); repeat the process at a 90-degree angle to the east to establish an east baseline; repeat, if desired, for south and west baselines.
- **Alternative**: combinations of 5–12–13 or 8–15–17 or 20–21–29 will also produce a right angle.
- The row of stakes off the southwestern corner of a 10-foot grid system would be labeled 0N, the second row would be labeled 10N, the third row 20N, etc. The western row would be labeled 0E, the next row east 10E, third row east 20E, etc. Each stake has a designation written nN/nE from the datum point.

EXCAVATION GRID, SETTING UP WITH RIGHT ANGLE

- Use a "jiffy right angle."
- Place the corner of the angle on the unit control point.

- Using a compass, align one arm of the angle to magnetic north.
- Level the angle and install a stake or spike at the north and east ends of the angle.
- Invert the angle outward so the ends touch the north and east unit markers and install a northeast corner unit marker.

EXPEDIENT GRID, SETTING UP

- Stake #1 (surveyor's lathe) is at the datum point.
- Stake #3 is along the desired line of sight.
- While one person sights from stake #1 to stake #3, a third person installs stake #2 halfway in-between.
- Stake #5 is set in line with #2 and #3.
- Stake #4 is set by eye, etc.
- A 90-degree angle can be turned at any point using a surveyor's right-angle prism or by sighting along straightedges nailed together to form a horizontally mounted right-angled cross.

FAUNAL COLLECTION, ANALYSIS, AND IDENTIFICATION

- Screen to find specimens.
- Remember that faunal remains found in association with features are likely to be the result of human activities. If you can identify this during excavation, this is ideal. Finding the specimen in the screen is out of context.
- You can separate bone, shell, insect parts, etc.
- Try to determine invertebrate or vertebrate from the specimen(s).
- Sort into categories such as 1) large tubular bones, 2) small tubular bones, 3) flat bones, and 4) irregular bones.
- Record that the specimen is "cultural" unless definitively identified as "noncultural," e.g. in a complete skeleton or nest.
- Some elements may be identifiable to taxon (family, order, genus, species) by an expert or specialist. This is often done in the laboratory, by comparison with a reference collection.
- Quantification also takes place in faunal analysis, in the laboratory.

FEATURE RECORDING

Besides feature type, measurements, and drawings, these are kinds of information generally needed about features that are excavated.

- Excavation procedure: be specific.
- Portion excavated: which portion and why.
- General description: feature type and subjective statement about the constructional quality of the feature.
- Degree of preservation: generally excellent, good, or poor; state cause of deterioration and amount of damage.
- Cause and amount of deterioration: for example, weathering, intentional dismantling, animal disturbance.
- Description of how feature was constructed: description of materials used and description and interpretation of the sediment the feature was in.
- Thermal alteration: record the presence or absence of fire-reddening or charring and its extent if present.
- Sooting: record and describe the presence or absence of sooting on the feature.
- Description of modification: record and describe the presence or absence of changes to the feature.
- Artifacts and samples recovered: a general list by stratum.
- Interpretation of use history: use, remodeling, and abandonment context interpretations.
- Interpretation of associated features: list any features within this feature and any features that worked in conjunction with this feature (e.g. hearth and deflector).

FEATURES GUIDELINES

General

- Many features are first recognized through some change in color or texture in the matrix. Features are generally things not brought back to the laboratory.
- Please note that features include materials which have decomposed in place and are only recognizable as an anomaly (e.g. wooden artifacts, organic refuse). Clusters or concentrations of artifacts for a specific activity may also be considered a feature.

LISTS AND CHECKLISTS

- When a feature is discovered, it must be carefully exposed. Leave it in situ, pedestaling the feature, so that it can be excavated in its proper stratigraphic context. You want to determine the horizontal and vertical extent and characteristics of the feature.
- Err on the side of calling something a feature.
- Record in detail. Assign a feature (serial) number.
- Any artifacts or samples taken from the feature area should be given a feature provenience, tagged and bagged separately from other artifacts found in nonfeature parts of the level.
- Artifact clusters or concentrations are defined through point provenience.
- Once exposed, the feature must be measured in three dimensions and its precise provenience mapped horizontally (plan view) and vertically. It is important to show its associations with other objects and features.
- Prepare a label and a special finds form.
- Photograph and draw. You might use a provenience drawing square.
- If the feature extends into the level below or into an adjacent unit, the pedestal is not removed until all associations are recorded.

Specific features

- **Burial:** See **Burial excavation and observations.**
- **Ditch:** Once the outer edges of a ditch have been determined, a perpendicular trench is cut at the outer edges and dug until the depth of the ditch is discovered. Then the trench is extended into the ditch itself to determine its stratigraphy and shape.
- **Floor:** Carefully scrape horizontally to determine composition, density, and dimensions. Record features. A floor may be detectable by its feel (hard-packed).
- **Hearth, oven, fire pit:** carefully clear the earth with a whisk broom and trowel until it is fully exposed; then measure, map, photograph/sketch, and record. Note amount of ash, evidence of food remains. You may want charcoal for dating purposes.
- **Pit, posthole, robber trench:** you will detect these by color contrast between them and the surrounding soil. Measure and map on horizontal plan, especially for diameter. Clean area carefully, looking for associated postholes or pits. Continue to excavate only a few centimeters, leaving the earth around these features in place to reveal the stratigraphy. Draw the section. Record in detail the shape and contents. You may want a wood sample for carbon-14 dating.

- **Wall:** Brush the top clean. Measure. Photograph and draw to scale on horizontal plan. You may need to cut a trench perpendicular to both sides of the wall to expose all the features of the wall. Patterns of masonry and other relevant data (material, construction, etc.) need to be observed and recorded. After everything is documented, you will continue to excavate and look for other floor levels associated with the wall. If a second lower floor is found, then another trench perpendicular to the first trench is dug. The wall(s) remain until their relationship with structures lying below can be determined.

FIELD CLOTHING LIST

blaze-orange clothing (if in the woods during hunting season or in low-visibility or high-traffic area)
hat
raincoat
sunglasses
sweater or overcoat
wash-and-wear clothing (light-colored long-sleeve cotton work shirt, jeans or khaki pants)
waterproof clothing
work gloves
work shoes or boots (though heavy boots are not suitable for soft-floored sites)

FIELD CONSERVATION INITIAL STEPS

- Be very careful with the artifacts. Follow the director's policies regarding how to handle or sample lithics, ceramics, organic materials, etc.
- In general, handle artifacts as little as possible. If you clean artifacts you will remove residues that may be important for laboratory evaluation. If some field-cleaning is called for, use soft paintbrushes or toothbrushes, a bulb syringe, or small sprayer or atomizer.
- Consider wearing latex gloves to prevent contamination, especially for artifacts that may undergo dating, chemical, biological, or physical analysis techniques.

- It is better to repair artifacts in the laboratory under optimal conditions.
- When faced with stabilization problems in the field, consider whether a stabilizing agent or preservative is reversible. If any chemicals are used in the field, records should be kept of what was used and the methods by which the chemicals were applied.
- Bag larger or heavier artifacts separately from smaller and more fragile artifacts.
- Use stiff containers for very fragile artifacts.
- Bag separately those artifacts and ecofacts which may be subjected to special laboratory analysis or dating techniques.
- If artifacts are damp when bagged, poke a couple of tiny holes in the bag so they can dry out and so mold and fungus do not grow.
- Make a note on the tag if an artifact requires immediate or special attention.
- Use bubble wrap, acid-free paper, aluminum foil, etc. for special packing needs.

FIELD ETIQUETTE

- No obscene language or behavior.
- No sexual harassment.
- No threatening behavior or fighting.
- Address questions to your supervisor.
- Be courteous and enthusiastic toward visitors. If you are unsure about answering a question, refer the question to your supervisor.
- Be very careful around walls of and top edges of units.
- Develop good equipment habits. Clean items at the end of the day.
- Do not eat or drink in your unit.
- Do not presume that it is ok to step into someone else's unit.
- Keep meticulous records.
- Refrain from unnecessary jabber.
- Stay organized and keep your work area clean.

FIELD VEHICLE EQUIPMENT LIST

(for an extended trip or in an isolated area)

191

3-in-1 oil
adjustable pliers
assorted nuts, bolts, screws, etc.
ax
ball-peen hammer
blanket
brake fluid
breaker bar for socket wrench
bucket
car repair manual
carburetor cleaning spray
carburetor rebuild kit
cellular telephone
circuit tester
combination wrench set
compression tester
crescent wrench set
crowbar
distributor cap
duct tape
electrical connectors
electrician's tape
engine oil flush
epoxy or super glue
extinguisher
extractor set
feeler gauges
flares
flashlight
flat, round, triangular files
gas pump
gasket paper
gasket sealer
gear puller
hacksaw
hand cleaner
heavy-duty ignition wire
hex wrench set
hydraulic jack
hydrometer
impact wrench drive
inner tubes and inner tube repair
    kit

jumper cables
light-duty accessory wire
liquid white-out
lug wrench
machete
metal chisel
metal drills
metal punch
mounted tires, two
needle-nose pliers
oil
oil filler spout
oil filter wrench
oil pump
paper towels
Phillips screwdrivers
piece of carpet
plug wires
points, two sets of
putty knife
quick-start spray
radiator flush
radiator leak stop
rags
rear-end transmission oil
rip saw
sandpaper
sheepherder's jack
shovel
siphon tube
slot screwdrivers
socket extensions
socket U-joint
socket wrench set
socket wrench step down/up
spare belts
spare filters, multiple
spare fuses
spare gaskets
spare hoses
spark plug gauge
spark plug socket for wrench
spark plugs, two sets of

Tach/dwell meter
timing chain
timing light
tire pressure gauge
tire pump
torque wrench
towing chain
towing rope
tube patch kit
U-joints

valve spring depressor
vehicle manual
vise-grip pliers
water
water pump
WD-40
wheel bearing grease
wheel chocks/jack blocks
wire/sheet metal cutter

—— FIELDWORK COMPETENCE GUIDELINES ——

Fieldworkers should become competent in the following:

using a grid at an archaeological site
using measurement in the excavation of a unit and in plotting the
    provenience of artifacts and features
excavating a unit according to instructions, keeping the walls
    straight and floor level
recognizing various categories of artifacts
drawing a basic wall profile
mapping artifacts and features in a unit
using a trowel and shovel properly
screening materials in the field
understanding the delicate nature of some artifacts, such as charcoal
labeling bags properly and identifing artifacts
keeping meticulous records
keeping daily excavation notes
cleaning and caring for field equipment

—————— FIRST AID KIT ——————

Ace bandages
adhesive tape roll
antacid
antibiotic ointment
antiseptic soap
aspirin/acetaminophen

Band-Aids
burn ointment
cellular telephone
cold packs
cotton balls/cotton swabs
epi pens and antihistamine tablets

first-aid manual
gauze bandages and roll
ground sheet
hydrogen peroxide
insect repellent
matches
medication alert
mild laxative
mild sedative
motion-sickness medication
paper cups/measuring spoons
personal prescriptions
poison-ivy medication
razor blades

rubbing alcohol
safety pins
salt tablets
scissors
sheets/towels/blankets
smelling salts
snakebite kit (freeze kit)
splints
sterile gauze pads, two sizes
sunburn lotion
tourniquet
triangular bandage
tweezers/needle/thread
water purification tablets

— FLAKED STONE ARTIFACT IDENTIFICATION —

(some types of stones used for flaked artifacts and descriptions helping to identify them)

- Basalt: a dense dark gray fine-grained igneous rock.
- Chalcedony: a milky or grayish translucent to transparent quartz, a flint-like stone with a waxy appearance.
- Chert: fine-grained rock with semi-glossy finish, is usually white, pinkish, brown, gray, or blue-gray in color.
- Flint: a hard kind of stone; a form of silica more opaque than chalcedony.
- Jasper: an opaque form of quartz; red or yellow or brown or dark green in color.
- Obsidian: acid or granitic glass; usually dark, especially black, but transparent in thin pieces.
- Opal: a translucent mineral consisting of hydrated silica of variable color.
- Quartz: a hard glossy mineral – when clear and colorless it is called rock crystal; milky quartz is milky white; smoky quartz is brown and cloudy; rose quartz is a pale red color; sugar quartz is the color of brown sugar.
- Quartzite: a compact granite rock composed of quartz sandstone, commonly white, yellow, or red.
- Rhyolite: a fine-grained light colored volcanic rock, colors from white, through gray, and yellow to reddish-pink.

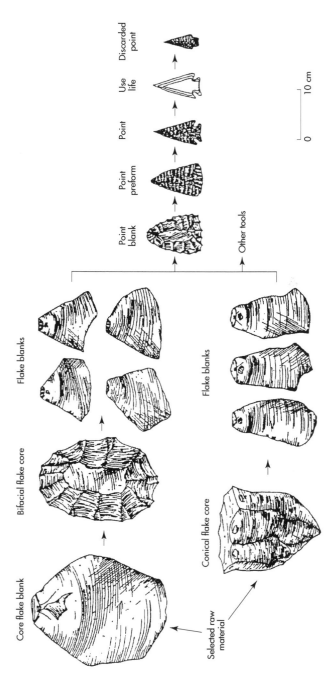

Figure 3.6 Flaked stone artifacts. (Mark Q. Sutton and Brooke S. Arkush, Figure 11: A core reduction/tool production sequence and use-life continuum, p. 42 from *Archaeological Laboratory Methods: An Introduction*, Third Edition. Dubuque, IA: Kendall/Hunt Publishing, 2002. Copyright © J. J. Flenniken)

Core flake blank

Selected raw material

Bifacial flake core

Conical flake core

Flake blanks

Flake blanks

Point blank

Point preform

Point

Use life

Discarded point

Other tools

0   10 cm

FLORA COLLECTION, ANALYSIS, AND IDENTIFICATION

- Most plant remains will be found in the screening process or from soil samples in the field.
- Seeds and charcoal may be found in screening. Soil samples must also be taken – for dating, retrieval of small samples, retrieval of pollen or phytoliths, and characterization of the soil. A large soil sample is recommended.
- Plant remains in association with features are likely the result of human activities, so you must also take control samples from nearby contexts for comparison.
- Special samples may be taken in the field for pollen and phytoliths.
- The first identification is done by sorting into seeds, plant parts, charcoal, shell, bone, insect parts, pigment, lithic debitage and artifacts, etc.
- A comparative collection of plant specimens is very helpful. An experienced archaeobotanist may be consulted for further classification and identification.

GLASS ATTRIBUTES

coating
color (amber/brown, amethyst/purple, black, blue, clear, dark green, green, red/pink, white/milk glass)
composition (potash-lead glass, potash-lime glass, soda-lime glass)
cutting
enameling
engraving
etching
gilding
inclusions
molding (contact, optic, pattern, press)
painting
staining
superimposition (glass applied to glass)
thickness

■ Are there differences in the smoothness on different parts of the rock? If it is equally smooth all over, it is unlikely to have been used for milling or grinding.

■ Does the surface glint or shine when held up to strong light at eye level? This may indicate smoothing by human action.

■ When viewed with a magnifying glass (10X), is the smoothness limited to the higher parts while the lower parts are unsmoothed? This is a characteristic of ground stone.

■ Is there a transition between the smooth part and the rest of the rock, almost like an edge? This, too, is a characteristic of ground stone.

■ Does the rock have an unnatural shape, but looks more purposefully shaped?

■ Use your sense of touch to aid you in the identification. If it is really smooth, combined with one or more of the above characteristics, it likely indicates human action.

Describing ground stone

Shape

concave	rectangular
convex	rough
cross-section	round
flat	rounded
irregular	smooth
other	square
oval	triangular
plan view	

Shape of distal end
flattened
other
pointed

Surface scars
long
other
rounded

LISTS AND CHECKLISTS

HEARTH IDENTIFICATION

- Look for discoloration in the rocks used to line the firepit.
- Look for charcoal remains which have turned the soil beneath the hearth area dark – reddened or blackened soil or rocks must be investigated.
- Leave any stones or discolored soil in place as you use a brush to sweep away loose soil.
- When you have located the hearth, expose the top completely by brushing away the soil, watching for any micro-artifacts.
- Look for cooking and eating utensils, bones, and food remains.
- Halt excavation until the size, shape, and location of the hearth is recorded.
- Photograph and draw the hearth.
- You may be instructed to excavate the material from one side of the hearth, leaving the other half intact to provide a vertical profile of the deposits.
- Charcoal samples should be removed, which will indicate the type of wood used.
- After the hearth has been excavated and everything recorded, the area adjacent to it is excavated – looking for utensils, food remains, bones, etc.

HISTORICAL DOCUMENTS, USEFUL

family records (Bibles, correspondence, diaries, diplomas)
institutional records (church records, educational records, newspapers)
public records (cemetery records, census records, court and probate
  records, federal mortality schedules, land records, military
  records, tax lists, vital statistics records)

INDIVIDUAL STRATA, DEFINING

- Supply list: guides for describing the basic characteristics of soils and sediments, sample bags and containers, hand lens, Munsell color chart, water bottle, rules/tapes, graph paper, notebook, writing instruments.
- What are the obvious changes in color, texture, gravel content, and soil structure in the profile? Use the point of a trowel to

stab a profile and note how the tool penetrates the face of the exposure.

- Are there textural differences within any stratum defined on the basis of color? Are there structural differences within any stratum defined on the basis of color and texture? You are looking for internal textural and structural differences to distinguish divisions or different types of B horizons.
- Where are large artifacts, clusters of artifacts, placed fill, features, architectural elements, or anomalies in the profile? These need to be in your drawing of the profile. Note the points of origin of undisturbed features and the vertical distribution of large or heavy artifacts on the face of the profile. Inscribe the strata boundaries and features with the point of the trowel on the face of the exposure – or otherwise delimit them. Clean the profile where it was disturbed for testing and then photograph and draw the profile.

KNIVES, SHARPENING

- Use a wet or dry sharpening stone.
- Place the stone flat on a stable surface.
- Holding the knife by its handle, put the blade at a 10- to 25-degree angle to the stone.
- Draw the knife toward you and across the stone.
- Repeat process on the other side of the blade.

LEATHER/SKINS/TEXTILES/CORDAGE FIELD CONSERVATION

- Keep away from light and heat.
- Carefully brush off dust or dirt.
- Support the item from underneath and handle it minimally.
- If wet or waterlogged, keep wet and store in a polyethylene bag or in polyethylene sheeting with a fungicide.
- If dry and/or brittle, wrap carefully in acid-free tissue paper.
- If consolidation is unavoidable, spray on a thin solution of PVA and wrap in tissue paper, using a splint for support.
- Pseudomorphs, the carbonized fragments of textiles on metal objects or sherds, should be left in place and protected, then brought to the attention of a conservator.

- Excavating a level by quadrants may give more control over artifact provenience. It can substitute for point provenience, especially when the latter would be impractical.
- Each quadrant must be excavated, screened, and documented individually.
- Pull a tape between two adjacent corners and hold it there. Find the midpoint between the corners on the tape.
- Hold the string of a suspended plumb bob at the midpoint, with the plumb bob touching the ground.
- Place a nail, spike, or surveying pin at this point.
- Repeat for the other walls.
- Find the unit's center point by pulling a tape diagonally across the unit between two opposite corners and following the procedure used for the side walls.
- There are now five points on the floor of the unit.
- Anchor one end of a string to the nail at the center point of the north wall, pull it taut, and wrap it around the nail at the unit's center, then around the nail for the center of the south wall. The unit is divided in half.
- Do the same for west to east; the unit is now divided in quadrants.
- When digging, establish the base of the level, using the string lines for guidance.
- Each quadrant is treated as if it were a level within the unit – for measurement and data collection. The matrix is screened, bagged, tagged, and catalogued separately from the other quadrants in the level.

LITHICS FIELD CONSERVATION

- Stone can be affected by corrosive acids (e.g. fertilizer), acid rain, air pollution, plant life (e.g. lichens), and salt.
- If you use a tool to remove something from stone, it should be of a material softer than the stone. Dirt should be removed with a soft brush.
- If a stone has salt on its surface, allow it to dry and gently dust off the salt with a soft brush. If the crystals re-form, then immerse in a tub of distilled water and use a soft brush to remove the crystals after some time has passed.

- For insoluble salts, you can try a 2% solution of hydrochloric acid on the area. If you soak the stone, then check it frequently.
- If a stone has a crumbling or cracked surface, consolidation may be required (thin solution of PVA). A thin coat that is completely absorbed should be followed by a thicker coat.
- Flakes should be bagged separately to avoid their grinding against other artifacts and lose use-wear information.
- Leave items unwashed to preserve for residue analysis.

LITHICS IDENTIFICATION CHART

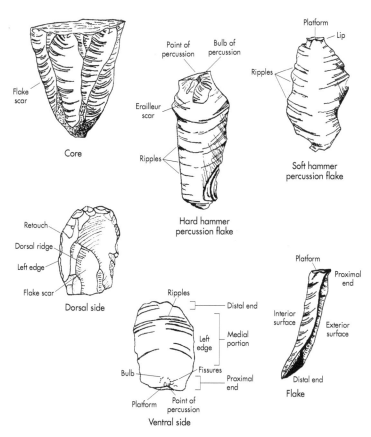

Figure 3.7 Lithics identification chart. (Norena Shopland "Identifying Worked Flint," *Archaeological Finds*, Tempus Publishing, 2005. Copyright © PAS. Reprinted by permission of Norena Shopland and The Portable Antiquities Scheme)

LOCATING A SITE WITHIN A SECTION

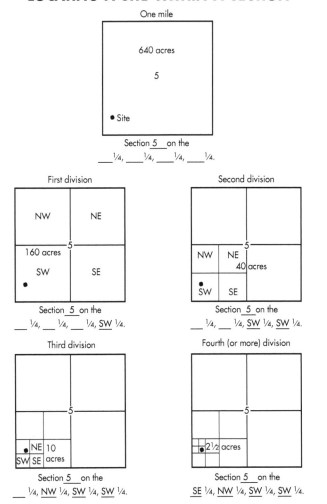

Figure 3.8 Locating a site within a section (from the Office of the State Archaeologist; State of Iowa. Copyright © The Office of the State Archaeologist of Iowa. Reprinted by permission)

MASONRY AND BRICK DESCRIPTION TERMS

- Bed joint: horizontal joint between masonry.
- Galleting: pebbles inserted into mortar joints as protection or decoration.

- Glazed bricks, projecting headers, vitrified headers: decorative devices.
- Honeycomb: designed with missing alternate bricks, either for decoration, ventilation, or access.
- Lacing course: a row of tiles or bricks used to reinforce a masonry feature.
- Mortar: a plastic building material that hardens and is used in masonry or plastering.
- Perpend: vertical joint between ends.
- Rustication: use of chamfered joints.
- Stopped end: a finish with closers like half headers set in the penultimate course.
- Toothing: the use of gaps or projections in alternate courses.
- Tumbling in: designed with bricks set at a diagonal angle to create a buttress against it.

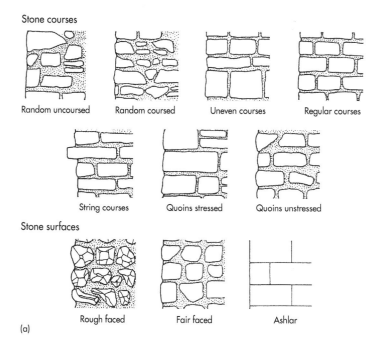

(a)

Figure 3.9a Stone courses and finishing. (Steve Roskams, Figure 20: Stone courses and finishing, based on the Museum of London system, p. 187 from *Excavation.* New York: Cambridge University Press, 2001. Copyright © 2001 by Cambridge University Press. Redrawn and reprinted with permission of the author and Cambridge University Press)

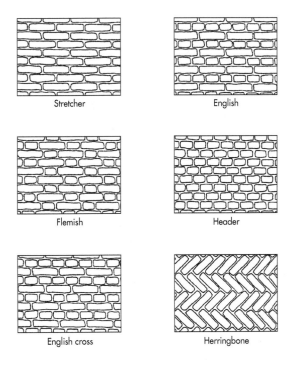

Stretcher

English

Flemish

Header

English cross

Herringbone

(b)

Figure 3.9b Brick bonds. (Steve Roskams, Figure 21: Common brick bonds, based on the Museum of London system, p. 188 from *Excavation*. New York: Cambridge University Press, 2001. Copyright © 2001 by Cambridge University Press. Redrawn and reprinted with permission of the author and Cambridge University Press)

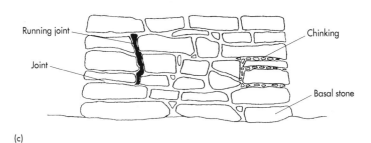

Running joint

Chinking

Joint

Basal stone

(c)

Figure 3.9c Masonry wall attributes. (Figure 3, p. 61 from *The Crow Canyon Archaeological Center Field Manual [HTML Title]*. Crow Canyon Archaeological Center, 2001a. Copyright © 2001 by Crow Canyon Archaeological Center. Reprinted by permission)

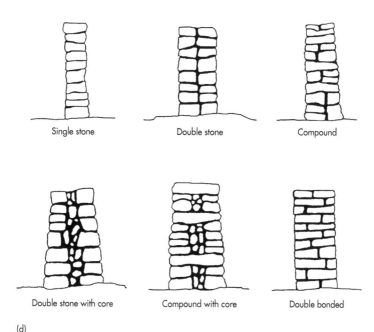

(d)

Figure 3.9d Wall cross-section types. (Figure 4, p. 62 from *The Crow Canyon Archaeological Center Field Manual [HTML Title]*. Crow Canyon Archaeological Center, 2001a. Copyright © 2001 by Crow Canyon Archaeological Center. Reprinted by permission)

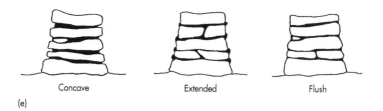

(e)

Figure 3.9e Mortar forms. (Figure 6, p. 64 from *The Crow Canyon Archaeological Center Field Manual [HTML Title]*. Crow Canyon Archaeological Center, 2001a. Copyright © 2001 by Crow Canyon Archaeological Center. Reprinted by permission)

MEASUREMENT EQUIPMENT

Various combinations are chosen, depending on whether you are measuring distance, direction, or both.

100-meter reinforced tape (steel ribbon)
20-meter reinforced tape
30-meter reinforced tape
alidade
chain
compasses
dumpy level
electronic distance measuring equipment (various types, e.g. Total Station, GPS, distance meter)
field notebook with waterproof paper
hand level
pencils, pens, erasers
plane table
plumb bobs
prism, prism mount, prism pole
range poles
spirit level
stadia
surveyor's pins
telescope
theodolite
transit
trundle wheel or perambulator

METAL ARTIFACT ANALYSIS STEPS

decoration analysis (repoussé, tracing, pointille, engraving, stamping, overlay/plating, inlay, damascening, enameling, cloisonné, granulation, filigree, spinning, etc.)
determination of manufacturing technique (cast? wrought?)
function analysis
material analysis (alloy? ore? native?)
measurement and density assessment
shape analysis

METAL DETECTOR USE

- Sweep the detector 1–2 inches above and across the unit to be excavated. Whenever the detector signals that a metal object lies below the surface, a small flag should be planted at that point.
- There are two basic types of detector – transmitter receiver and beat frequency oscillator. The transmitter receiver is the easiest to operate.
- Those with smaller search coils detect objects of every size at shallow depths; larger coils are for detecting large objects at greater depth.
- Use earphones to better detect the signal variations. Earphones also block out the sound of high winds and other extraneous noises.

METAL FIELD CONSERVATION

- Metals are rarely found native; most are found in the form of ores.
- Some metals may deteriorate as soon as they are exposed to air or material containing acids.
- Before disturbing broken or fragile objects, make sure you draw and photograph them.
- Iron is often rusty, and brass, bronze, and copper are covered with a greenish crust of copper carbonates over copper oxides and chloride.
- Do not pull metal objects out of the ground because it is often impossible to determine their strength and they can easily break. Carefully clean around the object and pedestal it, undercut the object, and then gently lift it out.
- To prevent further corrosion in the field, keep the metal dry and pack it with silica gel.
- Particularly fragile artifacts should be put in rigid containers for transport to the laboratory.
- Keep all metals dust-free, in low humidity, and in acid-free packaging. Do not touch unless absolutely necessary.
- Resist the temptation to clean coins in the field.
- Do not put metal in plastic bags as moisture will soon accumulate.
- All metal should be cleaned in the laboratory. If you try to remove corrosion in the field, you will likely irreparably damage the object. Do not wash metal artifacts in the field or try to repair them.

- Collecting oral histories is most often done in the form of an audio or video taped interview.
- As the interviewer, it is often wise to meet with the teller(s) before-hand and go over the process with them.
- Have them sign an Oral History Form.
- One might start the session before the recording begins by explaining how the interview will proceed, and then asking a few questions to tantalize the teller's memories.
- It should not be a dialogue, but should be a selection of stories from a teller prompted by short questions.
- An oral history interview should include the following information:

  date of recording
  place of recording
  name of story, if applicable
  full name of interviewee/storyteller
  your name as "collector" or "interviewer"
  a list of key words to help researchers identify the subjects, places, and people involved. If the subject is addressed in any detail, include it.
  Personal History Release Form

- Consider the following discussion areas for the taped interview:

  childhood days
  schooling
  occupations and work life
  religious experiences
  community events and involvement
  political involvement
  transportation modes and experiences
  crafts, folk arts, customs, traditions
  encounters with the law
  folktales, legends, and superstitions
  musical experiences or talents
  experiences and involvement with war
  memorable characters and/or incidents
  marital experiences: first child, first date, wedding plans, etc.
  timeline of their life

PHOTO MENU BOARD

- A black slotted menu board is used with white plastic letters to spell out the site, unit, etc. for in-photograph labeling for unit profile and feature photographs.
- Set the board up to give: site number, unit number, unit coordinates, feature number *or* compass direction of profile, depth *or* horizontal location, date.
- Keep the letters in small plastic bags, maybe separate ones for the different types of information on the board. Letters should be kept separate from numbers.
- Certain parts of the menu board can be set up ahead of time. Frequently used words like "unit," "profile," or "feature" can be kept in separate bags to facilitate set-up.

PIT IDENTIFICATION

- Pits are intentionally dug or natural holes in the ground that were filled with rubbish/debris or used for storage. They may extend through a number of strata.
- Darkened soil or variations in soil color and texture may indicate a pit or indicate the disturbance of surrounding soil horizons when the pit was dug.
- The top of the pit should be exposed and recorded in the same manner as with hearths.
- One method is to leave the pit undisturbed and to dig the surrounding material through strata until only the pit is left. This will work if the pit is small and extends only through one or two strata.
- If the pit is large and/or extends through a number of strata, then it can be dug one side at a time or in quarters/quadrants.
- The artifacts in a pit may have been disturbed and the excavator will have to determine if this is the case.
- Regardless of the method used, a pit is considered a stratum by itself and the material within it is assigned additional strata as needed.

PLANE TABLE MAPPING EQUIPMENT

aerial photographs
alidade (with pins, screwdriver
   for adjustment)
altimeter
beam compass
binoculars
brown paper for covering map
   sheet
brush (sable or camel's hair)
   for lenses
calculator
color cloth or flags for station
   signals
colored pencils, crayons
colored tape for stadia points
erasers
hatchet
manufacturer's instruction
   books
mathematical tables
measuring tape
nails

notebooks
paper
pencils (TH–9H)
pens
pens and ink
Philadelphia rod
plane table
plane table sheets
pliers with wire cutters
plumb bobs
scale for plotting points
solar ephemeris
stadia rod
stereoscope
straightedge
surveying text
taping pins
taping scale
tracing material
triangulation and level survey
   data
tripod with cap

POINT PROVENIENCE PROCEDURE

- This method gives the most control over one's data because the exact location of each artifact, its context and association, is recorded.
- Decide if the artifacts will be mapped-and-pulled as they are found, or pedestaled-and-left-in-place until the level has been completed. The latter is the most time-consuming.
- Work cleanly, opening only a small area at a time, mapping artifacts.
- If you are using a Total Station, it will speed up the recording process. The angle turned off a point of reference, distance from the instrument position to the artifact, and artifact elevation would be recorded for every artifact.

- If you are using a theodolite, you can take provenience measurements on more than one point of the artifact.
- A mapping frame may aid the recording of a large number of artifacts.
- Each artifact recorded by point provenience is assigned a unique number, tagged and bagged individually.

Map-and-pull:

- Start at one wall and skim a small area with a trowel. Either record each artifact as found or wait until a number of them are found.
- Constantly screen the matrix. Anything found in screening will be assigned a general level provenience.
- Work your way across the floor of the unit until you reach a closing depth, as you would for any level.

Pedestaling:

- Work in the smallest area possible before expanding.
- Use a trowel or even smaller tools.
- Start by excavating a very narrow trench down to the base of the level along one side wall. You will vertically slice the unexcavated face of the level from one side of the unit to the other. This will let you see artifacts and stratigraphic changes before you get to them with the trowel.
- Fully expose the top of each artifact.
- Make gentle vertical cuts in the excavation floor and remove the matrix around the artifact, making a pedestal. Clear the matrix to the base of the level. This is repeated for each artifact.
- If you cannot extend the excavation to the base of the level due to the density of artifacts, you will have to meticulously clear out loose matrix.
- When you have exposed as much as possible, do the mapping, drawing, and photography.

--------- **POLLEN SAMPLE COLLECTION** ---------

- Clean the outer surface of the unit profile. Sample within one stratum of the profile rather than mixing strata.
- Avoid taking samples from hearths or other features in which there is ash or charcoal or other evidence of burning.

- Use a clean trowel.
- Start sampling from the bottom of the profile and work toward the top.
- Move the trowel laterally, following the plane of the stratum.
- Collect 0.5–1 liter (or quart) of material.
- Clean the trowel between samples.
- Put the sample in a sterile, leakproof container. Add a few drops of fungicide if the sample is damp.
- Label each sample.

POST MOLD IDENTIFICATION

- A cast or mold will exist wherever wood has been used as a post in the ground. The soil around a post is packed and will retain its shape even after the wood has disintegrated.
- The soil around a post will have a slightly different color and texture.
- Inside the ring of packed soil, the decayed or organic matter will likely be darker than the packed soil surrounding it.
- When a circle like this appears, digging should halt and the location and size of the post mold should be recorded.
- Consider these methods: 1) dig around the mold from at least three sides until the bottom is reached – then search the surrounding area for signs of other posts; 2) assume it is a post mold and attempt to find others before continuing to excavate the first.
- Post molds can indicate a large structure, fence, or site – so also look for indications of walls and floors.

POTENTIAL FIELD HAZARDS

animal bites
cave-ins
climate extremes, exposures, exhaustion, dehydration, cramps; skin cancer
cuts, abrasions, bruises
excessive pollen, dust; allergic reactions to airborne particles; airborne disease
falls
fire and burns

hazardous underground utilities
hazardous wastes, chemicals
hunting season exposure
insect bites, allergic reactions to stings, Lyme disease
lightning strikes
location or accommodations hazards
miscellaneous
obscurity of site and remoteness from emergency services
poisonous plant exposure
strains and sprains
toxic waste dumps
vehicular traffic

POWERS' SCALE OF ROUNDNESS FOR GRAINS

Class	1	2	3	4	5	6
	Very angular	Angular	Sub-angular	Sub-rounded	Rounded	Well rounded
High sphericity	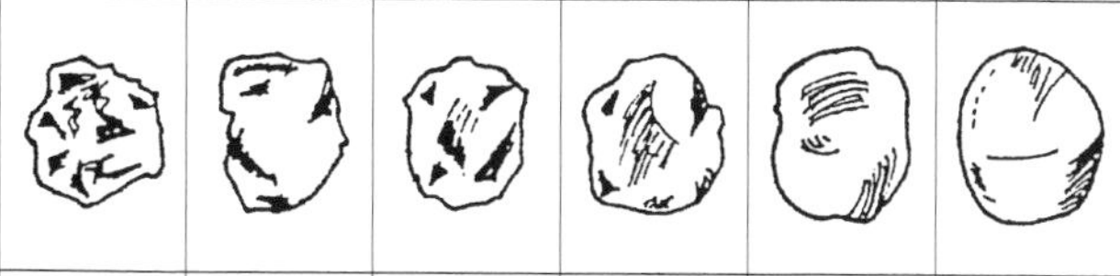					
Low sphericity	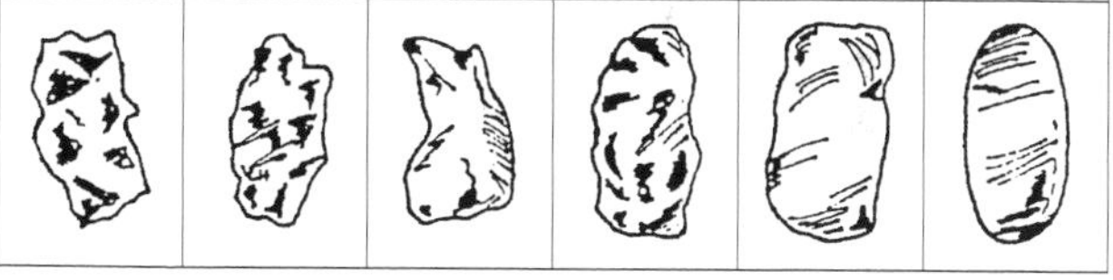					

Figure 3.10 Powers' Scale of Roundness. (A. Barraclough, Quaternary sediment analysis: a deductive approach at A-level. Powers' scale of roundness, pp. 15–18 from *Teaching Geography* 17(1), 1992. Copyright © 1992 by The Geographical Association. Reprinted by permission)

RADIOCARBON DATING, SOURCES OF ERROR

contamination before sampling
contamination during or after sampling
context of deposition (when formation processes of context are not
  fully understood)
date of context

RECONNAISSANCE EQUIPMENT

aerial photos
altimeter
backpack
boots
camera, film, tripod
clinometer
compass
first aid kit
flagging
mapping board
maps
metal tags
notebook
pencils, pens, erasers
permanent marking pens
pocket stereoscope
pocket tape/ruler
site record forms
snakebite kit
topographical maps
water bottle

ROCK AND MINERAL
IDENTIFICATION CHART

Table 3.1 Rock types

General rock type	Texture – average size of minerals	General color and/or composition – Miscellaneous observations	Rock name
IGNEOUS ROCKS Interlocking homogenous crystalline texture – no preferred orientation to the mineral grains	Fine grained – Extrusive, volcanic	Felsic – Light colored	Rhyolite
		Intermediate	Andesite
		Mafic – Dark colored	Basalt
	Medium grained – Dikes, sills, etc.	Felsic – Light colored	——
		Intermediate	Dacite
		Mafic – Dark colored	Diabase
	Coarse grained – Generally intrusive	Felsic – Light colored	Granite
		Intermediate	Diorite
		Mafic – Dark colored	Gabbro
		Ultramafic	Peridotite
	Glassy	Dark to black – felsic (DOES NOT follow normal color index)	Obsidian
	Frothy	Felsic – Light colored	Pumice
		Mafic – Dark colored	Scoria
SEDIMENTARY ROCKS Consolidated detrital clasts, chemical precipitates, and/or biological residue	Coarse fragments	Rounded clasts	Conglomerate
		Angular clasts	Breccia
	Sand sized fragments	Clean quartz (w/feldspar?)	Sandstone
		Dirty w/rock fragments and clay	Graywacke
	Fine grained – cannot see individual clasts	Nonfoliated, "clay the size"	Siltstone
		Foliated – "clay the material"	Shale
	Chemical – fine grain	Soft – passes fizz test	Limestone
		Hard – fails fizz test	Chert
	Fossiliferous	Mostly shall fragments	Coquina
METAMORPHIC ROCKS Interlocking non-homogenous crystalline texture – commonly with a preferred orientation to the mineral grains	Foliated, very fine grained – no visible minerals	Dull – passes "tink test"	Slate
		Foliated, shiny due to increased size of micaceous minerals (almost see them)	Phyllite
	Foliated – medium to coarse grained	Individual mineral grains visible. Major mineral(s) included as name modifiers	Schist (ex. Mica Schist)
	Color banded	Alternating layers of light (felsic) and dark (mafic) minerals	Gniess
	Distinct layering – often highly folded and contorted	Alternating layers of felsic igneous rock (light) and mafic gniess (dark)	Migmatite
	Non-foliated with non-oriented grains	Soft – passes fizz test	Marble
		Hard – fails fizz test	Quartzite
		Interlocking hornblende crystals	Amphibolite

215

■ The best samples are those found in situ that can be linked to meaningful associations. A clean trowel or knife blade, aided by tweezers, should be used to pick up the material. Handling organics with the hands can lead to contamination by body oils. The sample should be placed in a foil pouch, plastic or glass vial, or polyethylene bag. If the sample is wet, it should be allowed to dry thoroughly before being packed for shipping or storage. Do not let dust or dirt contaminate the material while drying.

■ The sample should be clearly labeled and placed in a second collecting bag, also labeled. Information should be recorded at the time of collection about possible associations, evidence of any disturbance, expected significance of date of sample, name of sampler, exact position and depth, unit and level, name and number of site, method used for collecting, any conservation treatment (to be avoided!), condition of the sample when collected, and species of plant or wood.

■ Try to collect as much as possible if radiocarbon dating is anticipated.

■ For AMS samples, microstratigraphic techniques are necessary. Note burrows, tree root cavities, ancient soil stumps, soil cracks, and other human factors noted in the matrix.

■ Sediment soil: collect sediment and/or soil from representative strata, levels, or features. This can be used to determine chemistry, decomposed materials, human activities, natural stratigraphy, particle size, and trace elements.

■ Column samples: collect incremental and constant volume samples of matrix and its inclusions down the wall of an excavation. This can be used to determine chemistry, cultural stratigraphy, decomposed materials, degree of post-depositional movement of artifacts, human activities, natural stratigraphy, particle size, and trace elements.

■ Flotation: collect sample or constant volume of matrix from excavation levels, collect sample or all of feature matrix. This can be used for reconstruction of local environment and subsistence and for recovery of micro-artifacts, especially floral and faunal remains.

■ Bulk sample: collect volume of matrix from an excavation level or strata or feature. This can be used as an archival sample of matrix or be held for future analyses.

- Pollen/phytolith: collect sediment from newly exposed deposits on level floors or in features, inside of side walls, or beneath artifacts. This can be used to identify decomposed botanical remains and reconstruct the local environment. Use clean implements and store in dry, sterile containers.
- (Samples for dating purposes can be collected during any type of fieldwork.)
- Oxidizable carbon ratio: collect organic sediments from buried soil or feature. This can be used to determine the age of strata or feature.
- Optically stimulated luminescence: collect sediment from unexposed portions of level floors or side walls. This can be used to determine the age of strata or features. These are best collected by specialists.
- Thermoluminescence: collect burned or heated lithic artifacts or clay, ceramics, and sample of associated sediment. This can be used to determine the age of strata or feature.
- Paleomagnetism or archaeomagnetism: collect burned sediments, clay, or rock preserving their compass/magnetic orientation in situ in the matrix. This can be used to determine the age of relevant strata or feature.
- Radiocarbon/carbon-14/dendrochronology: collect wood and wood charcoal. This can be used to determine the age of relevant strata or feature. Use a clean trowel, wrap the sample in aluminum foil and place inside a clean plastic or glass container.

SAMPLING DEEP-SITE EXCAVATION

- Gather information on number, depth, extent of subsurface zones by making stratigraphic probes.
- Create sample stratification of the site.
- Excavate sample test units.
- Classify sample text units by layer to determine activity categories and the relations between the layers.
- Expand the excavation based on this classification to improve the representation of activity categories in each layer.

- Decide the types of archaeological data to be collected.
- Decide what sampling strategy best fits the research design, e.g. one must sample in clusters to look for patterns and frequency changes.
- If using cluster sampling, decide the size and shape of sampling unit.
- Decide the type of cluster sampling type, simple (all items in each category are collected or counted as they occur within cluster) or nested (where subsample units are necessary).
- Decide on probabilistic (for defining patterning; uses prior knowledge of site) or nonprobablistic (for contextual variability; uses mathematical probability theory), depending on the type of information desired.
- If using probabilistic sampling, then decide how to control for bias – choosing simple, systematic, systematic unaligned, or stratified random sampling.
- Decide what percentage of the whole is to be sampled and the sample size.

General:

existing knowledge
objectives of the survey
population to be sampled
data to be collected
degree of precision required
method of measurement
frame
sample selection
pre-test
organization of fieldwork
summary and analysis of data
information useful for future surveys

SAMPLING TECHNIQUES

bulk sampling
column or core sampling
haphazard sampling
purposeful or judgment sampling
random sampling
systematic sampling

SCREEN MESH CHART

230 = 0.06 mm, 0.00236 in
120 = 0.12 mm, 0.00472 in
100 = 0.15 mm, 0.00591 in
60 = 0.25 mm, 0.00984 in
40 = 0.42 mm, 0.01654 in
35 = 0.50 mm, 0.01969 in
20 = 0.85 mm, 0.03346 in
18 = 1 mm, 0.03937 in
10 = 2 mm, 0.07874 in
6 = 3.35 mm, 0.13189 in
5 = 4 mm, 0.15748 in

LISTS AND CHECKLISTS

SCREENING

- Choice of screen size is dependent on the data you need in order to answer your research questions – and by time constraints.
- The standard screen size for archaeology is $1/4$-inch mesh; smaller screen size of $1/8$ and $1/16$ inch mesh may be used depending on what is being excavated.
- Matrix may be shaken through the screen or pushed through it by hand (wearing gloves to prevent injury) or carefully with a tool (wood preferred to metal).
- Use a trowel with caution so you do not damage artifacts.
- Screen can damage artifacts, even lithics and ceramics, so be careful.
- Smaller loads of matrix in screening improves the chances of spotting artifacts before and during sifting.

■ Simple water screen may be done, using a hose or buckets of water and a screen on rigid stand – useful for breaking down problem sediments and soils (large amounts of clay, very moist matrix). You must also factor in drying time.

SEDIMENT TEXTURE TESTS

Do consistence testing with a 1 inch cube of sediment because the sample size will influence how easily it breaks. Select one value in each of the categories given, based on the following descriptions of those values (adapted in large part from the USDA Soil Survey Manual).

■ **Consistence (dry):** a measure of resistance to pressure. Select an air-dry clod and break it between the thumb and forefinger or in the hand.
■ Loose: noncoherent.
■ Soft: soil mass is weakly coherent and fragile; breaks to a powder or individual grains under slight pressure.
■ Slightly hard: weakly resistant to pressure; can be broken between thumb and forefinger.
■ Hard: moderately resistant to pressure; can be broken in the hand without difficulty but is barely breakable between thumb and forefinger.
■ Very hard: very resistant to pressure; can be broken in the hand only with difficulty and is not breakable between thumb and forefinger.
■ Extremely hard: extremely resistant to pressure; cannot be broken in the hand.

■ **Consistence (moist):** this is the cohesion of the sediment particles when pressure is applied; conduct test with a small amount of moisture dispersed throughout the sample.
■ Loose: noncoherent.
■ Very friable: crushes under gentle pressure.
■ Friable: crushes easily under gentle to moderate pressure between thumb and forefinger.
■ Firm: crushes under moderate pressure between thumb and forefinger, but resistance is distinctly noticeable.
■ Very firm: crushes under strong pressure; barely crushable between thumb and forefinger.

- Extremely firm: crushes under very strong pressure; cannot be crushed between thumb and forefinger.

- **Stickiness (wet):** stickiness refers to the tendency of an object to adhere to other objects. The sample should be completely moistened but not overly wet. To determine stickiness, sediment is pressed between the thumb and forefinger, and its adherence is noted using the following guidelines:
- Nonsticky: after release of pressure, practically no sediment adheres to thumb or forefinger.
- Slightly sticky: after pressure, sediment adheres to thumb and forefinger but comes off one or the other rather cleanly; does not appreciably stretch.
- Moderately sticky: after pressure, sediment adheres to both thumb and forefinger and tends to stretch somewhat before pulling apart.
- Very sticky: after pressure, sediment adheres strongly to both thumb and forefinger and is decidedly stretched when digits are separated.

- **Plasticity (wet):** plasticity is the property of sediment that enables it to change shape continuously under the influence of applied stress and to retain the impressed shape on removal of that stress. Roll the sediment between the thumb and forefinger, and observe whether or not a wire or thin ribbon of sediment can be formed.
- Nonplastic: no wire or ribbon is formed.
- Slightly plastic: wire or ribbon can be formed, but sediment mass is easily broken.
- Moderately plastic: wire or ribbon can be formed, and moderate pressure is required for the sediment mass to break.
- Very plastic: wire or ribbon can be formed, and much pressure is required for the sediment mass to break.

- **Molded Ball (wet):** Molded ball refers to the ability of the sediment to be molded into a shape and not rupture under applied stress. Roll the sediment in the palms to form a ball. Observe the ball's resistance to breakage when stress is applied with a finger.
- None: a ball cannot be formed.
- Very weak: ball crumbles when touched with a finger.
- Fragile: ball doesn't crack or break when touched gently.
- Strong: ball doesn't crack or break when touched and handled freely.

- Very strong: can be formed into any shape and will not break even under rough handling and heavy pressure.

- **Ribbon (wet):** Ribboning also is a test of the stability of sediments. Extrude the sediment between the thumb and forefinger until the ribbon breaks, then measure the ribbon. Definitions are based on the length of the ribbon formed.
- None: no ribbon can be formed.
- Slight: ribbon is less than 2.5 cm long.
- Medium: ribbon is between 2.5 and 5 cm long.
- High: ribbon is longer than 5 cm.

- **Smoothness/grittiness (wet or dry):** refers to the abrasiveness or lack of abrasiveness you feel when kneading sediments to determine the presence of fine sediments and/or sand. For field determination, rub the sediment between the thumb and forefinger or between the palms of the hands.
- Gritty: many grains are felt.
- Smooth: very little grittiness is felt.
- Neither gritty nor smooth: smooth feeling, but some grains can be felt.

SHELL ANALYSIS STEPS

- Attempt to identify the taxa either by consulting field guides for the region or by consulting a specialist, such as a marine biologist.
- Once the genera and species have been determined, the artifacts must be classified – using an established typology (if available) for the area or region from which the artifacts have been recovered.
- Send to the laboratory for a thorough description.

SOIL ANALYSIS CHECKLIST

- Color: Munsell Soil Color Chart.
- Constituents: mineral or stone found in the soil.
- Nature of soil: general description of compact/loose, dark/light, moist/dry, etc.

- Particle size: Wentworth or Tyler scale.
- Shape: angular, subangular, subrounded, rounded.
- Texture: smooth, fine, rough, sharp; composition, e.g. earth and ashes, surface humus, etc.

SOIL ANALYSIS PROCEDURE

A ped is a unit of soil structure such as a prism, block, or granule, which is formed by natural processes, in contrast with a clod, which is formed artificially.

- Determine nature of soil: hold ped of soil between your thumb and forefinger. Record one of the following: loose (you have trouble picking out a single ped and the structure falls apart before you handle it), friable (the ped breaks with a small amount of pressure), firm (the ped breaks when you apply a good amount of pressure and dents your fingers before it breaks), or extremely firm (the ped cannot be crushed with your fingers).
- Basic texture descriptions: sand (large, gritty), silt (medium, soft, silky, floury), clay (small, sticky, hard to squeeze).
- To make a finer distinction about texture: place some soil from a horizon (about the size of a small egg) in your hand, and, using the spray mist bottle, moisten the soil. Let the water soak in and then work the soil between your fingers until it is the same moisture throughout. Once the soil is moist, try to form a ball.

1. If the soil forms a ball, then test for clay. If it is really sticky, hard to squeeze, stains your hands, has a shine when rubbed, forms a long ribbon (5+ cm) without breaking, call it a clay. Then, wet a small pinch of the soil in your palm and rub it with a forefinger. If the soil feels very gritty, it is either sandy clay, sandy clay loam, or sandy loam. If it feels very smooth and not at all gritty, it is either silty clay, silty clay loam, or silt loam. If it feels only a little gritty, then it is either clay, clay loam, or loam.
2. If the soil is somewhat sticky, is somewhat hard to squeeze, forms a medium ribbon (between 2–5 cm), call it a clay loam. Then, wet a small pinch of the soil in your palm and rub it with a forefinger. If the soil feels very gritty, it is either sandy

clay, sandy clay loam, or sandy loam. If it feels very smooth and not at all gritty, it is either silty clay, silty clay loam, or silt loam. If it feels only a little gritty, then it is either clay, clay loam, or loam.

3. If the soil is soft, smooth, easy to squeeze, at most slightly sticky, forms a short ribbon (less than 2 cm), call it a loam. Then, wet a small pinch of the soil in your palm and rub it with a forefinger. If the soil feels very gritty, it is either sandy clay, sandy clay loam, or sandy loam. If it feels very smooth and not at all gritty, it is either silty clay, silty clay loam, or silt loam. If it feels only a little gritty, then it is either clay, clay loam, or loam.

4. If the soil forms a ball but no ribbon and is very gritty, texture is loamy sand.

5. If the soil forms a ball but no ribbon and is very soft and smooth with no gritty feeling, texture is silt.

6. If the soil does not form a ball and falls apart in your hand, texture is sand.

─────────────── SOIL SAMPLES ───────────────

■ If stratigraphy in the form of ash, shell lenses, etc., occurs, a sample should break at those points of stratigraphic contact. Shell and ash concentrations should not be mixed in a single sample.

■ Before starting the sampling, draw the side wall where the sample is to be taken.

■ By placing a piece of material at the bottom of the unit and holding a bag directly below the sample to be taken, the desired section of earth may be removed with a trowel.

■ Collect soil in horizontal lines across a profile face.

■ Take large soil samples at certain depth intervals and also within features. Optimally they should be 1,500–2,000 grams in weight. Label each sample carefully.

SOIL TYPES' EFFECTS ON MATERIALS

Acid soil's effect on

antler, bone, ivory: poor preservation
ceramics: reasonable preservation, calcareous fillers dissolve
copper alloys: bad corrosion
cotton, linen, wood: poor preservation
glass and glazes: reasonable preservation, leaching of alkalis
hair, horn, leather, wool: slow deterioration of protein
iron: bad corrosion
lead: poor preservation
shell: poor preservation
silver: poor preservation
stone: good preservation; etching; dissolution of limestone and marble

Acidic and waterlogged soil's effect on

antler, bone, ivory: poor preservation
ceramics: reasonable preservation, calcareous fillers dissolve
copper alloys: good preservation
cotton, linen, wood: good preservation
glass and glazes: reasonable preservation
hair, horn, leather, wool: good preservation
iron: good preservation
lead: good preservation
shell: poor preservation
silver: good preservation
stone: poor preservation

Alkaline soil's effect on

antler, bone, ivory: good preservation
ceramics: poor preservation; dissolution of basic structure; insoluble salt encrustation
copper alloys: good preservation
cotton, linen, wood: poor preservation
glass and glazes: poor preservation; dissolution of basic structure
hair, horn, leather, wool: poor preservation
iron: good preservation
lead: poor preservation
shell: good preservation

silver: good preservation
stone: good preservation; insoluble salt encrustation

Alkaline waterlogged soil's effect on

antler, bone, ivory: poor preservation
ceramics: poor preservation; dissolution of basic structure; insoluble
   salt encrustation
copper alloys: good preservation
cotton, linen, wood: good preservation
glass and glazes: poor preservation
hair, horn, leather, wool: good preservation
iron: good preservation
lead: good preservation
shell: poor preservation
silver: good preservation
stone: insoluble salt encrustation

Arctic soil's effect on

all materials: good preservation

Desert soil's effect on

antler, bone, ivory: good preservation
ceramics: good preservation; possible wind erosion
copper alloys: good preservation
cotton, linen, wood: good preservation
glass and glazes: good preservation; possible wind erosion
hair, horn, leather, wood: good preservation
iron: good preservation
lead: good preservation
shell: good preservation
silver: good preservation
stone: good preservation; possible wind erosion

Saline soil's effect on

antler, bone, ivory: poor preservation; soluble salts
ceramics: poor preservation; soluble salts
copper alloys: bad corrosion
cotton, linen, wood: extreme dehydration

glass and glazes: poor preservation
hair, horn, leather, wool: extreme dehydration
iron: bad corrosion
lead: reasonable preservation
shell: poor preservation; soluble salts
silver: slight salinity good, high salinity poor
stone: poor preservation; soluble salts

STONE TOOL PARTS

blade
bulb of percussion
compression rings
core
core tool
cortex
direction of force
dorsal surface

eraillure (small secondary flake) scar
flake
flake scar
profile
removed flake
striking platform
ventral surface
waste flake

STRATIGRAPHIC/NATURAL-LEVEL EXCAVATION METHOD

- Natural levels are excavated when the stratigraphy is clearly defined and can be followed during excavation.
- You can determine whether the stratigraphy is naturally or culturally derived by studying the basic characteristics of the soil and sediments.
- In addition to the geologically defined strata, you may observe lenses (thin lines of deposit) within a layer – which can also be the result of natural or cultural activities.
- These make it hard to follow the natural stratigraphy.
- The rule is to remove a layer until you get to something that is not like that layer. Look closely for changes in texture, color, soil structure, and moisture content of the soil and sediment.
- If you are bulk proveniencing, you may not observe the changes in stratigraphy until later and then you will have to document those changes. The most important records are the profile drawing of the excavation walls and photographs of them.

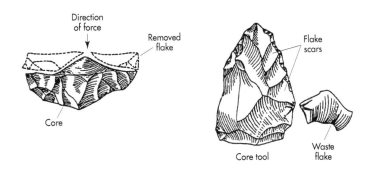

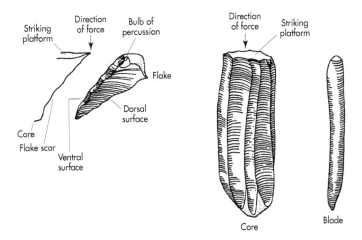

Figure 3.11 Stone tool parts terminology. (Kenneth Page Oakley, Figure 10.1: Terminology used in describing lithic core, flake and blade tools reflecting manufacturing technology. [After Oakley 1956. By courtesy of the British Museum {Natural History}], p. 356 from *Man the tool-maker*, third edition. London: British Museum {Natural History}, 1956. Copyright © 1956 by The Trustees of The British Museum. Reprinted by permission of The British Museum)

(a) Segment method

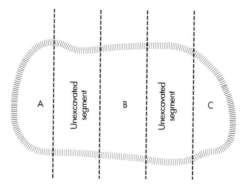

Segment (A, B, C) excavated through earthwork.
Unexcavated segments serve as controls.

Figure 3.12a Segment excavation method. (Philip C. Hammond, The Excavation of Mounds and Other Earthworks: A. Segment Method, from *Archaeological Techniques for Amateurs*. New York: Van Nostrand, 1963. Copyright © 1963 by Philip C. Hammond. Reprinted by permission of the author)

(b) Quadrant method

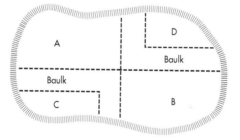

Quadrants (A, B, C, D) excavated, with control
baulks unexcavated

Figure 3.12b Quadrant excavation method. (Philip C. Hammond, The Excavation of Mounds and Other Earthworks: B. Quadrant Method, from *Archaeological Techniques for Amateurs*. New York: Van Nostrand, 1963. Copyright © 1963 by Philip C. Hammond. Reprinted by permission of the author)

- The profile map should be at a scale that permits all relevant details to be shown; a scale of 1:10 is preferable for most features and structures.
- Use a map stamp if available.
- The face to be documented should be "cleaned" by scraping with a trowel. It should be shaved as smooth and vertical as possible. As nearly as possible, it should be directly under the string indicating the edge of the excavation unit. When cutting a face back in this manner, try to collect artifacts according to the same strata in which the unit was excavated.
- Photograph the face as nearly level and square-on as possible. If it is not possible to photograph the entire face with one exposure, take more than one shot and overlap them. Photographs of profiles show much more detail when taken on a cloudy day or when shaded with plastic sheeting. To enhance the color contrast, dampen the profile with a handheld water sprayer. Always take at least one color and one black-and-white photograph of a stratigraphic profile that has *not* been dampened, scored with a trowel, or modified in another way. Record in the photo log how the face was modified.
- Draw the profile by measuring from the leveled string line. It should be as taut as possible and not touch anything except the end anchors.
- Measuring up and down, perpendicular to the level line, map in the stratigraphic breaks, the medium and large inclusions, and the boundaries of the profile. Also draw in lenses and pockets of gravel. Draw inclusions that protrude from the profile face as though the inclusions were sliced off flush with the profile face.
- Measure in the boundaries of the profile accurately. Do not draw ruler-straight vertical edges on the profile. Label the modern ground surface, label what is outside the profile on both sides (usually unexcavated), and label what is under the bottom of the profile.
- Label the strata with letter designations, starting from the topmost stratum. Provide a key for symbols used on the map.
- Record the elevation of the level string line you measured from.
- Complete the appropriate recording form.

STRUCTURAL REMAINS GUIDELINES

- Investigate the building types of the area before excavation.
- When a structural feature is discovered during excavation, special care should be taken.
- Small tools and a whisk broom should be used.
- Features should be photographed in the best possible light.
- Drawings should be made.
- The structural remains should be fully documented.

SUPERVISOR CHECKLIST

planning
surveying (measuring, plotting, mapping)
excavation and collection
stratigraphy analysis
artifact analysis
recording (field notebooks, photography, drawing)
conservation
cataloging
reporting the data

SURFACE OBSERVATIONS CHECKLIST

- Above-ground structures or features: grave markers, rock alignments or petroforms, standing structures, etc.
- Drainage: patterning in extremely dry or wet areas, substantial subterranean features, etc.
- Sediment/soil color: patterns of color, unnatural colors for the context, etc.
- Topography: look at abandoned roadbeds, caves, depressions, dumps, graves, modified rock, mounded areas, placed fill, rock shelters, structures, unnatural patterns, unusual ways that the land rises or falls, very straight or angled streams, etc.
- Vegetation: field edges, lack of growth, look at introduced species, lush growth over features, patterned growth, species out of context, etc.

project or site name/designation
landowner name and address
measure or estimate of site size
type of site, feature, or cluster
current use of site
visibility of site
surface conditions
topographic setting
architectural evidence
exposure/slope direction (compass bearing) and degree/percent
soil type
vegetation cover
evidence of previous disturbances
evidence of destruction or vandalism
proximity to water and distance to it
relationship to drainage
size and shape of site, feature, cluster
clusters or patterns of artifacts on a site
evidence of horizontal stratigraphy
degree of integrity of context
documentation of find-spots for artifacts or samples collected
number, size, and types of artifacts observed but not collected
number and types of photographs taken
number and types of illustrations drawn

SURVEYING EQUIPMENT LIST

Abney level or clinometer
arrows
ax
backpacks
binoculars
cellular telephone
chains
chalk, greasy and white
clipboards

LISTS AND CHECKLISTS

compasses (or pocket transits)

cross-staff or optical square

drawing board

dumpy level, plane table and alidade, theodolite, or transit – and
tripod

erasers

field notebook

forms

graph paper

grid stakes

hammers, large and small

indelible ink pens

knife

leveling rod

levels (hand, line, spirit)

machete

maps (government survey, USGS, UTM counter)

markers

nails (stake tacks or spads, PK nails)

paint for stakes

pencils (mechanical), pencil sharpener

permits

photographic equipment (including extra film)

photographic scale

plastic bags, cloth sacks

plastic neon tape or ribbons

plumb bobs

portable sifter

protractor

ranging poles

reinforced tapes, steel tapes (50 m)

rulers, especially 2–3 m flexible rule

shovels (including pointed-end)

small measuring tapes (3 m, 5 m, or 10 m)

stakes or pegs

stiff brushes, whisk brooms

string, cord

survey forms

surveyor's pins

Total Station or EDM – and tripod

trowels

walkie-talkie radio sets

aluminum foil
batteries
candle
cellular telephone
cord
emergency food or chocolate
emergency poncho
fire starter
flashlight
flint
knife (Swiss army)
magnifying glass
matches
needle and thread
orienteering style compass
paper

pencil
personal first aid kit
personal identification
pin-on compass
plastic sheet
razor blades
rescue blanket
safety pins
signal mirror
space blanket
waterproof matches
water-purifying tablets
whistle
wire saw
zip-lock bags

TELESCOPE SETUP AND USE

- Determine what type of focusing mechanism the telescope has. Small telescopes use one of two basic types – you either move the eyepiece, or you move the primary mirror.
- Check for an eyepiece-movement focusing mechanism. It will be either a geared system or a simple sliding eyepiece.
- Turn a wheel or pair of wheels in a geared system, called rack and pinion. As you turn the wheel, the eyepiece moves closer to or farther away from the primary mirror or lens. A rack-and-pinion focus is better than a sliding or twisting focus.
- Most refractors and Newtonian reflectors use a rack-and-pinion focus.
- Slide or turn the eyepiece in a slide-focusing system. This action moves the eyepiece closer to or farther from the main lens of the telescope. Sometimes, a locking screw will keep the telescope from slipping out of focus. Small refractors and lower-cost reflecting telescopes use slide-focusing mechanisms.
- Look for a screw knob on the back of a telescope whose focus mechanism moves the mirror. Turn the knob to shift the mirror forward or backward. This focus method is very common in

standard Schmidt Cassegrain and Maksutov-style telescopes. Set up the telescope. Avoid direct bright lights, which will keep you from seeing faint objects.

- Select the item to focus on.
- Use the finder telescope to center the item in the telescope. With most new telescopes, you will have to align the finder scope (see the instructions for your telescope) with the main telescope.
- Once you discover which direction sharpens the image, continue in that direction until you achieve the best view.

THEODOLITE/TRANSIT/DUMPY LEVEL SETUP

- Place the tripod on the ground at the point (called the instrument point, IP) from which measurements are to be taken and spread the legs, extending them so they are level.
- Adjust the tripod over the point, so that the upper plate is horizontal and level.
- Firmly affix the transit to the tripod.
- Position the tripod with the plumb bob, allowing the plumb bob to be just a little above the point.
- Level the head by gently adjusting the legs without changing the position of the plumb bob.
- Push each leg firmly into the ground while observing the plumb bob.
- Adjust the plumb bob to .01 m over the point.
- Re-level and adjust the transit on the tripod so that it is directly over the IP.
- Level the transit with the leveling screws by checking through 360 degrees of rotation. Start with the plate bubble parallel to the two leveling screws. To adjust, simultaneously turn one screw clockwise and the other counter-clockwise until level. Rotate the telescope 90 degrees and re-level the instrument. Then repeat in 90-degree increments until the plate bubble remains in the same position throughout the entire circle. Check the level bubble before each reading. Sun shining on a transit will heat and expand the sunny side, requiring a re-leveling of the instrument.
- Sight the other known point, called the Backsight Point (BS), with the horizontal angle set at 0. On electronic transits, there is a button labeled "0SET" to be pushed when it is sighted on the BS. Most older non-electronic transits have two horizontal

motions. Use the upper motion to set the horizontal reading to 0, then use the lower motion to sight on the BS.

■ You are now ready to begin using the transit. Using the two points (the IP and the BS), with a known horizontal distance between them (which establishes what's known as the baseline), you can map existing features with only one helper by reading horizontal angles to each feature from both points. You also can use this method to determine heights (elevation) by reading horizontal and vertical angles from both points.

THEODOLITE/TRANSIT/DUMPY LEVEL USE

This is very general. It is not possible to present a detailed discussion of how to operate every type under all field conditions.

■ The user records the horizontal angle between a reference point (e.g. true north) and the desired survey point.

■ The respective angles from the site datum to a series of survey stations are determined by reading the fine graduations on a Vernier scale(s) (modern instruments compute and display this).

■ Sight along a line (ray) to the target point; the angle between true north and the target point is read by observing the position of the Vernier index in reference to the underlying graduated horizontal circle (read in degrees on the horizontal circle or as minutes and seconds on the Vernier scale).

■ Angles can be used to calculate distance by trigonometry.

■ When sighting the backsight point, use as a target a vertical pointed pole or plumb bob placed directly over the BS point.

■ Sight on the pole or plumb bob string with the horizontal cross-hair as close to the point as possible to ensure that the vertical cross-hair reflects the true angular position of the point.

■ Unlock the horizontal and vertical circle screws, sight your next point and record the horizontal (and vertical) angle in your field book.

■ Reading one angle with the telescope in both direct and reversed (plunged) positions will compensate for minor instrument errors and minor setup errors; if the difference between the two is great, correct the instrument or remedy the setup error and repeat – average the two readings to arrive at a more accurate value.

- Watch for errors in recording the values in your field notebook; transposition of numbers and reading errors are the most common.
- To ensure greater accuracy: read, record, check reading, check recording.

TIMBER/JOINTING DESCRIPTION TERMS

brace or shore: a member, usually diagonally set, which props up a structure
joist: base for a floor or ceiling
lap: joining piece for end or face of one timber for the face of another
member: essential part of a framed structure
mortise and tenon: a tongue set into a slot cut into the edge or face of another timber
plank: part of horizontal or vertical surface
plate: horizontal member for a structure
post: vertical member
stake: pointed vertical member
tie-back: a piece joined to a plate or principal vertical member to prevent movement

TREE-RING SAMPLE COLLECTION

- When wood or charcoal is found during excavation, it should be evaluated for its potential for tree-ring dating as soon as possible; a potentially datable sample contains a minimum of 30 to 40 rings. All potentially datable samples should be collected as promptly as possible after being exposed. If for some reason it is impossible to collect a sample soon after exposure, it should be covered with either damp soil or plastic. When left exposed to the air or direct sunlight, these samples deteriorate rapidly.
- Great care should be taken in the exposure and handling of tree-ring samples. A potential sample should be exposed carefully with small hand tools. Pedestaling the sample during exposure can be helpful in collecting a specimen as intact as possible. In order to date a tree-ring sample to the year the tree died, some bark must be present on it. Thus, the exterior surface of the

sample is of supreme importance in getting the most interpretable dating results.

- Each sample should be wrapped securely with cotton string to hold it together as it dries. The optimum amount of string depends on the size and condition of the sample. The sample does not need to be completely encased in string to be stabilized, and completely encasing a sample in loose string serves no purpose. One effective method is to wrap string around the sample first lengthwise and then around the smaller dimension. The latter loops draw against the former loops and keep them taut. The ends of the string should be tied in a bow.

- Do not place the sample in any container or wrapping other than a paper bag. Use an unused paper bag when possible, and label it legibly. After the sample is bagged, it is a good idea to keep it in the shade (especially in hot, dry weather) until it can be transported to the lab.

- If a long segment of a timber is found, it is not necessary to collect the entire specimen. A 10- to 20-cm-long sample that includes the most complete cross-section is desirable.

- Charred specimens are more likely to be datable than uncharred specimens, owing primarily to the shrinkage and distortion that occurs during the desiccation of uncharred specimens. So in the case of partly burned logs, it is best to obtain a sample from a section that has been completely carbonized.

- Multiple fragments from one specimen may be collected for any of the following reasons: 1) to be sent all in one bag to the tree-ring lab for analysis (for example, if you have multiple fragments from one piece of wood and cannot tell which is the most complete); 2) to be used as a vegetal sample; 3) to be curated for future analysis (write that on the bag).

- In most cases, tree-ring samples will be collected as point-located artifacts (if a sample is collected from a posthole, however, it may not be point located, because full provenience information will be recorded as part of the feature recording). To point-locate a tree-ring sample that is larger than a nodule, an elevation should be taken beneath each end of the sample. The horizontal location of the sample should be recorded either by plotting it on an appropriate map or by recording the grid coordinates of both ends of the sample. The diameter of the sample should also be recorded. An interpretation of the origin of the sample (e.g., roof support post, fuel wood, doorway lintel) is also helpful for evaluating any dates that may result.

- Create a receding upward slope to the sides at the top and step in the trench at a lower level. Sloping is digging back trench walls at an angle to eliminate the possibility of collapse. The angle of the receding upward slope stabilizes the material. Sloping can be time-consuming and expensive.
- Alternatively, prop the sides of the trench with scaffolding or a vertical framework, held by cross-members and extendable as the work proceeds. Use a ladder for access, not the framework.
- Modular shoring and sheeting can be purchased for this use. They can be removed for repeated use on future projects. They are made of steel, aluminum, and plastics, have hydraulic bracing systems, and can accommodate excavations of a wide range of trench sizes. The type of system used depends on many factors, including soil conditions and the width and depth of the excavation.

TRENCHING TYPES

Trenches are long, narrow excavation units used to view stratigraphy, collect a sample for building a chronology, locate features, and determine site boundaries. Trenching can be destructive and does not give broad exposure – and it can be dangerous.

backhoe trench: used to identify subsurface deposits and features when surface visibility is low or there are time constraints
slit trench: most common; used to provide vertical exposure
step trench: long and with steps going down, used for mounds or deeply buried deposits
wall trenches: used next to architectural features to outline walls

TROWELING METHOD

- For clay-like and sticky deposits, trowel across the proposed line of intersection – because different layers will often break away from each other.
- For sandier and less cohesive deposits, trowel down the line.

LISTS AND CHECKLISTS

- Pay attention to cleanliness and working methodically from the known edges toward the unknown ones.
- Work systematically backwards, pulling the material onto the unexcavated part at one's knees.
- The weight of the body is needed over the trowel for energetic work; squatting or kneeling is best and sitting is not recommended.
- Use a kneeling pad or wear knee pads for protection.
- Use the side of the trowel to remove loose or thin deposits.
- Use the point of the trowel to remove soil from the vertical face at the edge of the deposit.
- Use the point of the trowel to maximize the preservation of artifact finds.
- Use the side of the trowel to clean and reveal strata.

UNIT, COMPLETION OF

- Draw the profile of at least two adjoining walls.
- Record the profile of all four walls.
- A coring device, auger, or posthole digger can be used in the floor of the unit to extend the record of stratification if necessary. In the case of an auger or posthole digger, screen the matrix.
- Leave a modern token, like a penny from the current year, in a bag at the base of the unit for future diggers.
- Backfill.

UNIT, EXCAVATION OF

It is important to prevent cave-ins, preserve the corner stakes, and record meticulously and accurately.

- Photograph or make a plan drawing of the unit surface. The surface contours should be plotted on the site map.
- As each level, natural or arbitrary, is completed, the floor and walls of the unit should be scraped clean and inspected for cultural features, soil changes, or natural disturbances.
- Whenever possible, units are excavated down to the base of the site to sterile subsoil.

Natural levels/Natural stratigraphic level method

- Determine the opening or ground elevations for the perimeter of the unit, using a line level suspended on a string anchored at the base of the nail on the datum.
- Position yourself adjacent to the point to be measured.
- Hold an extended folding rule, putting the 0 on the point to be measured, holding it vertically.
- Pull the string taut and with the level centered, adjust so the bubble is centered. Where the taut line intersects the rule, that is the elevation reading. Take elevation readings for all corners of the unit and its center point.
- You may take a core sample from within the boundary of the unit at this time.
- Whether you are to dig in natural or arbitrary levels, do not do so mechanically. If there is a major change in a level, you may want to analyze and terminate it.
- Cut the side walls using the taut string as a guide. The top layer is removed with a flat shovel to get a straight cut down. Do not go deeper than the presumed depth of your first stratum.
- Begin removal of the first level, working down each wall to the base of the first natural stratum before working into the center of the unit.
- Look for changes in color, texture, and structure of the matrix.
- Stop when you notice a change in the color or texture of the wall or floor. Also stop when you encounter a feature or evidence of an occupational surface in the stratum.
- Do not let digging get too far ahead of the screening.
- Do not mix materials from different levels or contexts in the screening.
- Note frequency and distribution of artifacts and variations in the matrix.
- Take special note of features and heavy artifacts and map their location.
- All artifacts from the same level are assigned the provenience for that level and are tagged as such when bagged.

Arbitrary levels/Unit-level method

- The base of such a unit will be determined strictly by depth measurements. The depth of the level is adjusted to the surface elevations of the unit, which will determine whether the level's floor is flat or contoured.

- If a level floor is desired, then you must determine a single standard elevation – either the average of the surface elevations, the highest point, or the lowest point. You then proceed at a certain amount below datum from that reference point.
- Start in a corner with a trowel. Keep checking the below-datum reading (with line level and ruler) until you reach the desired amount below datum. Repeat for each corner. Then continue between the corners.
- If you are following the surface contours, then the base of the excavated level will be an arbitrary measure below each of the unique readings for the opening of the level.
- Instead of having to measure with the line level and ruler, you simply measure down from the surface with a ruler or tape.

——— VERTICAL-FACE EXCAVATION METHODS ———

- Control face: troweling done against a vertical control face composed of a vertical cut (the material being removed), a horizontal surface (the material being left), and the contact (perpendicular juncture between) done in 2–5 cm levels across square. Each slice moves a defined amount of the control face with each pass, exposing more of the surface and removing more of the cut.
- Control front: a line of control faces cross-cutting adjoining excavation units with close attention paid to the adjoining units.
- Single vertical face: unit or contiguous series of units sliced with a vertical cut, horizontal area, and a contact area.
- Step-trenching/level-stripping: excavation in a staggered series of vertical faces at successive depths, which looks like steps in cross-section.

4

Mapping, Drawing, and Photographing

This chapter touches on three different areas that help the archaeologist describe the physical setting, features, and artifacts. There are instructional and refresher topics, lists of terms and symbols, and checklists for supplies, among other things.

Without the careful drawing and mapping of artifacts, features, stratification, etc., a site would be meaningless. Accurate drawing and mapping influences the way a site will be studied and presented in publications. Photographs of the site and excavated artifacts are supplemented by scale drawings, which can emphasize relevant details in ways not generally possible in photographs. Line drawings of maps, an overall site plan, vertical sections, architectural reconstructions, and drawings of finds are often published in excavation reports. These drawings can offer more detail and may be less expensive than photography. Mapping and drawings are the key to successful final publication on the excavation and subject.

Photography of excavations is very important. It acts as verification and is also a link between all recording systems. Photographs offer day-to-day analysis and progress of the site from survey through excavation. It is important for the archaeologist to understand photographic equipment, care for it, and learn how to create photographic logs as a check on techniques, supplies, coverage, etc.

CONTENTS

243

——— **AERIAL PHOTOGRAPHS, READING** ———

The identification of features on a photograph is not difficult if the following facts are remembered. The view that is presented by the aerial photograph is from above and, as a result, objects do not look familiar. Objects that are greatly reduced in size appear distorted. Most aerial photography is black and white, and all colors appear on the photograph in shades of gray. Generally speaking, the darker the natural color, the darker it will appear on the photograph.

The identification of features on aerial photographs depends upon a careful application of five factors of recognition. No one factor will give a positive identification; it requires the use of all five.

- **Size.** The size of unknown objects on a photograph, as determined from the scale of the photograph or a comparison with known objects of known size, gives a clue to their identity. For example, in a built-up area the smaller buildings are usually dwellings, and the larger buildings are commercial or community buildings.
- **Shape (pattern).** Many features possess characteristic shapes that readily identify the features. Man-made features appear as straight or smooth curved lines, while natural features usually appear to be irregular. Some of the most prominent man-made features are highways, railroads, bridges, canals, and buildings. Compare the regular shapes of these to the irregular shapes of such natural features as streams and timber lines.
- **Shadows.** Shadows are very helpful in identifying features since they show the familiar side view of the object. Some excellent examples are the shadows of water towers or smoke stacks. As viewed directly from above, only a round circle or dot is seen, whereas the shadow shows the profile and helps to identify the object. Relative lengths of shadows also usually give a good indication of relative heights of objects.
- **Shade (tone or texture).** Of the many different types of photographic film in use today, the film used for most aerial photography, except for special purposes, is panchromatic film. Panchromatic film is sensitive to all the colors of the spectrum; it registers them as shades of gray, ranging from white to black. This lighter or darker shade of features on aerial photographs is known as the tone. The tone is also dependent on the texture of the features; a paved highway has a smooth texture and produces an even tone on the photograph, while a recently plowed field or a marsh has a rough, choppy texture and results in a rough or grainy tone. It is also important to remember that similar features may have different tones on different photographs, depending on the reflection of sunlight. For example, a river or body of water appears light if it is reflecting sunlight directly toward the camera, but appears dark otherwise. Its texture may be smooth or rough, depending on the surface of

the water itself. As long as the variables are kept in mind, tone and texture may be used to great advantage.

- **Surrounding objects.** Quite often an object not easily recognized by itself may be identified by its relative position to surrounding objects. Large buildings located beside railroads or railroad sidings are usually factories or warehouses. Identify schools by the baseball or football fields. It would be hard to tell the difference between a water tower next to a railroad station and a silo next to a barn, unless the surrounding objects such as the railroad tracks or cultivated fields were considered.

Before a vertical photograph can be studied or used for identification of features, it must be oriented. This orienting is different from the orienting required for the construction or use of the point designation grid. Orienting for study consists of rotating the photograph so that the shadows on the photograph point toward yourself. You then face a source of light. This places the source of light, an object, and its shadow in a natural relationship. Failure to orient a photograph properly may cause the height or depth of an object to appear reversed. For example, a mine or quarry may appear to be a hill instead of a depression.

Conventional signs in archaeological drawing

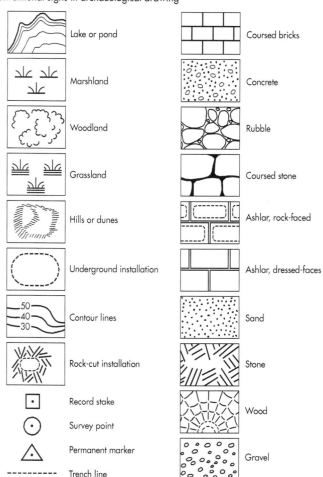

	Lake or pond			Coursed bricks
	Marshland			Concrete
	Woodland			Rubble
	Grassland			Coursed stone
	Hills or dunes			Ashlar, rock-faced
	Underground installation			Ashlar, dressed-faces
	Contour lines			Sand
	Rock-cut installation			Stone
	Record stake			Wood
	Survey point			Gravel
	Permanent marker			
	Trench line			

Figure 4.1 Archaeological drawing symbols

MAPPING, DRAWING, AND PHOTOGRAPHING

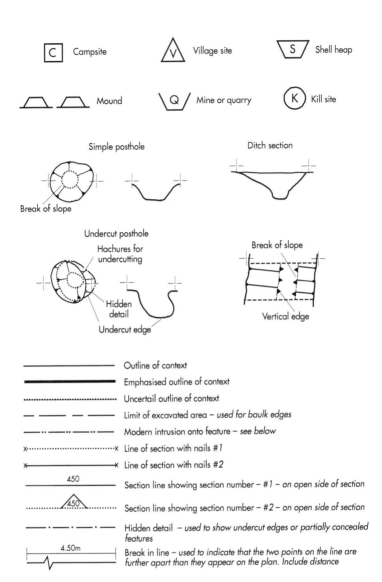

Figure 4.1 Continued

248

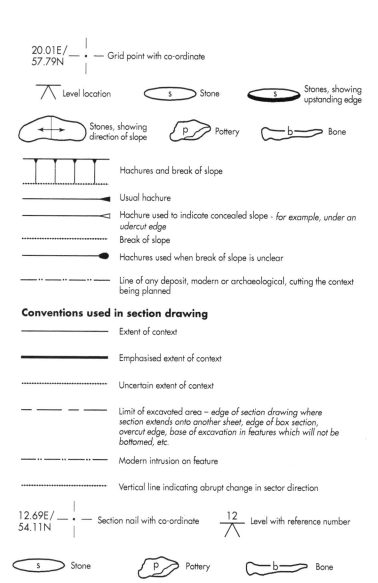

20.01E/ — • — Grid point with co-ordinate
57.79N

Level location

Stone

Stones, showing upstanding edge

Stones, showing direction of slope

Pottery

Bone

Hachures and break of slope

Usual hachure

Hachure used to indicate concealed slope - *for example, under an udercut edge*

Break of slope

Hachures used when break of slope is unclear

Line of any deposit, modern or archaeological, cutting the context being planned

Conventions used in section drawing

Extent of context

Emphasised extent of context

Uncertain extent of context

Limit of excavated area – *edge of section drawing where section extends onto another sheet, edge of box section, overcut edge, base of excavation in features which will not be bottomed, etc.*

Modern intrusion on feature

Vertical line indicating abrupt change in sector direction

12.69E/ — • — Section nail with co-ordinate
54.11N

12
—⟋⟍— Level with reference number

Stone

Pottery

Bone

Figure 4.1 Continued

Conventions used in elevation drawing in addition to section conventions

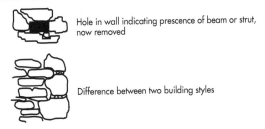

Hole in wall indicating prescence of beam or strut, now removed

Difference between two building styles

Conventions representing common deposit types

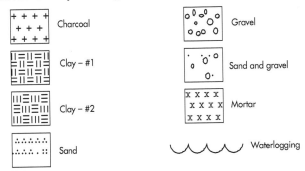

Charcoal

Clay – #1

Clay – #2

Sand

Gravel

Sand and gravel

Mortar

Waterlogging

Labelling conventions

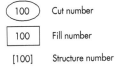

Cut number

Fill number

Structure number

Figure 4.1 Continued

——— ARCHAEOLOGICAL DRAWINGS ———

- Elevation drawing: straight-on view of exposed feature surface.
- Isometric drawing: portrays features in three dimensions to illustrate technology; can be computer-generated.
- Perspective drawing: reconstruction of feature, structure, etc., often three-dimensional.
- Plan drawing: scaled depiction for horizontal relationships of features and associated artifacts.

- Profile drawing: portrays the outline of a feature, also included in section drawing.
- Scaled drawing: plan and cross-section views for strata, features, artifact/ecofact distributions.
- Section drawing: wall depiction of stratigraphic sequence of matrices, features, and associated artifacts/ecofacts.

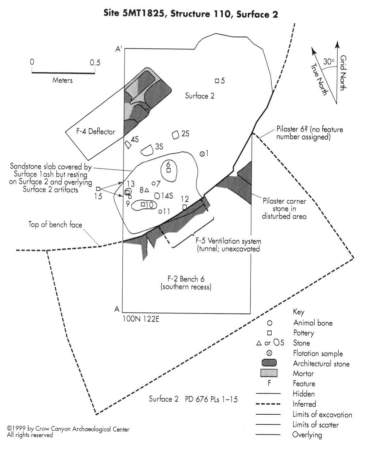

Site 5MT1825, Structure 110, Surface 2

MAPPING, DRAWING, AND PHOTOGRAPHING

Figure 4.2 Archaeological drawings. (Site 5MT1825, Structure 110, Surface 2, from *The Castle Rock Pueblo Database.* Crow Canyon Archaeological Center, 2001b. Copyright © 2001 by Crow Canyon Archaeological Center. Reprinted by permission)

- The architectural plan shows all four stakes and the layer or stratum as a whole.
- The plan can be traced on transparent paper to later superimpose the development of different structures or the position of artifact collections.
- All architectural elements must be accurately represented by their length, height, and thickness.
- If there is a pronounced slope, this must be represented by contour plans in addition.
- Artifact collections and features should be accurately measured and plotted; a drawing frame can be of assistance.

DRAFTING, DRAWING, AND MAPPING EQUIPMENT LIST

architect's metric scale
black India ink
calipers
calculator
cleaning powder
cotton swabs
direction arrows
drafting brush
drawing board
drawing pens with several nibs
ellipse (centimeter)
erasers
erasing shield
field notebook
flexible curves
folder and storage tubes for drawings
French curves
graph paper (centimeters, millimeters)
line level
masking tape
mechanical pencils with (soft black) leads
nails (6″ and 1″)
pencil sharpeners, sandpaper block, or lead pointer

pencils (variety from 3H to 7H; generally, soft black leads for drawing)
planning frame(s) (generally 1 m × 1 m)
plumb bob
polyurethane foam or carpet piece
protractor
razor blade and/or scissors
rulers (centimeter, scale)
string
tapes (hand; 30 m, 50 m, or 100 m)
tracing paper (Mylar)
transfer lettering and numbering
triangle (transparent 30–60–90 degree)
T-square

—— DRAWING A PLAN WITH OFFSETTING ——

- You may need to draw by "offsetting" features with tapes.
- Establish a reference line to draw from: align your tape with the grid if it exists; if no grid, locate the site and a reference line on a USGS or Ordnance Survey map.
- Work with another person if possible, with one person drawing and the other measuring.
- Measure points on the feature by putting nails with neon tape where you want to take a coordinate and then offset to your reference line tape.
- Establish the coordinate of each nail, take measurements of strategic points of the feature and transfer the coordinates to a plan.

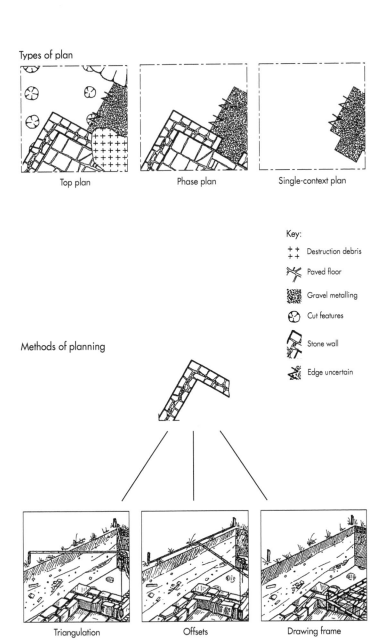

Types of plan

Top plan

Phase plan

Single-context plan

Key:

+ +
+ +   Destruction debris

        Paved floor

        Gravel metalling

        Cut features

        Stone wall

        Edge uncertain

Methods of planning

Triangulation

Offsets

Drawing frame

Figure 4.3 Plan types and planning methods. (Steve Roskams, Figure 9: Examples of different plan types and planning methods, p. 138 from *Excavation*. New York: Cambridge University Press, 2001. Copyright © 2001 by Cambridge University Press. Redrawn and reprinted with permission of the author and Cambridge University Press)

■ Many site plans are drawn at a 1:20 scale with 5 cms on the page representing 1 m of a unit. If you use a planning frame, at 1:20 each cm square on the graph paper equals one 20 cm square outlined by the strings on the planning frame.

■ Assemble your drawing board, drawing film or paper, pencil, sharpener, eraser, planning frame, measuring tape, etc.

■ Site north should always be at the top of the drawing, show an arrow and N to locate your plan horizontally, label the appropriate grid points with their coordinates from the site grid or take EDM readings on the corners of your planning frame or along your tape and mark these on the plan.

■ Take appropriate levels to illustrate differences in height over your feature and its relationship to surrounding features and mark these on the plan.

■ Mark the corners of your planning frame lightly on the drawing paper.

■ Try drawing the easy things first, like the outline of the context.

■ Add a planning index with the site name, site number, scale, date, plan/section identification, initials of drawer; also use the conventional symbols to show 1) which plans adjoin your plan on the same level and 2) which plans lie directly over and under your plan.

Drawing specific types of feature:

■ If a feature is large, stretch a tape aligned to the grid across the top of the feature and use a plumb bob to position nails in the feature along the alignment of the grid; then lower the planning frame into the feature.

■ Try to prop the frame so that it is level. If you cannot lower the frame into the feature or it will not balance over the top, try using planks or rods to support the planning frame.

■ Determine the extent of color changes, slopes, etc. that need to be drawn.

■ If unable to use a planning frame, measure in the feature using a hand tape.

MAPPING, DRAWING, AND PHOTOGRAPHING

DRAWING A SKELETON

- If you have limited time, lie enough planning frames over the area to cover it. Record the corner coordinates of the frames. Set yourself up above the skeleton for both photographing and drawing. Take levels and record them on the drawing.
- Skeletons are normally drawn at 1:10.
- Stretch a tape over the skeleton on one side and lie the frame(s) over it – with neither the tape nor the frame(s) touching the skeleton.
- Use a plumb bob to establish the position of the bones within the grave.
- Measure the lengths of the bigger bones, then the small.
- Supine extended skeletons generally get five levels: skull, ribcage, pelvis, knees, and feet. The base and top of grave cut levels are also recorded.

DRAWING FRAME USE

- The frame's string intervals should match the scale adopted for planning; if drawing at 1:20, it is best to place the string at 0.20 m intervals so that each grid square formed by the string in the frame equals a 10 mm square on paper.
- If the ground is quite irregular, a smaller frame may work best; frames 1 m × 1 m work in most instances.
- Stand vertically above the frame, using a plumb bob if the frame is set far from the surface being drawn; it has to be level (use spirit level) and positioned as near the ground as possible.
- One or more corners of the frame may have to be supported; adjustable legs are advised.
- Record the edge of the unit and most of its surface detail.
- Consider color-coding different types of find.
- Delineate areas of wear or increased compaction.
- Represent the vertical dimension by a combination of spot heights (the number and position of these depends on the degree of irregularity of the surface) and hachures.
- Number the spot heights in a running sequence specific to the unit.
- Contour lines may be added, but this can also be done on the computer.

MAPPING, DRAWING, AND PHOTOGRAPHING

256

DRAWING FROM A DIGITAL PHOTOGRAPH

The rest of this article is written with the expectation that the reader will have become somewhat familiar in advance with the following chapters in the Corel® Painter 7™ manual: The Workspace, Basics, Painting, Applying Art Materials, Cloning and Tracing, Using Layers, and Printing.

The first step in beginning one of my digital drawings is to prepare an image file that will serve as a reference for the actual drawing:

• **Assemble the reference material in digital form.** This can be done using photos from a digital camera; alternatively photographic prints and slides can be scanned onto a CD by a photo-imaging house (sketches and other non-photo material can also be scanned).

For those of you who don't want to work from photographs, I would recommend thumbnailing a rough sketch of the planned work in Painter including major lines and solid shapes, resizing it to the final size (see below), and substituting this file each time the reference photo is mentioned below.

• **Edit.** Most photos benefit from at least some cropping and color, brightness, and contrast adjustments. Some require more work, such as moving or removing objects or collaging several photos together.

• **File format.** The final file can be an Adobe Photoshop® Psd or a Tiff. A Psd can be opened in Painter and used as such or saved as a Riff, Painter's native format. (Photoshop cannot read Riffs, but Painter can save them as Psds for Photoshop.)

• **Mode.** If you plan to make your final output an IRIS print, work in RGB mode, as the IRIS atelier often likes to control the CMYK conversion.

• **Working resolution.** It is important to experiment with Painter to find what working resolution produces a personally acceptable brushstroke. To my eye Painter yields the most pixel information at a drawing resolution of 75 ppi but the whole image looks better when printed as if it had been drawn at a higher resolution, 150 or 225 ppi for example. So a 20 × 30" image might translate into drawing at 60 × 90" @ 75 ppi and resizing the final to 20 × 30 @ 225 ppi.

• **Output size and resolution.** The amount of memory in your computer is one major factor in deciding how large the work is to be and at what resolution. The other is the nature of the machine that will output the final image; each printer has an optimal resolution (number of pixels per inch) and a maximum paper size.

MAPPING, DRAWING, AND PHOTOGRAPHING

An example would be an IRIS printer that prints at 300 ppi on a maximum sheet size of 35 × 47″, maximum image size of 33 × 45″. 33″ × 300 pixels is 9,900 pixels by 45″ × 300 pixels or 13,500 pixels × 3 (for 24-bit color depth), which makes approximately a 400 megabyte file. That is too big for most artists' computers and for the IRIS I use, which can't take much over 100 megabyte files.

The solution to this problem is to draw the image at half size and have the IRIS atelier resize it up once it's inside the machine; 33 × 45″ @ 150 ppi is 95.6 MB.

• **Proof the reference file.** It is a good idea to print the reworked reference photograph at the final size on your desktop color printer. The image can be broken into sections that will fit on letter or legal-size paper; the printed sections are then trimmed and taped together to reassemble the image. This is an important final step in determining that scale, composition, color, and value choices are correct. Once the reference file is established, prepare the workspace.

• **Palettes.** In Painter, open the following palettes and arrange them so they take up the least amount of screen space: Controls, Brushes, Tools, Objects (open the Layers section), and Art Materials (open Papers and Colors).

• **Monitor workspace layout.** Open the file that contains the copy of the reference photograph and drag the edges until it occupies half the space that remains after opening the palettes. Create an empty Riff file of the same size as the reference file. Drag its edges until it occupies the other half of the work space. This file will become the drawing.

• **Establish the look of the drawing.** Select a paper texture from Painter's Papers palette, a color from the Colors palette, and a brush or pencil or piece of pastel from the Brushes palette. To do a digital drawing, for example, select "Dry Media/Charcoal," black for a color, and any one of a number of papers. "Synthetic Super Fine" is a good basic paper, as is "Rougher." "Watercolor" makes great rocks, while "Scratchy" works well for tree trunks.

• **Registration marks.** With the drawing file active, on the canvas in some part of the image that will remain white when the drawing is finished, create an X for a registration mark with a 1-pixel "Flat Pen" brush with the "Straight Lines" button checked on the Draw Style end of the Controls: Brush palette.

On the layers palette, create a new layer, zoom in to about 500%, and make a second registration mark precisely on top of the first (this is because layers can get accidentally out-of-alignment; do this every time you create a new layer).

• **Begin drawing on the new layer.** The strokes will look like blacks marks on white paper, but they will actually be black marks on a transparent layer with the white of the canvas showing through. Do not draw on the canvas itself or you will curtail the advantages of working with layers.

If you accidentally draw on the canvas, you can select it all, edit/copy, and edit/paste onto a new layer; then fill the canvas with white. You will have to keep this layer on the bottom of the stack because it is not transparent.

• **Drawing with white over dark.** In digital drawing, negative spaces can be drawn positively; for example, lots of small white flowers on a dark plant are easier to create and look much more alive when done as white marks over a dark background (instead of drawing the black all around the edges of each of the white flowers). When using white over black, it is important to remember to check "Invert" on the Papers palette or the strokes will look mushy.

• **Using layers to separate colors, lines, tones, solids, and paper textures.** When drawing with white over darks, it is a good idea to put the white on a separate layer because it soon becomes confusing as to whether it is under (on the canvas) or over the black layer. If the whites are all on their own layers, toggling the layers' eye icons will show where they are.

It is also a good idea is to keep fine lines, broad lines, solids, tones, and secondary paper textures, both for black and for white, each on its own separate layer. This greatly simplifies revisions, because you can redraw or add to one without affecting the others.

Be sure to lock your layers, except for the one you're drawing on to avoid mixing lines and tones or blacks and whites accidentally. Try not to have more than a couple overlapping tone layers done with the same paper texture or the texture will look corrupted.

If many multiple layers makes your file too big for your machine, create separate files for each category: colors, lines, tones, solids, and secondary paper textures. When done, collapse the layers in these files into one layer and Edit/Copy, Edit/Paste it into the main drawing. (Here's where the registration marks come in.) Save an uncollapsed version of the files in case of revisions.

The hardest thing about drawing on a computer is not being able to see both close-up and far away at the same time.

You can see the paper texture best at 100% zoom, but you can't see how your pencil strokes are relating to the overall image. If you zoom out to see the whole image, you can't see what you're doing with your pencil. Partly, experience helps overcome this, but there are also some strategies for dealing with it.

• **Best zoom levels for drawing large images.** Broad areas of tone done with big brushes can be done zoomed way out or "Zoomed To Fit." Fine details done with small brushes are best done anywhere from 200–300% zoomed-in.

• **Using the reference photo.** The reference photograph is an invaluable aid in orienting you within the drawing and in helping you to keep your brushstrokes in sync mentally with the overall image. This is why the initial work you do on the photograph is such a key component of the digital drawing process.

Whichever technique described below is employed, it will accomplish the same thing as projecting a slide onto a wall or a drawing surface, only it's a lot more convenient; it avoids cartooning; and the photo doesn't fade.

Here are my suggestions:
Split the workspace: having the photograph and the drawing side-by-side on the monitor lets you gauge the overall effectiveness of how you're drawing.

Tracing paper option: This enables you to be accurate about the shape and placement of objects. Designate the reference photo as the clone source in the File menu. When you wish to view the reference photo under the drawing as if you were using a lightbox, click the tracing paper icon in the vertical scroll bar (upper right corner of the file window). If it seems preferable to devote the whole of the workspace to the drawing, minimize the reference photo and maximize the drawing and click "Hide Palettes" in the Window section of the program's menu bar. Tracing paper will still work.

Photo on a layer: Copy the reference photo, paste it as a separate layer into the drawing, and drag it to the bottom of the stack. The opacity of the reference photo layer can be adjusted to make the drawing marks show up better. When the drawing is finished, delete the reference photo. The only disadvantage to this alternative is that it makes the file-size larger.

How to spot-check your values: Make a black-and-white version of the photograph, created with "Grayscale" Mode in Photoshop or by running a black-and-white Two-Point Gradient on it in Painter. If you set the black-and-white version as the clone source and clone a spot of it into the drawing with the Straight Cloner brush, you can see if your tones are too light or too dark. Then hit "Undo" to get rid of the cloned piece of the photo.

Cartoon layer: For objects that are not decipherable at the zoom level at which you need to draw, create a layer for a cartoon and cartoon the object with a smallish (5 pixel) Flat Color Pen and a contrasting color (red is good) at whatever zoom level you can best see it. Then go to your drawing layer with the cartoon visible but locked and draw the object at the most comfortable zoom. You may want to adjust the transparency of the cartoon layer to make it just barely visible so as not to obscure parts of your brushstrokes.

Proof the drawing: As the drawing progresses, it is a good idea to proof it full-size from time to time as the ultimate strategy for being able to see what you've been doing. Make all the layers that are not part of the drawing, such as the photo or the cartoon, invisible and then save the file as a Tiff. A box will appear warning you that the layers will be merged with the canvas; say "OK."

Close Painter and open Photoshop. Go to "Preferences" in the File menu, select "General" and then "Interpolation: Bicubic." Open your drawing file and resize it (this works better than resizing in Painter). Edit-Copy/File-New/Edit-Paste sections of the drawing that are the right size to print on your proofing printer and stick the sections together with double-sided Scotch™ tape.

SAVE! SAVE AS!
I should have said this a lot sooner. Save your photographs and drawings frequently to prevent losing a morning's work to a crash or power failure.

• **Save and rename.** Every time you make a major change or at least every three or four working sessions, save and then "Save As" and give the file a new name.

• **Save to a CD.** Once a week or so, it pays to save the latest versions of the file to a write-able CD-ROM. That way if a virus eats your hard-drive, you still have your drawing.

• **File-naming system.** Give the piece a title, let's say "Sunset," and then add the date and time: "Sunset020926_1053" (translates as "Sunset" as it existed on September 26, 2002 at 10:53 am – use military time for PM).

Numeric numbering allows your files can be automatically sorted by name in the order that the drawing progressed, making it easy to revert to an earlier version if necessary. You will never overwrite a file that way because the same minute never comes around twice.

• **Keep a notebook.** It helps to have a record of what you did to each file. It's not unusual to get toward the end of a long project and discover that you have somehow corrupted part of the drawing, left a patch of cloned photo in or forgotten to invert the paper when drawing with white, etc. Being able to go back to an earlier version and clone in a section or Edit-Copy/Edit-Paste whole layers from before the corruption means you don't have to totally go back to square one to fix things.

• **Final save.** Once the drawing is finished, burn the file onto 3 CDs (one for the studio, one for the safety-deposit box, and one for the atelier).

DRAWING SCALES

- Establish the scales used for various types of drawings for the project, e.g. feature plans at 1:20, sections and elevations at 1:10, site plans at 1:20.
- 1:1 This is seldom used in fieldwork.
- 1:2, 1:4, 1:5 Used to draw finds that will not be removed from the site.
- 1:10 Ten centimeters on the ground are equivalent to one centimeter on the plan. This is used primarily for sections and elevations, also profiles and complex small deposits as well as for skeletons.
- 1:20 Used primarily for feature plans, site plans, and sometimes for large complex sections.
- 1:50 Used for complete site plans reduced from 1:20 originals, for simple sites with little stratification, and large simple sections and profiles.
- 1:100 Used for site plans taken from 1:20 or 1:50 originals, but much detail is lost. Also used for sketch drawings in large-scale survey work when brief sketch is acceptable.
- 1:200, 1:250, 1:500 Used to draw site or location plans.
- 1:2,500, 1:10,000 Used to locate sites from survey work. These correspond with USGS and Ordnance Survey maps.

DRAWING SMALL FINDS

- If the small find is less than .20 m at its widest point, you may draw it at 1:1 or 1:5 rather than the usual 1:10. Use 1:10 if you are including context.
- Annotate the drawing as it requires more detail and description than archaeological features.

EARTH TYPES IN SECTION DRAWINGS

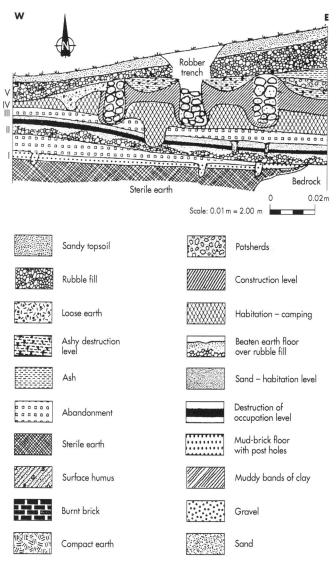

Figure 4.4a Stratigraphy drawing symbols. (Martha Joukowsky, Figure 7.5: Stratigraphic vertical section of a multilevel site, p. 154 from *A Complete Manual of Field Archaeology.* Englewood Cliffs, NJ: Prentice Hall, 1980. Copyright © 1980 by Martha Joukowsky. Reprinted by permission of Simon & Schuster Adult Publishing Group)

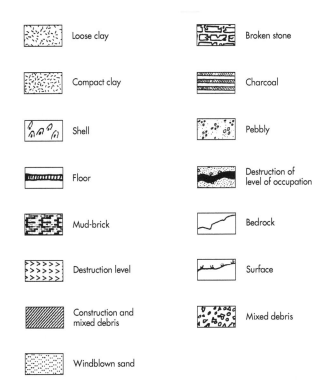

Figure 4.4b Section drawing symbols. (Martha Joukowsky, Figure 9.11: Symbols for various types of earth used in section drawings, from *A Complete Manual of Field Archaeology*. Englewood Cliffs, NJ: Prentice Hall, 1980. Copyright © 1980 by Martha Joukowsky. Reprinted by permission of Simon & Schuster Adult Publishing Group)

——— FEATURE MAPPING AND DRAWING ———

- Features should be drawn to scale, then reduced for the plan.
- Most features are first plotted using a protractor for angle measurements and scale to ascertain extent and shape.
- Before drawing a feature on a plan, it is a good idea to draw a rough sketch.
- Visualize the shape of a feature as a series of straight lines that are connected; once the spatial coordinates of the endpoints of these lines have been determined and placed on a map, drawing in the feature's outline is relatively easy.

- Draw the boundaries of features with a black line.
- Map the exposed horizontal portion of the feature.
- A feature that is an artifact cluster may be best drawn using a frame.
- Large artifacts within the bounds of a feature will require locating additional points in order to accurately portray them.
- Measurements taken off unit corners and side walls may be sufficient for outlining many features.
- Consider the use of hatching, stippling, colors, or a combination to distinguish between features.
- Any symbols or colors used should be meaningful and standardized.
- Every drawing should contain all relevant information that is described in the field record.

ILLUSTRATION INSTRUCTIONS

(for those times when line drawings of artifacts are done in the field)

- Annotate the drawing sheet with the artifact number and/or type series number, date, illustrator's initials, unit number, find spot, level, etc.
- Drawings done in the field should be logged.
- Many artifacts are drawn in outline and in section/profile; decoration should be drawn and labeled.
- All artifacts should be drawn according to conventions.
- All drawings are scale and require exact measurements of all dimensions.

LABELING SITE GRIDS

- Grids work on a system of "eastings" measured from west to east and "northings" measured from south to north. Measurement starts at the datum point.
- Do not label the datum point as 0E0N because if your site later extends to the south or west of the original grid, you will be working with negative grid points.
- Start instead at 100E 100N or a larger figure that allows for expansion.

- From the datum point, label the eastings from west to east. Then label northings from the datum point.
- If you use wooden pegs, write on them with a permanent marker. If you use plastic or metal grid pegs, permanently mark on a finds label or neon tape that is tied securely to each peg.
- You may find it useful to identify each 10-meter square or other logical area separately as A, B, C, etc.
- Prepare a sketch plan of the site that shows site north, the grid, the outline of the units, etc.

MAKING A SITE MAP

To make a site map, you need to know direction, horizontal distance, and vertical distance.

Determining direction (by compass or surveying instruments)

First, here is how to use a compass:

- Hold the base plate compass flat in front of your chest so that the compass needle floats freely and points to magnetic north. (The only thing a compass needle can do is point to magnetic north.)
- Rotate the entire compass housing until the needle sits within the orienting arrow stenciled onto the base of the compass housing (usually the orienting arrow is red). The zero degree mark on the compass housing and the north end of the needle should be aligned – they now point to magnetic north.
- Keep the orienting arrow and the compass needle pointing north. Twist the base plate until the direction-of-travel line points exactly at the distant landmark you wish to move toward. Double-check to make sure everything is still properly aligned.
- Note the exact number of degrees marked on the compass dial where the direction-of-travel line intersects the compass dial. That number of degrees is the direction to the distant landmark.

Determining horizontal distance (by pacing, taping, stadia, or electronic transit)

■ Pacing is only approximate, so taping or using a vehicle's odometer may be advised.

■ Two methods of taping: breaking tape (measure short segments while keeping the tape horizontal) or slope reduction (measure directly down a slope and reduce slope distance to horizontal distance by trigonometric calculations). See **Taping procedures**

Determining vertical distance (breaking tape, Abney level, electronic transit)

See **Taping procedures**

■ Identify the site reference point, which is the approximate center of the site (to be marked with a metal tag or other marker) and which is the central point for mapping.

Radial method
■ Stand on the site datum point.
■ Mark its position at the center of the map, determine true north, and take a bearing or azimuth to the first feature.
■ Put the bearing on the map with a protractor.
■ Pace the distance from the datum point to the feature and scale this on the map (e.g. 1 cm = 1 m).
■ Plot the feature and return to the datum point.
■ Repeat the procedure until the site is mapped.

Intersection/triangulation method
■ Stand on the site datum point (point #1).
■ Lay out a line 30 m long to true north (or another direction if you prefer) and establish point #2.
■ Take bearings on the feature (F-1) from both points #1 and #2 – the point where the two bearings intersect establishes the approximate location of F-1.
■ Tape the distances from points #1 and #2 to F-1 if you need accuracy.
■ The accuracy also increases when you take three or more bearings (azimuths) that converge on F-1, forming the "surveyor's triangle of error."
■ This whole procedure is immeasurably easier with the use of electronic data measuring equipment.

MAPPING, DRAWING, AND PHOTOGRAPHING

The scale used for most US topographic mapping is 1:24,000. USGS maps at this scale cover an area measuring 7.5 minutes of latitude and 7.5 minutes of longitude and are commonly called 7.5-minute quadrangle maps.

Most of Alaska has been mapped at 1:63,360, with some populated areas also mapped at 1:24,000 and 1:25,000.

Maps at 1:24,000 scale are fairly large and provide detailed information about the features of an area, including the locations of important buildings and most campgrounds, ski lifts, and water mills. Footbridges, drawbridges, fence lines, and private roads are also shown at this scale.

Small-scale maps (1:250,000 and smaller) show large areas on single map sheets, but details are limited to major features, such as boundaries, parks, airports, major roads, railroads, and streams.

Maps scaled at 1:150,000 are published privately for a variety of states in an *Atlas and Gazetteer* series by the DeLorme Mapping Company. There is more detail in topography compared to maps at the 1:250,000 scale.

The 1:62,500 scale map shows topography in greater detail and covers a fairly extensive area. This is used more for counties. Road systems are shown in greater detail, some structures are depicted, and the contour interval is smaller which provides for a more realistic depiction of the landscape.

MAPPING, DRAWING, AND PHOTOGRAPHING

MAP SYMBOLS

BATHYMETRIC FEATURES

Area exposed at mean low tide: sounding datum line***	
Channel ***	
Sunken rock***	

BOUNDARIES

National	
State or territorial	
County or equivalent	
Civil township or equivalent	
Incorporated city or equivalent	
Federally administered park, reservation, or monument (external	
Federally administered park, reservation, or monument (internal)	
State forest, park, reservation, or monument and large country park	
Porest Service administrative area*	
Forest Service ranger district*	
National Forest System land status, Forest Service lands*	
National Forest System land status, non-Forest Service lands*	
Small park (county or city)	

BUILDINGS AND RELATED FEATURES

Building	
School; house of worship	
Athletic field	
Built-up area	
Forest headquarters*	
Ranger district office*	
Guard station or work center*	
Racetrack or raceway	
Airport, paved landing strip, runway, taxiway or apron	
Unpaved landing strip	
Well (other than water), windmill or wind generator	
Tanks	
Covered reservoir	
Gaging station	
Located or landmark object (feature as labeled)	
Boat ramp or boat access*	
Roadside park or rest area	
Picnic area	
Campground	
Winter recreation area*	
Cemetary	

COASTAL FEATURES

Foreshore flat	Mud
Coral or rock reef	Reef
Rock, bare or awash; dangerous to navigation	

COASTAL FEATURES – continued

Groups of rocks, bare or awash	
Exposed wreck	
Depth curce; sounding	-18 23
Breakwater, pier, jetty, or wharf	
Seawall	
Oil or gas well; platform	

CONTOURS

Topographic
Index	6000
Approximate or indefinite	
Intermediate	
Approximate or indefinite	
Supplementary	
Depression	
Cut	
Fill	
Continental divide	

Bathymetric
Index***	
Intermediate***	
Index primary***	
Primary***	
Supplementary***	

CONTROL DATA AND MONUMENTS

Principal point**	3-20
U.S. mineral or location monument	USMM 438
River mileage marker	Mile 69

Boundary monument
Third-order or better elevation, with tablet	BM 9134 BM 277
Third-order or better elevation, recoverable mark, no tablet	5628
With number and elevation	67 4561

Horizontal control
Third-order or better, permanent mark	Neace Neace
With third-order or better elevation	BM 52 Pike BM393
With checked spot elevation	1012
Coincident with found section corner	Cactus Cactus
Unmonumented**	

Vertical control
Third-order or better elevation, with tablet	BM 5280
Third-order or better elevation, recoverable mark, no tablet	528
Bench mark coincident with found section corner	BM 5280
Spot elevation	7623

GLACIERS AND PERMANENT SNOWFIELDS

Contours and limits	
Formlines	
Glacial advance	
Glacial retreat	

MAPPING, DRAWING, AND PHOTOGRAPHING

Figure 4.5 Map symbols. (Map symbols, topographic. Reprinted from the U.S. Geological Survey, www.usgs.gov/)

LAND SURVEYS

Public land survey system
Range or Township line
Location approximate
Location doubtful
Protracted
Protracted (AK 1:63,000 scale)
Range or Township labels — R1E T2N
Section line
Location approximate
Location doubtful
Protracted
Protracted (AK 1:63,000 scale)
Section numbers — 1 - 36
Found section corner
Found closing corner
Witness corner — WC
Meander corner — MC
Weak corner*

Other land surveys
Range or Township line
Section line
Land grant, mining claim, donation land claim, or tract
Land grant, homestead, mineral, or other special survey monument
Fence or field lines

MARINE SHORELINES

Shoreline
Apparent (edge of vegetation)***
Indefinite or unsurveyed

MINES AND CAVES

Quarry or open pit mine
Gravel, sand, clay, or borrow pit
Mine tunnel or cave entrance
Mine shaft
Prospect — X
Tailings — Tailings
Mine dump
Former disposal site or mine

PROJECTION AND GRIDS

Neatline — 39°15'
Graticule tick — 90°37'30" 55'
Graticule intersection
Datum shift tick

State plane coordinate systems
Primary zone tick — 640 000 FEET
Secondary zone tick — 247 500 METERS
Tertiary zone tick — 260 000 FEET
Quaternary zone tick — 98 500 METERS
Quintary zone tick — 320 000 FEET

Universal transverse mercator grid
UTM grid (full grid) — 273
UTM grid ticks* — 269

RAILROADS AND RELATED FEATURES

Standard guage railroad, single track
Standard guage railroad, multiple track
Narrow guage railroad, single track
Narro guage railroad, multiple track

RAILROADS AND RELATED FEATURES – continued

Railroad siding
Railroad in highway
Railroad in road
Railroad in light duty road*
Railroad underpass; overpass
Railroad bridge; drawbridge
Railroad tunnel
Railroad yard
Railroad turntable; roundhouse

RIVERS, LAKES, AND CANALS

Perennial stream
Perennial river
Intermittent stream
Intermittent river
Disappearing stream
Falls, small
Falls, large
Rapids, small
Rapids, large
Masonry dam
Dam with lock
Dam carrying road
Perennial lake/pond
Intermittent lake/pond
Dry lake/pond — Dry lake
Narrow wash
Wide wash — Wash
Canal, flume, or aqueduct with lock
Elevated aqueduct, flume, or conduit
Aqueduct tunnel
Water well, geyser, fumerole, or mud pot
Spring or seep

ROADS AND RELATED FEATURES

Please note: Roads on Provisional-edition maps are not classified as primary, secondary, or light duty. These roads are all classified as improved roads and are symbolized the same as light duty roads.

Primary highway
Secondary highway
Light duty road
Light duty road, paved*
Light duty road, gravel*
Light duty road, dirt*
Light duty road, unspecified*
Unimproved road
Unimproved road*
4WD road
4WD road*
Trail
Highway or road with median strip
Highway or road under construction — Under Const
Highway or road underpass; overpass

Figure 4.5 Continued

270

ROADS AND RELATED FEATURES – *continued*		SURFACE FEATURES – *continued*	
Highway or road bridge; drawbridge		Sand or mud	
Highway or road tunnel		Disturbed surface	
Road block, berm, or barrier*		Gravel beach or glacial moraine	
Gate on road*		Tailings pond	
Trailhead*			

SUBMERGED AREAS AND BOGS

		TRANSMISSION LINES AND PIPELINES	
Marsh or swamp		Power transmission line; pole; tower	
Submerged marsh or swamp		Telephone line	
Wooded marsh or swamp		Aboveground pipeline	
Submerged wooded marsh or swamp		Underground pipeline	

VEGETATION

Woodland	
Land subject to inundation	
Shrubland	
Orchard	
Vineyard	

Max Pool 43

SURFACE FEATURES

Mangrove

Levee	

Figure 4.5 Continued

MAPPING INSTRUMENTS

Abney level
alidade (telescope) and plane table
Global Positioning System/GPS
magnetic compass (hand-bearing or sighting, baseplate or protractor/
  orienteering, or pocket transits)
other electronic distance measurement instruments
stadia rod
total station
transit

MAPPING, DRAWING, AND PHOTOGRAPHING

271

MAPPING SCALES AND AREAS

Scale 1:X	Feet/ inch	Inch/ mile	Acres/ sq inch	Sq miles/ sq inch
100	8.3	633.60	0.0016	0.000002
120	10.0	528.00	0.0023	0.000004
200	16.7	316.80	0.0064	0.000010
240	20.0	264.00	0.0092	0.000014
250	20.8	253.44	0.0100	0.000016
300	25.0	211.20	0.0143	0.000022
400	33.3	158.40	0.0255	0.000040
480	40.0	132.00	0.0367	0.000057
500	41.7	126.72	0.0399	0.000062
600	50.0	105.60	0.0574	0.000090
1,000	83.3	63.36	0.1594	0.000249
1,200	100.0	52.80	0.2296	0.000359
1,500	125.0	42.24	0.3587	0.000560
2,000	166.7	31.68	0.6377	0.000996
2,400	200.0	26.40	0.9183	0.001435
2,500	208.3	25.43	0.9964	0.001557

Scale 1:X	Feet/ inch	Inch/ mile	Acres/ sq inch	Meters/ inch
2,400	200	26.40	0.92	61.0
3,000	250	21.12	1.43	76.2
3,600	300	17.60	2.07	91.4
4,000	333	15.84	2.55	101.6
4,800	400	13.20	3.67	121.9
5,000	417	12.67	3.99	127.0
6,000	500	10.56	5.74	152.4
7,200	600	8.80	8.26	182.9
8,400	700	7.54	11.25	213.4
9,600	800	6.60	14.69	243.8
10,000	833	6.34	15.94	254.0
12,000	1,000	5.28	22.96	304.8
15,000	1,250	4.22	35.87	381.0
15,840	1,320	4.00	40.00	402.3
18,000	1,500	3.52	51.65	457.2
20,000	1,667	3.17	63.77	508.0
24,000	2,000	2.64	91.83	609.6
30,000	2,500	2.11	143.48	762.0
40,000	3,333	1.58	255.08	1016.0

MAPPING, DRAWING, AND PHOTOGRAPHING

MAPS FOR ARCHAEOLOGICAL SITES

Types of maps

- Regional map: depicts archaeological sites within region, showing relationship of site to natural landscape; can use available topographic maps at suitable scales as base maps, then prepare simply by adding the relevant archaeological data.
- Site map/site record map: small-scale map depicting the site in detail; sometimes good-quality, large-scale maps may be available for a site which contain accurate topographic data (e.g. contour information) and these can be converted to site maps by simply plotting the location of archaeological features on them.
- Site plan/site excavation map: a survey map showing the site and surrounding area with features and using conventional symbols; this is used to present the results of excavation – the sequence following a feature before, during, and after excavation.
- Topographic map with main elevations, 3-D aspects of land forms and using conventional symbols.

Basic kinds of maps

- Sketch maps: made without instruments, often during feasibility studies or archaeological reconnaissance, to record the general characteristics of a site.
- Compass maps: made with pocket-transit compass and tape for a reasonably accurate planimetric map.
- Aerial photograph maps: planimetric maps made by tracing ground features from an aerial photograph, though scale of the photograph affects the quality.
- Instrument maps: the preferred method for archaeological mapping, using total station or transit/theodolite or alidade/plane table.

Site mapmaking general guidelines

- Site maps can be made with surveying instruments or through triangulation with tapes or with a plane table and alidade.
- Establish points of reference to which subsequent measurements of distance and angles will be related.
- Position the points so you see the greatest number of things to be mapped and also make sure there is a clear line of sight between them.

MAPPING, DRAWING, AND PHOTOGRAPHING

- Map must contain archaeological and topographic features, location of source areas of surface collections and the limits to all excavations.
- Draw the map with a scale in meters.
- Include title block, survey date, reference grid, north arrow, bar scale, magnetic declination, initials of map-maker, explanation of symbols, etc.
- Make sure true north is pointing upward.
- Draw in pencil.
- Final drawing will be done with India ink or a stylus permanent-ink drawing pen (e.g. Micron) with all pencil lines erased.
- Final lettering may be done by hand or transfer lettering.

──── PHOTOGRAPHIC EQUIPMENT LIST ────

accessory shoe
arrow or trowel (for pointing north)
batteries for camera and flash unit
black-and-white scales
cameras (digital, Polaroid, reflex)
directional arrow
exposure meter
film (which should be stored in cool place)
filters
flash unit
grey card
lens hoods
lens shade
lenses, including zoom lens
light meter
photo menu board with letters and numbers *or* chalkboard with chalk
photography log book
reflectors
remote-control shutter release
shade cloth
spirit level
tripod

- Store the film in a cool place.
- You can never have too many photographs. Take at least one color and one black-and-white photograph every time and include a calibrated north arrow whenever possible.
- Each exposure must be recorded in the photo log at the time the photo is taken.
- Use indirect lighting to get higher-quality photographs. Photos taken in cloudy weather work out well. If that is not possible, the shaded effect can be created by using plastic sheeting.
- Focus the item of interest by looking around the periphery for extraneous items that may detract from the item.
- It is important to keep the lens clean, hold the camera steady, and focus.
- Protect the camera from heat, dampness, dust, and dirt.
- Put a bar scale in the photograph, parallel to the side or base.
- The subject of photography can and possibly should be photographed at different times of day.
- Consider taking several exposures at different settings for photographs of great importance. This is called bracketing; take exposures one stop above and one below the meter's reading.
- When photographing successive levels of a unit, always orient the photos in the same direction, so the series of photos makes sense.
- When photographing a feature, the light meter reading should be done by the feature.
- If a feature is partly in the sun, you may need to either shade the entire feature or provide more lighting to the shaded part. Reflectors can help with shadows.
- All features should be photographed individually after excavation/exposure is complete.
- Photographs must show the relationship of artifacts to the feature or burial.
- Photographs must show the relationship of a feature to a broader area of context, e.g. a room or feature's place within a block excavation.
- All stratigraphic profiles to be mapped should be photographed. The photo should be taken as level and square-on as possible. If it is impossible to include the entire face in one photograph, take multiple, overlapping shots. Indirect lighting is especially

MAPPING, DRAWING, AND PHOTOGRAPHING

important for stratigraphic profile photos. To enhance color contrast, you can dampen the profile by carefully spraying it with water from a hand sprayer. If you elect to do this, remember that this is additional photo documentation; you must always take at least one color and one black-and-white shot of a stratigraphic profile that has not been dampened, scored with a trowel, or altered in any other way. If you take this type of additional photo, record on the photo log how the face was altered.

- When excavation in a structure is complete, multiple final photos from different angles should be taken of whatever architecture is exposed, such as walls and floor. These shots should be taken on a cloudy day if possible.
- Unusual artifacts found in situ, whether in fill or on a surface, should be photographed.
- Take working photos of participants, tour groups, and staff people occasionally.
- Each roll of film should get a unique log number and a record must be kept of each exposure.
- Process the film as soon as possible.

PHOTOGRAPHS TO BE TAKEN

(depending on the director's instructions)

artifacts and other finds in situ
daily record of excavation, by unit
detail of features
detail of stratigraphic profiles
panoramic and general site views
phase photographs
publicity photographs (participants, group tours, staff people)

PHOTOGRAPHY, DIGITAL

These are basic steps for taking digital photographs outdoors.

- Use automatic exposure for most outdoor scenes.
- Override automatic exposure when the scene is much lighter or darker than middle gray.

- Increase exposure to lighten a scene; decrease exposure to darken a scene.
- Override automatic exposure when the sun is behind or on one side of the scene to be shot.
- Override automatic exposure when light reflects off of bright sand or snow.
- Experiment with overriding automatic exposure for high-contrast scenes.
- Use a light meter to determine the appropriate aperture setting and shutter speed.
- Adjust the aperture setting and shutter speed in small steps.
- Shoot a picture and preview it to evaluate settings. Adjust as necessary and shoot again.
- Try shooting from several angles; you can delete the worst choices on the spot.

PLANE TABLE USE

- Set the plane table up over the datum point.
- Attach the drafting material to the table surface.
- Center the table over the datum, using a plumb bob suspended from the bottom of the tripod.
- Level the plane table using the built-in level or a small carpenter's level.
- Draw a north–south meridian on the drafting film/paper and an east–west baseline.
- Orient the plane table to true north by placing a compass (adjusted for magnetic declination) on the north–south line.
- Place a triangular engineer's scale on the north–south meridian and use it to sight along the north line.
- Have someone run the tape out along the north line for the desired distance and have them put a stake in at that point. Place grade stakes or wire flags at intervals along this line.
- Turn a 90-degree angle to set up the baseline running east. Align the engineer's scale or alidade along the east–west line on the drafting material and sight along the line (foresight) to a stadia rod.
- Have someone place a stake at E30 on the line of sight.
- Install as many stakes or flags along the meridian and baseline as needed.

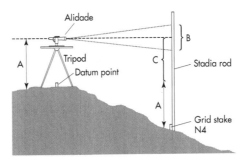

Figure 4.6 Determining distance and difference in elevation using an alidade and plane table. (Thomas R. Hester, Harry J. Shafer, and Kenneth L. Feder, Figure 9.30: Determination of distance and difference in elevation using an alidade and plane table (mounted on a tripod), p. 220 from *Field Methods in Archaeology*, Seventh Edition. New York: McGraw-Hill, 1997. Copyright © 1997 by Thomas R. Hester, Harry J. Shafer, and Kenneth L. Feder. Reprinted by permission of The McGraw-Hill Companies)

- Draw a line along the beveled edge of the alidade baseplate scaled to represent the actual distance and plot the position of the stake on the map.
- You can expand this indefinitely by marking the datum point with a stake or wire flag, then set up the plane table at a new station, such as N30.
- Orient the table by taking a backsight on the previous datum point. This is done by placing the sighting guide exactly along the meridian and sighting back (south) to the datum point. Rotate the plane table so you are sighting directly at that datum point. Secure the table rotation lock, then turn a 90-degree angle east from N30, tape east and establish N30/E30.
- Use this same procedure if you are using an instrument like an alidade.

PLOTTING CONTOUR LINES

- Controlling point method: surveyor obtains the elevation of each grid stake and plots this information on the site map; contour then interpolated using the known elevations of the grid points as controlling points.

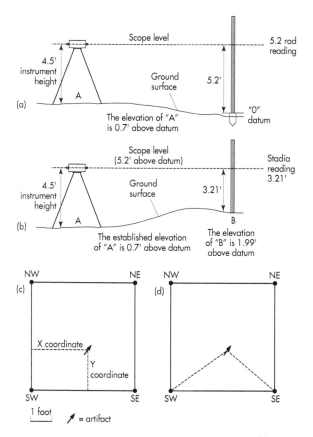

Figure 4.7a Determining elevation with a stadia rod off an elevation datum or benchmark. (Martha Joukowsky, Figure 6.54: Determining elevation with a stadia rod off an elevation datum or benchmark, p. 154 from *A Complete Manual of Field Archaeology*. Englewood Cliffs, NJ: Prentice Hall, 1980. Copyright © 1980 by Martha Joukowsky. Reprinted by permission of Simon & Schuster Adult Publishing Group)

Figure 4.7b Determining elevation with a stadia road from a point of known to a point of unknown elevation. (Martha Joukowsky, Figure 6.55: Determining elevation with a stadia rod from a point of known elevation to a point of unknown elevation, p. 154 from *A Complete Manual of Field Archaeology*. Englewood Cliffs, NJ: Prentice Hall, 1980. Copyright © 1980 by Martha Joukowsky. Reprinted by permission of Simon & Schuster Adult Publishing Group)

Figure 4.7c and d Determining spatial coordinates: (c) the distance to the center of an artifact from Y, X; (d) triangulating from two corners. (R. M. Stewart, Figure 9.21: Determining the spatial coordinates of an artifact on an excavation floor, p. 256 from *Archaeology Basic Field Methods*. Dubuque, Iowa: Kendall/Hunt, 2002. Copyright © 2002 by Kendall/Hunt Publishing Company. Reprinted by permission of the publisher)

- Radial method: plumb the plane table over the site benchmark and read the elevations outward/downhill in the cardinal directions and at 45 degrees in each quadrant – yielding eight "rays" along which points of known distance and elevation are plotted and each contour line connects points of the same elevation.
- Trace contour method: rodperson places the rod at a trial location, surveyor directs rodperson uphill or downhill until the rod reading indicates the desired contour interval.
- Note: contours can be approximated (interpolated) by referring to the contour lines on the appropriate USGS quadrangle and transferring them to the site record map, augmenting with direct observation.

―――――――――― **PLUMBING A LINE** ――――――――――

(plumbing and marking tape lengths)

- A plumb bob is used to locate the measurement point on the tape vertically above a fixed marker or to place taping pins to mark tape lengths.
- Each end point of a measurement is marked by placing the plumb bob string over the tape and securing it with one thumb.
- For adding and subtracting tapes, the rear measuring point (i.e. the starting point) is adjusted to the nearest whole meter (e.g. 14 m) such that the graduated portion of the tape at the forward end straddles the closing point.
- The plumb bob is "dropped" and a taping pin is placed vertically below the plumb bob point (i.e. perpendicular to the tape).
- To measure distance between fixed points: the plumb bob is "dropped" and the string is adjusted along the tape length until the plumb bob point is vertically above the fixed point.
- To read the tape, the string of the plumb bob is used to mark the tape measurement points.
- For fully graduated and subtracting tapes, the measured distance is the difference between the rear (RMP) and forward (FMP) measurement points.

PROFILE/SECTION DRAWING INSTRUCTIONS

- Most sections are drawn to 1:10, but some simple sections may be recorded at 1:20 or 1:50. Profiles are the simplest form of section drawing and are drawn in the same way as a section, but show only the outline of a feature.
- When you are drawing a section too large for one sheet, split the section equally between two sheets. Get your drawing supplies together.
- The profile should be as vertical as possible (check with plumb bob) and clean from top to bottom.
- It may be useful to spray with water to bring out slight color differences.
- You must establish a level line from which measurements are taken in order to draw a profile accurately. Anything can be firmly anchored in the ground at the surface over the profile to be drawn and a taut, leveled string attached. The string should slightly overhang the face of the profile to make measurements more convenient.
- Use a line level to level the string.
- Get the graph paper, pencils, etc. for drawing.
- Choose a scale for the drawing to accommodate the length and width of the profile.
- Pick a horizontal line on the graph paper to represent the level line you established. Draw in that line.
- Position a folding rule or tape along the top of the profile, with "0" at one edge.
- If the top of the profile is sloped, pull a tape along the leveled string and with a plumb bob, drop measured points onto the ground at a regular interval, marking the points with nails.
- Take measurements down from the level line to points along the boundaries of strata, features, etc.
- You will also measure the points where an individual boundary line meets the edge of the cleaned profile or excavation wall and points between so you can draw the boundary by "connecting the dots."
- Some people delineate the boundaries of strata with continuous lines, but others use colors, especially colors accurately depicting the real coloration.
- You will also draw the top of the profile.
- Each point requires two measurements – a horizontal one from the "0" end of the tape and a vertical one from the level line.

MAPPING, DRAWING, AND PHOTOGRAPHING

- Work with one boundary at a time, from the top of the profile to the bottom. It is best to draw in the top and bottom of the section and the limits of the sides, then fill it in with strata, features, etc.
- You might find it useful to put a drawing frame in vertically.
- On the basic drawing, label the strata, features, etc. Describe each stratum, feature, etc.
- The drawing should have a title block (project, site, provenience or spatial location of profile, date, illustrator's name, catalog number, scale, north arrow, key to symbols, descriptions of strata, features, etc.

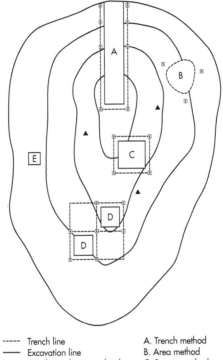

-----	Trench line	A. Trench method
——	Excavation line	B. Area method
▫	Trench or other record stake	C. Square method
⊙	Temporary plotting stake	D. Checkerboard method
▲	Surveyor's permanent marker	E. Sounding

(a)

Figure 4.8a Excavation plot plan. (Philip C. Hammond, Excavation plot plan and techniques, from *Archaeological Techniques for Amateurs*. New York: Van Nostrand, 1963. Copyright © 1963 by Philip C. Hammond. Reprinted by permission of the author)

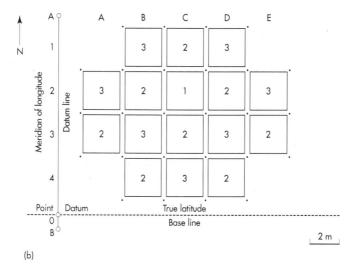

(b)

Figure 4.8b Grid excavation plan. (Martha Joukowsky, Figure 6.10: Alternate grid excavation plan, p. 345 from *A Complete Manual of Field Archaeology*. Englewood Cliffs, NJ: Prentice Hall, 1980. Copyright © 1980 by Martha Joukowsky. Reprinted by permission of Simon & Schuster Adult Publishing Group)

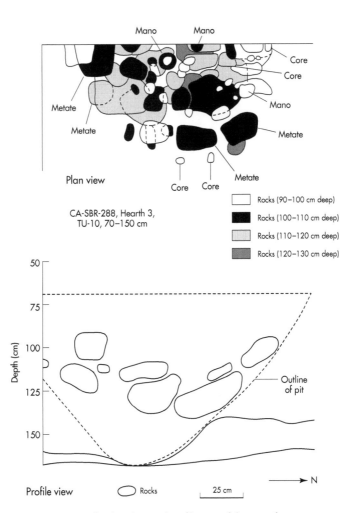

Figure 4.8c Example of a plan- and profile-view of the same feature on a map. (Mark Q. Sutton and Brooke S. Arkush, Figure 112: Example of a plan- and profile-view map of the same feature on a map, p. 323 from *Archaeological Laboratory Methods: An Introduction*, Third Edition. Dubuque, IA: Kendall/Hunt Publishing, 2002. Copyright © 2002 by Kendall/Hunt Publishing Company. Reprinted by permission of the publisher)

Site 5MT1825, Structure 104, Stratigraphic Profile

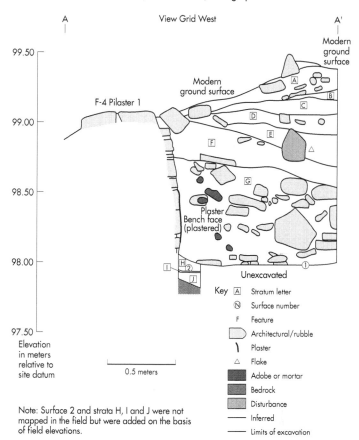

A   View Grid West   A'

Modern ground surface

99.50

Modern ground surface

F-4 Pilaster 1

99.00

98.50

Plaster
Bench face
(plastered)

98.00

Unexcavated

Key

- A Stratum letter
- Ⓝ Surface number
- F Feature
- Architectural/rubble
- Plaster
- △ Flake
- Adobe or mortar
- Bedrock
- Disturbance
- Inferred
- Limits of excavation

97.50

Elevation
in meters
relative to
site datum

0.5 meters

Note: Surface 2 and strata H, I and J were not
mapped in the field but were added on the basis
of field elevations.

Figure 4.8d Example of a profile-view. (Site 5MT1825, Structure 104,
Stratigraphic profile, from *The Castle Rock Pueblo Database*. Crow Canyon
Archaeological Center, 2001b. Copyright © 2001 by Crow Canyon
Archaeological Center. Reprinted by permission)

SCALE OF DRAWINGS, CHANGING
WITH A PHOTOCOPIER

Photocopy down to the size required and then, if needed, trace them. Most drawings will have to be photocopied at least twice to get to the desired scale. Remember that photocopiers distort drawings. Center the drawing in the photocopier and also measure between grid points on the final scaled-down drawings to make sure the distance is at the correct scale.

Scaling from	First at	Then at	Then at	Then at
1:10 to 1:20	> 50%	~	~	~
1:20 to 1:50	> 50%	> 80%	~	~
1:20 to 1:100	> 50%	> 50%	> 80%	~
1:50 to 1:20	< 50%	< 80%	~	~
1:50 to 1:100	> 50%	~	~	~
1:50 to 1:200	> 50%	> 50%	~	~
1:100 to 1:200	> 50%	~	~	~
1:10,000 to 1:25,000	> 50%	> 80%	~	~
1:25,000 to 1:10,000	< 50%	< 80%	~	~

Changing scale without a photocopier is best done by drawing two sketch scales, one above the other, of the scale of the original drawing and the scale of the new drawing. Then outline, for example, a 5 cm × 5 cm on a 1:20 plan and a 2 cm × 2 cm on a 1:50 plan.

SCALED MAP FOR ARTIFACTS

- Create this type of map to show the location of certain artifacts.
- Determine the exact location of the artifact.
- Establish the dimensions of the unit on a piece of graph paper.
- Label the map with its provenience, subject matter, etc. Include a north arrow and scale and a key to symbols.
- Use an engineer's scale or drawing compass to plot the artifact's spatial measurements onto the map.
- Draw a larger artifact to scale by first determining its center point on the map, then measuring the length and width of the piece. With the engineer's scale, recreate the artifact's shape from the center point, using the measurements.

- Number the artifact's location. The number links the position on the map to spatial coordinates and the artifact itself.

———— SINGLE-CONTEXT PLANNING ————

- This method is used for complex features and stratigraphy, mainly on urban sites. It presumes the total removal of each deposit.
- Every context gets its own plan – a pre-excavation plan, sections, and post-excavation plan for cut features like ditches, hearths, pits, and postholes and pre-excavation and post-excavation plans for floor layers.
- Running sections may be drawn across a site to record deposits as they are taken away.

———— SPECIAL SECTION DRAWING INSTRUCTIONS ————

- For an uneven section or an outstanding feature within a section, you will need to place extra nails in the section to ensure that it is drawn to the same level. You will need to include the coordinates of every nail that is on a change of angle and annotate the section drawing, showing which way each facet of the section faces.
- For drawing a horizontally or vertically stepped section, you will need several section strings with the start of each string directly underneath the end of each previous section string.
- To draw the interior or exterior surface of a curved structure, establish a section line as near to the top of the feature as possible. Take levels around the inside of the feature and join the dots on the drawing. Pick a convenient number on the tape and hold it on the section line. Set the tape up vertically and tautly (with a plumb bob) and draw 10 cm on either side of it. Repeat at 20 cm intervals around the inside or outside of the feature, making sure that the selected point on the tape is always on the section line.
- To draw an elevation or wall fairly quickly, set up your section line as close to the bottom of the elevation as possible. Using the largest planning frame available, put its base on the section line. Ensure that the strings of the frame are vertical using a plumb bob. Use something to balance the frame if necessary.

SURVEYING SYMBOLS

△	Triangulation station	⟨	Center
⊙	Transit traverse point	₵	Center line
▣	Stadia station	na.	nail
B.M	Bench mark	tk.	Tack
Stk	Stake	cb.	Curb
Spk	Spike	F.S.	Foresight
—·—	fence	B.S.	Backsight
▬	Fence showing posts on side	H.I.	Height of instrument
	Line of building	⊼	Optical instrument
S.B.	Stone-bound	↑N	True North
Tel.	Telephone pole	↑	Magnetic North

Figure 4.9 Surveying abbreviations and symbols. (Martha Joukowsky, Figure 5.47: Common abbreviations and symbols used in surveying notes, p. 93 from *A Complete Manual of Field Archaeology*. Englewood Cliffs, NJ: Prentice Hall, 1980. Copyright © 1980 by Martha Joukowsky. Reprinted by permission of Simon & Schuster Adult Publishing Group)

Taping on level ground

Lining in
- Mark the line at both ends and at intermediate points as necessary.

Applying tension
- The rear tapeperson calls "tape" when reaching end of tape.
- The forward tapeperson is lined in holding the zero end of the tape.
- Tape should be straight and held at the same elevation.
- A specified tension is applied to the tape.

Plumbing (of suspended tapes)
- Required when obstacles or surface irregularities make it undesirable to lay the tape on the ground.
- Tape is held in a horizontal position with a plumb bob over the point used to mark the tape length.

Marking tape lengths
- The rear tapeperson holds the "100 ft" end of the tape over the rear (or first) point, and calls "stick" when ready.
- The forward tapeperson places a pin exactly opposite the zero mark on the tape, and calls "stuck" when the pin is in place.
- The pin location is checked by repeating the measurement (as many times as necessary).
- The forward tapeperson paces off 100 feet and the process is repeated until a final partial tape length is measured.

Reading the tape
- There are two types of tapes: adding tape – this is actually 101 feet long; cut tape – this is 100 feet long, and requires subtraction to use.
- Measure the distance.
- Double check measurement.

Recording the distance
- After the partial tape length has been measured, the rear tapeperson determines the number of full tape lengths by counting the number of pins collected.
- This number is called out to the forward tapeperson, who adds it to the partial tape distance, and records the total distance.

Taping on uneven or sloping ground

- On gentle slopes, hold the tape horizontal and use a plumb bob at one or both ends.
- On a steep slope, one method of finding horizontal distance is "breaking tape."
- Breaking tape involves measuring shorter distances one at a time to allow the tape to be held horizontal at or below chest height.
  - The forward tapeperson places a pin at a tape mark.
  - The rear tapeperson moves ahead and holds the tape mark at the pin while the forward tapeperson proceeds.
  - This is repeated until the full 100 foot distance is marked.

MAPPING, DRAWING, AND PHOTOGRAPHING

- The procedure is the same as when taping 100 foot lengths, only for shorter segments.
■ Taping downhill is preferable to and easier than taping uphill.

Taping on a steep slope

On steep slopes it is often better to measure along the slope and determine the angle of inclination or the difference in elevation.

TOPOGRAPHIC MAP, READING A

■ Interpreting the colored lines, areas, and other symbols is the first step in using topographic maps. Features are shown as points, lines, or areas, depending on their size and extent. For example, individual houses may be shown as small black squares. For larger buildings, the actual shapes are mapped. In densely built-up areas, most individual buildings are omitted and an area tint is shown. On some maps, post offices, churches, city halls, and other landmark buildings are shown within the tinted area.
■ The first features usually noticed on a topographic map are the area features such as vegetation (green), water (blue), some information added during update (purple), and densely built-up areas (gray or red).
■ Many features are shown by lines that may be straight, curved, solid, dashed, dotted, or in any combination. The colors of the lines usually indicate similar kinds or classes of information: brown for topographic contours; blue for lakes, streams, irrigation ditches, etc.; red for land grids and important roads; black for other roads and trails, railroads, boundaries, etc.; and purple for features that have been updated using aerial photography, but not field verified.
■ Various point symbols are used to depict features such as buildings, campgrounds, springs, water tanks, mines, survey control points, and wells.
■ Names of places and features also are shown in a color corresponding to the type of feature. Many features are identified by labels, such as "Substation" or "Golf Course."
■ Topographic contours are shown in brown by lines of different widths. Each contour is a line of equal elevation; therefore, contours never cross. They show the general shape of the terrain. To help the user determine elevations, index contours (usually every

fourth or fifth contour) are wider. The narrower intermediate and supplementary contours found between the index contours help to show more details of the land surface shape. Contours that are very close together represent steep slopes. Widely spaced contours, or an absence of contours, means that the ground slope is relatively level. The elevation difference between adjacent contour lines, called the contour interval, is selected to best show the general shape of the terrain. A map of a relatively flat area may have a contour interval of 10 feet or less. Maps in mountainous areas may have contour intervals of 100 feet or more. Elevation values are shown at frequent intervals on the index contour lines to facilitate their identification, as well as to enable the user to interpolate the values of adjacent contours.

■ Bathymetric contours are generally offshore since they show the shape and slope of the ocean bottom. They are shown in blue or black. Bathymetric contours are shown in meters at intervals appropriate to map scale and coastal profile, and should not be confused with depth curves.

■ Depth curves are shown along coastlines and on inland bodies of water where the data are available from hydrographic charts or other reliable sources. Depth figures, shown in blue along the curves, are in feet on older USGS maps and in meters on newer maps. Soundings, individual depth values, may also be shown.

5

Measurement and Conversion

Accurate and careful measurements are especially important in archaeology because the interpretation of data is based on the results of measuring and plotting. The purpose of measuring is to establish the exact position of artifacts, features, and other archaeological data so that maps and plans may be precisely prepared. Measuring helps to achieve excavation goals.

This chapter aids in calculations and measurements. Charts and instructions are offered for conversions. Much information is provided about setting up and using measuring equipment. Details of taking such measurements are discussed below, but those working in archaeology will gain further understanding from reading other field manuals and textbooks. Measuring may be the single most significant aspect of an excavation.

--- **CONTENTS** ---

MEASUREMENT AND CONVERSION

293

—— ALIDADE, CARE AND ADJUSTMENT OF ——

- Clean the lenses when necessary with a soft brush.
- Cushion the case when it is transported in a vehicle.
- If a sighted point shifts slightly in relation to the cross-hairs when the eye is moved, the cross-hairs must be focused precisely by the eyepiece ring after pointing the telescope to the sky. The telescope is then depressed to the original sight and refocused as necessary.
- If the alidade has been dropped, the set of cross-hairs needs to be checked by placing the alidade on a solid level surface, releasing the retaining ring and rotating the telescope firmly against its stop, sighting on a distant point and adjusting for parallax, and elevating the telescope with the tangent screw to see if the point sighted stays on the vertical cross-hairs. The cross-hairs can be rotated with the capstan screws.
- If the compass needle dips so much that it touches the window of the compass box, slide the balancing weight along the needle until it remains level.
- Lift by the pedestal, never the telescope.
- Lift the magnetic needle off its bearing when not in use.
- Place the alidade in its carrying box when not in use and do not leave it on the plane table unattended.
- To adjust the level so it is parallel with the telescope axis: center the bubble by moving the tangent screw, reverse the level end for end, turn the capstan screws on the level to bring the bubble back to center, center again with tangent screw, and reverse the level, repeating the procedure until the bubble stays centered when the level is reversed.
- Turn the shield of the striding level up and remove the level before placing the alidade in its case.

MEASUREMENT AND CONVERSION

AREA, CALCULATING

- Areas are calculated by multiplying two lengths and are generally reckoned in units of length squares (e.g. square yards, square meters).
- The basic formula for calculating area is length times width (LxW) if the area is a rectangle or square. If you are estimating the area for a rectangle you will always use LxW. If you are calculating the area for a square you can multiply the length of one side times itself, or (S^2).
- Before an area can be computed, it must be enclosed in a closed traverse. To do a rough survey, the measurements of a closed traverse are plotted to scale on graph paper and the number of squares are counted. Each square's area can be determined from the original scale.
- Another technique is to use a planimeter (an instrument for measuring the area of any plane figure by passing a tracer around its boundary line). The rough scale drawing is made and the planimeter measures the area on paper. (See also **Planimeter use**)
- Another technique is triangulation. All the areas of the traverse are divided into triangles, each triangle's area is computed (because you know the distances and angles), and the total is equal to the total area traversed.
- Other techniques are: double parallel distance, double meridian distance, and coordinate methods.

BASELINE/DATUM LINE, DATUM POINT, SITE BENCH MARK AND DATUM PLANE, SITE REFERENCE POINT, ESTABLISHING A

Make sure you get permission to install reference points on the site.

Baseline/datum line

- The baseline is drawn from the datum point and generally runs due N/S or E/W so that any extensions from it can be described easily. Some supervisors establish the baseline outside the excavation area while others use it to bisect the site. It should extend past the length of the site on both ends and the parallel lines that extend from its ends should also extend beyond the site on both ends.

■ The direction of the baseline is confirmed using a compass and a second stake driven into the ground at the end of the baseline. Additional stakes are set into the ground at intervals along the baseline, which will be used to mark off the grid squares.

■ The grid is constructed with either a level and transit or triangulation to lay out two lines at 90-degree angles from each end of the baseline. Stakes are driven in at intervals along these lines the same way they were placed along the baseline. The grid layout's accuracy is verified by measuring between the stakes and adding the measurement; the distance should always equal the length of the baseline.

■ The initial point of the datum line can be called "A" and its termination point "B." The datum point is "O" and all three points have their positions and elevations measured. None of these three points should be located in the area to be excavated.

■ Sometimes the N/S line is called the datum line and the E/W line is called the baseline. The latter is a true parallel of latitude from the datum point and, at every point, at right angles to the datum line.

Datum point

■ The datum point can be the same as the site reference point. The datum point has to be permanent as it is the reference point for any future work on the site.

■ If survey markers are not established on the site, you can create a permanent marker for the datum point. Use corrosion-resistant pipe set in concrete and install a brass-cap marker to the pipe. The datum point should give the name and address of the organization doing the work.

■ There are two types of datum point: central datum, located near the center of the site, from which the grid system is prepared (usually based on the rectangular Cartesian coordinate system with NE, SE, NW, SW quadrants); and off-site datum, located southwest of the site and outside its perimeter, from which the grid system is set out north and east (usually based on the X and Y coordinates of plane trigonometry).

■ If all the material cannot be mapped directly to the datum point, then secondary datums can be set up and measurements taken from them. These secondary datums are linked directly to the datum point.

- The datum point is assigned coordinate X (northing), Y (easting), and Z (elevation).
- All grid coordinates are given relative to the datum point. Each excavation unit will also have its own datum, which is tied to the site datum point. (You should consistently use one designated corner for this in all units.)
- If the datum point's elevation above mean sea level is not known, it can be arbitrarily assigned 100 m or any value large enough to permit elevations at all probable excavated points to be subtracted from that value without going into negative numbers.
- In a cave excavation, the datum point is generally located on the roof of the cave.

Site bench mark and datum plane

- If the datum point is lower than some parts of the site, establish a site bench mark on the highest point. Use a USGS bench mark on or near the site if possible. The vertical provenience of features uses the bench mark. The bench mark is also used to map the topography of the site by plotting contour lines on the map.

Site reference point

- This is the approximate center of the site and the central point for mapping. Its position must be located in reference to the USPLSS, Global Positioning System, or another locational system. It can be the same as the datum point.
- The site reference point is used as the internal reference point for mapping the site features. It is also the terminal point of the directions given to workers on the site.
- Use a prominent natural or cultural feature in a central location on the site. It can be temporary or permanent, depending on the needs of the project. Try for an established (monumented) section corner, USGS bench mark, or some other survey marker that is part of an established system. Its location may be indicated on the pertinent USGS 7.5-minute topographic quadrangle.
- If there is an established survey marker within a reasonable distance on the site, take compass bearings and measure the distance from the survey marker to the site reference point.
- Survey stakes made of polyvinyl chloride are good reference markers.

- When the grid is done, take reference measurements to each key point on the grid from permanent or semi-permanent features on the ground. Ideally, there should be three such measurements to each key point and it is better if they are kept short. The key points should include the datum and one or two points on the main lines and any others which seem important.

Note: The Ordnance Survey of the UK has established a series of bench marks all over and their positions and values are usually found on large-scale maps. If there is an OS bench mark near the site, it is best to link your work into an OS datum.

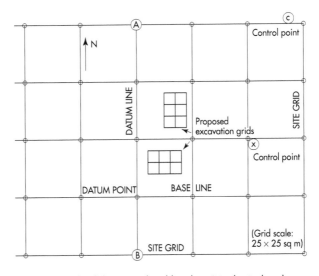

Figure 5.1 Example of datum, grid and baseline. (Martha Joukowsky, Figure 5.79: The datum line, grid, and base line provide an overall framework from which measurements for specific projects may be taken, p. 116 from *A Complete Manual of Field Archaeology*. Englewood Cliffs, NJ: Prentice Hall, 1980. Copyright © 1980 by Martha Joukowsky. Reprinted by permission of Simon & Schuster Adult Publishing Group)

The coordinate system

- A coordinate system is defined by three things: an origin, the directions of the axes, and a distance scale.
- The directions of lines in surveying fall in quadrants and are specified by bearings. A bearing is the smallest angle that a line makes with the reference meridian and cannot be greater than 90 degrees. A bearing is described by the quadrant it is in and its degrees from the N/S axis.
- Moving to the north or east is positive; moving to the south or west is negative.
- Angles are positive if they are measured from the positive side of the N axis and turn counterclockwise.
- A bearing is the smallest angle that a line makes with the fixed line of reference, a meridian. Bearings are measured in relation to the north or south directions of the meridian and put in quadrants with values of 0–90 degrees. From any position, a meridian may be true (passing through geographic north and south poles in relation to a point), magnetic (pointed at magnetic north), or assumed (approximation to true meridian). Bearings may also be one of these three, depending upon the reference meridian.
- Quadrant bearings are measured with these rules: all bearings are measured from the N/S axis; NE bearings are measured from north to east; SE bearings are measured from south to east; SW bearings are measured from south to west; and NW bearings are measured from north to west.
- The setting of the site's datum line should correspond to a north–south bearing, a fixed line of reference or meridian. You can use a compass to establish the bearing of the datum line. You should use true north (the direction of the geographical North Pole) in archaeology because it does not change over time.
- Using the Internet, you can now determine magnetic declination for any place on the earth since 1900. The National Geophysical Data Center offers two programs for calculating magnetic declination. One is called the Geomagnetic Field Synthesizer Program. There you are prompted to fill in a date and locational information for any part of the world. The program then returns both the horizontal and vertical declination. As a reminder, longitude values in the western hemisphere should be entered as negative. The Center also offers an online magnetic

MEASUREMENT AND CONVERSION

declination calculator program called Historical Declinations of the United States. This program is designed only for the conterminous US, but allows for a greater time span beginning in 1750 and running to 1995. This program only returns horizontal declination. Also, since this program only calculates in the western hemisphere, you enter the longitude as positive.

- If you prefer to have a simpler graphical reference, the US Geological Survey produces a map of the US showing lines of equal magnetic declination and annual change. Additional points of magnetic anomaly are also posted on this map. The map is revised every 5 years or so to compensate for the changes in the magnetic field.
- You can set a compass for local declination, per center of the pertinent USGS quadrangle, following the instructions given by the compass manufacturer.

Generally, here is how to take a compass bearing:

- Open the compass and angle the lid back; cup it firmly in one hand at waist height.
- Level the compass by centering the bull's-eye level and adjust the lid until the sighting tip and the point sighted appear in the mirror. The sighting arm may be turned upward as necessary.
- Rotate the leveled compass on a vertical axis until the mirror images of the point sighted and the sighting tip coincide with the axial line of the mirror.
- Check the bull's-eye level and read the bearing indicated by the white end of the needle. If the needle has not come to rest (it may not in old models not equipped with a damping mechanism), carefully estimate the center of its swing.
- Record the bearing and repeat the procedure as a check.

If the point sighted can be seen only at eye-level, or by a steep downhill sight, the procedure is as follows:

- Open the compass slightly with the lid up about 45 degrees and hold it with the sighting arm pointing toward the eye. Hold it about 1 foot (30 cm) from the eye so that the point sighted and the axial line of the mirror will both be in sharp focus.
- After leveling the compass by observing the bull's-eye level in the mirror, rotate it on a vertical axis until the point sighted is seen through the window in the lid.

- Checking to be sure the compass is level, bring the point sighted, the sighting tip, and the axial line of the window into coincidence.

- Read the bearing in the mirror and transpose it to a foresight before recording (e.g. N 20 degrees W becomes S 20 degrees E, or 340 degrees becomes 160 degrees). Transposition is necessary because the compass is oriented 180 degrees from its bearing sense. Repeat the procedure as a check.

- To find the true bearing from point A to point B on a sphere, project the chord AB on to the tangent plane of A. Call this projection AB'. The angle between AB' and the line segment pointing north in the tangent plane will be the true heading. The latter segment may be found by projecting the chord between A and the North Pole onto the tangent plane of A. In fact, with this method you may find the heading relative to any point, not just the "north" pole. This would be useful for finding the heading according to a real life compass which gives headings relative to magnetic north, not true north. For example, if you know the coordinates for magnetic north (which I don't, offhand) N, you could find the angle between the projection of AN and AB in the tangent plane of A – this would be the heading as measured by a "real" compass.

Calculating bearings from internal angles

- Start with a known bearing. Proceeding counterclockwise, the internal angles are written down. The angular closure is calculated and the internal angles are balanced so their sum equals 180 degrees. This balances the internal angles, angular closure, and bearings for all points of the traverse. These calculations should be double-checked.

Note: in a small enclosed site such as a rock shelter, it is very difficult to use a north–south bearing for the datum. Use the most convenient datum and indicate true north on your diagram.

- Put the leveling rod on the bench mark of known elevation, A1.
- Set up the measuring instrument at a turning point (a temporary intermediate point whose elevation is known and fixed during the measuring process).
- Take the leveling rod reading with a backsight on A1. This backsight added to the known elevation of A1 gives the height of the instrument.
- The leveling rod is then taken to point A2.
- Take a reading on this point and subtract from the instrument height. The difference between the readings for A1 and A2 gives the elevation of A2.
- The instrument is set in a new position and a backsight taken from this turning point to point A2. The process is repeated until a site control point is established.
- Each new bench mark represents accurate elevations which are tied to the final bench mark, the site control point. A minimum of three site control points, within sight of each other and not more than 100 meters apart, are the positions from which survey readings are taken. These points are given permanent stable markers and should lie outside the actual excavation area.

MEASUREMENT AND CONVERSION

COMPARATIVE TABLES OF WEIGHTS, MEASURES, TEMPERATURES (EQUIVALENTS)

Areas or surfaces

1 acre	43,560 square feet
1 acre	4,840 square yards
1 acre	0.405 hectare
1 are	119.599 square yards
1 are	0.025 acre
1 bolt length	100 yards
1 bolt width	45 or 60 inches
1 hectare	2.471 acres
1 mile square	1 section (of land)
1 square (building)	100 square feet
1 square centimeter	0.155 square inch
1 square decimeter	15.500 square inches
1 square foot	929.030 square centimeters
1 square inch	6.4516 square centimeters
1 square kilometer	247.104 acres
1 square kilometer	0.386 square mile
1 square meter	1.196 square yards
1 square meter	10.764 square feet
1 square mile	258.999 hectares
1 square millimeter	0.002 square inch
1 square rod, square pole, or square perch	25.293 square meters
1 square yard	0.836 square meter

10,000 square centimeters	1 square meter	1,000,000 square millimeters
100 ares	1 hectare	10,000 square meters
100 hectares	1 square kilometer	1,000,000 square meters
100 square meters	1 are	
100 square millimeters	1 square centimeter	
144 square inches	1 square foot	
160 square rods	1 acre	4,840 square yards / 43,560 square feet
30¼ square yards	1 square rod	272¼ square feet
40 square rods	1 rood	
6 miles square	1 township	36 sections / 36 square miles
640 acres	1 square mile	
9 square feet	1 square yard	1,296 square inches

Capacities or volumes

1 barrel liquid	31 to 42 gallons		
1 barrel, standard, cranberry	5,826 cubic inches	$86^{45}/_{64}$ dry quarts	2.709 bushels, struck measure
1 barrel, standard, for fruits, vegetables, and other dry commodities except dry cranberries	7,056 cubic inches	105 dry quarts	3.281 bushels, struck measure

1 board foot	a foot-square board, 1 inch thick	2,219.36 cubic inches
1 bushel (British Imperial) (struck measure)	1.032 US bushels, struck measure	
1 bushel (US) (struck measure)	2,150.42 cubic inches	35.239 liters
1 bushel, heaped (US)	2,747.715 cubic inches	1.278 bushels, struck measure
1 cord firewood	128 cubic feet	
1 cubic centimeter	0.061 cubic inch	
1 cubic decimeter	61.024 cubic inches	
1 cubic foot	7.481 gallons	28.317 cubic decimeters
1 cubic inch	0.554 fluid ounce	4.433 fluid drams
1 cubic meter	1.308 cubic yards	
1 cubic yard	0.765 cubic meter	16.387 cubic centimeters
1 cup, measuring	8 fluid ounces	1/2 liquid pint (US)
1 dekaliter	2.642 gallons	1.135 pecks
1 dram, fluid (British)	0.961 US fluid dram	0.217 cubic inch
1 gallon (British Imperial)	277.42 cubic inches	1.201 US gallons
1 gallon (US)	231 cubic inches	3.785 liters
1 gill	7.219 cubic inches	4 fluid ounces
1 hectoliter	26.418 gallons	2.838 bushels

3.552 milliliters	
4.546 liters	160 British fluid ounces
0.833 British gallon	128 US fluid ounces
0.118 liter	

305

1 liter	1.057 liquid quarts	0.908 dry quart	61.025 cubic inches
1 milliliter	0.271 fluid dram	16.231 minims	0.061 cubic inch
1 ounce liquid (US)	1.805 cubic inches	29.573 milliliters	1.041 British fluid ounces
1 ounce, fluid (British)	0.961 US fluid ounce	1.734 cubic inches	28.412 milliliters
1 peck	8.810 liters		
1 pint, dry	33.600 cubic inches	0.551 liter	
1 pint, liquid	28.875 cubic inches	0.473 liter	
1 quart (British)	69.354 cubic inches	1.032 US dry quarts	1.201 US liquid quarts
1 quart dry (US)	67.201 cubic inches	1.01 liters	0.969 British quart
1 quart liquid (US)	57.75 cubic inches	0.946 liter	0.833 British quart
1 tablespoon	3 teaspoons	4 fluid drams	½ fluid ounce
1 teaspoon	⅓ tablespoon	1⅓ fluid drams	

Cubic measure

1 cubic foot	1,728 cubic inches			
1,000 cubic centimeters	1 cubic decimeter	1,000,000 cubic millimeters		
1,000 cubic decimeters	1 cubic meter	1 stere	1,000,000 cubic centimeters	1,000,000,000 cubic millimeters
1,000 cubic millimeters	1 cubic centimeter			
27 cubic feet	1 cubic yard			

Lengths

1 angstrom	0.1 nanometer	0.0001 micrometer	0.0000001 millimeter	0.000000004 inch
1 cable's length	120 fathoms	720 feet	219 meters	
1 centimeter	0.3937 inch			
1 chain (engineers)	100 feet	30.48 meters		
1 chain (Gunter's or surveyor's)	66 feet	20.1168 meters		
1 decimeter	3.937 inches			
1 degree (geographical)	364,566.929 feet	69,047 miles	111.123 kilometers	
1 degree of latitude	68.708 miles at equator	69.403 miles at poles		
1 degree of longitude	69,171 miles at equator			
1 dekameter	32.808 feet			
1 fathom	6 feet	1.8288 meters		
1 foot	0.3048 meters			
1 furlong	10 chains (surveyor's)	660 feet	1/8 statute mile	201.168 meters
1 hand	4 inches			
1 inch	2.54 centimeters			
1 international nautical mile	1.852 kilometers	1.150779 survey miles	6,076.11549 feet	
1 kilometer	0.621 mile	3,281.5 feet		
1 league	3 survey miles	4.828 kilometers		

1 link (Gunter's or surveyor's)	7.92 inches	0.201 meter
1 link (engineer's)	1 foot	0.305 meter
1 meter	39.37 inches	1.094 yards
1 micrometer	0.001 millimeter	0.00003937 inch
1 mil	0.001 inch	0.0254 millimeter
1 mile	5,280 feet	1.609 kilometers
1 millimeter	0.03937 inch	
1 nanometer	0.001 micrometer	0.00000003937 inch
1 pica	12 points	
1 point	0.013837 inch	0.351 millimeter
1 rod, pole, or perch	16½ feet	5.029 meters
1 yard	0.9144 meter	
100 fathoms	1 cable length	
12 inches	1 foot	
3 feet	1 yard	
3 miles	1 league	5,280 yards
4 rods	1 chain 40 rods	1 furlong
5½ yards	1 rod, pole, or perch (16½ feet)	
6076.11549 feet	1 international nautical mile	
8 furlongs	1 statute mile	1,760 yards

15,840 feet
220 yards

660 feet

5,280 feet

308

Surveyor's chain measure

100 links	1 chain	4 rods	66 feet
7.92 inches	1 link		
80 chains	1 survey mile	320 rods	5,280 feet

Temperature conversion

From F to C: subtract 32, multiply by 5, divide by 9
From C to F: multiple by 9, divide by 5, add 32

Weights or masses

1 assay ton	29.167 grams	
1 bale	500 pounds in US	750 pounds in Egypt
1 carat	200 milligrams	3,086 grains
1 dram avoirdupois	27$^{11}/_{32}$ or 27.344 grains	1.772 grams
1 gamma	1 microgram	
1 grain	64.799 milligrams	
1 gram	15.432 grains	0.035 ounce, avoirdupois

1 hundredweight, gross or long	112 pounds		50.802 kilograms
1 hundredweight, net or short	100 pounds		45.359 kilograms
1 kilogram	2.205 pounds		
1 microgram	0.000001 gram		
1 milligram	0.015 grain		
1 ounce, avoirdupois	437.5 grains	0.911 troy ounce	28.350 grams
1 ounce, troy	480 grains	1.097 avoirdupois ounces	31.103 grams
1 pennyweight	1.555 grams		
1 pound, avoirdupois	7,000 grains	1.215 troy pounds	453.59237 grams
1 pound, troy	5,760 grains	0.823 avoirdupois pound	373.242 grams
1 ton, gross or long	2,240 pounds	1.12 net tons	1.016 metric tons
1 ton, metric	2,204.623 pounds	0.984 gross ton	1.102 net tons
1 ton, net or short	2,000 pounds	0.893 gross ton	0.907 metric ton
1,000 kilograms	1 metric ton		
10 centigrams	1 decigram	100 milligrams	
10 decigrams	1 gram	1,000 milligrams	
10 dekagrams	1 hectogram	100 grams	
10 grams	1 dekagram		
10 hectograms	1 kilogram	1,000 grams	
10 milligrams	1 centigram		

CONVERSION GUIDE

Unit	Multiplied by	Converts to this unit
abampere	1.00E+01	ampere
abcoulomb	10	coulomb
abfarad	1.00E+09	farad
acre	10	square chain (Gunter's)
acre	160	square rods
acre	100,000	square links (Gunter's)
acre	0.4047	hectare
acres	43,560	square feet
acres	4,047	square meters
acres	0.001562	square miles
acres	4,840	square yards
acre-feet	43,560	cubic feet
acre-feet	325,900	gallons
angstrom unit	3.94E–09	inch
angstrom unit	1.00E–10	meter
angstrom unit	0.0001	micron
astronomical unit	1.50E+08	kilometers
barrels (US, dry)	7,056	cubic inches
barrels (US, dry)	105	quarts (dry)
barrels (US, liquid)	31.5	gallons
barrels (oil)	42	gallons (oil)
bars	0.9869	atmospheres
bars	1,000,000	dynes/square centimeters
bars	10,200	kilograms/square meter
bars	1.00E+05	pascal
bars	2,089	pounds/square foot
bars	14.5	pounds/square inch
bolt (US, cloth)	36.576	meters
bucket (British, dry)	18,180	cubic centimeters
bushels (UK)	0.03636872	cubic meters
bushels (US)	0.03523907	cubic meters
bushels	1.2445	cubic feet
bushels	2,150.4	cubic inch
bushels	35.24	liters
bushels	4	pecks
bushels	64	pint (dry)
bushels	32	quarts (dry)
cable	0.10	mile (nautical)
cable	185.3	meters
caliber	0.01	inches

MEASUREMENT AND CONVERSION

Unit	Multiplied by	Converts to this unit
caliber	0.254	millimeters
calorie, gram (mean)	0.00396832	Btu (mean)
calorie	1.56E–06	horsepower-hour
calorie	1.58E–06	horsepower-hour (metric)
calorie (international table)	4.1868	joule
calorie (thermochemical)	4.184	joule
calorie (15°C)	4.1855	joule
calorie (20°C)	4.1819	joule
calorie (mean)	4.19002	joule
calorie (international) per hour	1.163E–03	watt
calorie (thermochemical)/ square centimeter minute	697.3333	watt per square meter
calorie	1.16E–06	kilowatt-hour
candle/square centimeters	3.142	lamberts
candle/square inch	0.487	lamberts
centares (centiares)	1	square meters
centigrams	0.01	grams
centiliter	0.3382	ounce fluid (US)
centiliter	0.6103	cubic inch
centiliter	2.705	drams
centiliters	0.01	liters
centimeters	0.03281	feet
centimeters	0.3937	inches
centimeters	0.00001	kilometers
centimeters	0.01	meters
centimeters	6.21E–06	miles
centimeters	10	millimeters
centimeters	393.7	mils
centimeters	0.01094	yards
centimeters-dynes	0.00102	centimeters-grams
centimeter-dynes	1.02E–08	meter-kilograms
centimeter-dynes	7.38E–08	pound-feet
centimeter-grams	980.7	centimeters-dynes
centimeter-grams	0.00001	meter-kilograms
centimeter-grams	0.07233	pound-feet
centimeters of mercury (0°C)	1,333.2239	pascal

Unit	Multiplied by	Converts to this unit
centimeters of mercury	0.01316	atmospheres
centimeters of mercury	0.4461	feet of water
centimeters of mercury	136	kilograms/square meter
centimeters of mercury	27.85	pounds/square foot
centimeters of mercury	0.1934	pounds/square inch
centimeters of water (4°C)	98.0638	pascal
centimeters/second	1.1969	feet/minute
centimeters/second	0.03281	feet/second
centimeters/second	0.036	kilometers/hour
centimeters/second	0.1943	knots
centimeters/second	0.6	meters/minute
centimeters/second	0.02237	miles/hour
centimeters/second	0.0003728	miles/minute
centimeters/second/second	0.03281	feet/second/second
centimeters/second/second	0.036	kilometers/hour/second
centimeters/second/second	0.01	meters/second/second
centimeters/second/second	0.02237	miles/hour/second
centipoise	1.00E-03	pascal second (Pa-s)
centistokes	1.00E-06	meter square/second
chain	792	inches
chain (engineer's or Ramden's)	30.48	meters
chain (surveyor's or Gunter's)	20.12	meters
chain (surveyor's or Gunter's)	22	yards
cheval vapeur (metric horsepower)	735.499	watt
circular mils	5.07E-06	square centimeters
circular mils	0.7854	square mils
circular mils	7.85E-07	square inches
circumference	6.283	radians
clo	0.2003712	kelvin square meter/watt
clusec	1.333224E-06	pascal cubic meter/second
cords	8	cord feet
cord feet	16	cubic feet
coulomb	3.00E+09	statcoulombs

Unit	Multiplied by	Converts to this unit
coulombs	1.04E−05	faradays
coulombs/square centimeters	64.52	coulombs/square inch
coulombs/square centimeters	10,000	coulombs/square meter
coulombs/square inch	0.155	coulombs/square centimeters
coulombs/square inch	1,550	coulombs/square meter
coulombs/square meter	0.0001	coulombs/square centimeters
coulombs/square meter	0.0006452	coulombs/square inch
cubic centimeter	3.53E−05	cubic foot
cubic centimeter	0.06102374	cubic inch
cubic centimeter	0.000001	cubic meter
cubic centimeter	1,000	cubic millimeter
cubic centimeter	1.31E−06	cubic yard
cubic centimeter	0.2815606	drachm (British, fluid)
cubic centimeter	0.2705122	dram (US, fluid)
cubic centimeter	2.20E−04	gallon (British, liquid)
cubic centimeter	2.64E−04	gallon (US, liquid)
cubic centimeter	0.001	liter
cubic centimeter	0.002113	pint (US, liquid)
cubic centimeter	0.001057	quart (US, liquid)
cubic feet	0.8036	bushels (dry)
cubic feet	28,320	cubic centimeters
cubic feet	1,728	cubic inches
cubic feet	0.02832	cubic meters
cubic feet	0.037037037	cubic yards
cubic feet	7.48052	gallons (US, liquid)
cubic feet	28.32	liters
cubic feet	59.84	pints (US, liquid)
cubic feet	29.92	quarts (US, liquid)
cubic feet/minute	472	cubic centimeters/second
cubic feet/minute	0.1247	gallons/second
cubic feet/minute	0.472	liters/second
cubic feet/minute	62.43	pounds of water/minute
cubic feet/second	0.646317	million gallons/day
cubic feet/second	448.831	gallons/minute
cubic inches	16.39	cubic centimeters (cc)
cubic inches	0.0005787	cubic feet
cubic inches	1.64E−05	cubic meters
cubic inches	2.14E−05	cubic yards

Unit	Multiplied by	Converts to this unit
cubic inches	0.004329	gallons
cubic inches	106,100	mil-feet
cubic inches	0.03463	pints (US, liquid)
cubic inches	0.01732	quarts (US, liquid)
cubic meters	28.38	bushels (dry)
cubic meters	1,000,000	cubic centimeters
cubic meters	35.31	cubic feet
cubic meters	61,023	cubic inches
cubic meters	1.307951	cubic yards
cubic meters	264.2	gallons (US, liquid)
cubic meters	1,000	liters
cubic meters	2,113	pints (US, liquid)
cubic meters	1,057	quarts (US, liquid)
cubic yards	764,600	cubic centimeters
cubic yards	27	cubic feet
cubic yards	46,656	cubic inches
cubic yards	0.7646	cubic meters
cubic yards	202	gallons (US, liquid)
cubic yards	764.6	liters
cubic yards	1,615.9	pints (US, liquid)
cubic yards	807.9	quarts (US, liquid)
cubic yards/minute	0.45	cubic feet/second
cubic yards/minute	3.367	gallons/second
cubic yards/minute	12.74	liters/second
cup (US)	236.5882	cubic centimeters
cup (UK)	2.841306E–04	cubic meter
curie	3.70E+10	decays per second
cusec hour	101.9407	cubic meter
cycle per second	1.0	hertz
days (mean solar)	86,400	seconds
days (sidereal)	86,164.09	seconds
debye	3.33564E–30	coulomb meter
decigrams	0.1	grams
deciliters	0.1	liters
decimeters	0.1	meters
degrees (angle)	0.01111	quadrants
degrees (angle)	0.01745	radians
degrees (angle)	3,600	seconds
degrees/second	0.01745	radians/second
degrees/second	0.1667	revolutions/minute
degrees/second	0.002778	revolutions/second
dekagrams	10	grams
deciliters	10	liters

Unit	Multiplied by	Converts to this unit
decameters	10	meters
dioptre	1.0	per meter
drachm (liquid) (UK)	3.551633E−03	cubic meter
drams (apoth. or troy)	0.1371429	ounces (avoirdupois)
drams (apoth. or troy)	0.125	ounces (troy)
drams (US, liquid, or apoth.)	3.6967	cubic centimeters
drams	27.3437	grains
drams	1.7718	grams
drams	0.0625	ounces
drops	0.01666	teaspoons
dyne/centimeters	0.01	erg/square millimeter
dyne/square centimeters	9.87E−07	atmospheres
dyne/square centimeters	2.95E−05	inch of mercury at 0°C
dyne/square centimeters	0.0004015	inch of water at 4°C
dynes	0.00102	grams
dynes	0.0000001	joules/centimeters
dynes	0.00001	joules/meter (newtons)
dynes	1.02E−06	kilograms
dynes	7.23E−05	poundals
dynes	2.25E−06	pounds
dyne centimeters	1.00E−07	newton meter
dyne/square centimeter	0.1	pascal (Pa)
dynes/square centimeter	0.000001	bars
electromagnetic unit of capacitance	1.00E+09	farad (F)
electromagnetic unit of charge	10	coulomb (C)
electromagnetic unit of current	10	ampere (A)
electromagnetic unit of inductance	1.00E−09	henry (H)
electromagnetic unit of potential	1.00E−08	volt (V)
electromagnetic unit of resistance	1.00E−09	ohm
electronvolt	1.6021917E−19	joule (J)
electrostatic unit of capacitance	1.112649E−12	farad
electrostatic unit of charge (franklin)	3.33564E−10	coulomb
electrostatic unit of current	3.33564E−10	ampere

Unit	Multiplied by	Converts to this unit
electrostatic unit of inductance	8.98755431E+11	henry
electrostatic unit of potential	299.7925	volt
electrostatic unit of resistance	8.98755431E+11	ohm
ell	114.3	centimeters
ell	45	inches
em (pica)	0.167	inch
em (pica)	0.4233	centimeters
erg/second	1	dyne-centimeters/second
ergs	9.48E–11	Btu
ergs	1	dyne-centimeters
ergs	7.37E–08	foot-pounds
ergs	2.39E–08	gram-calories
ergs	0.00102	grams-centimeters
ergs	3.73E–14	horsepower-hours
ergs	0.0000001	joules
ergs	2.39E–11	kilogram-calories
ergs	1.02E–08	kilogram-meters
ergs	2.78E–14	kilowatt-hours
ergs	2.78E–11	watt-hours
ergs/second	5.69E–06	Btu/minute
ergs/second	4.43E–06	feet-pounds/minute
ergs/second	7.38E–08	feet-pounds/second
ergs/second	1.34E–10	horsepower
ergs/second	1.43E–09	kilogram-calories/minute
ergs/second	1.00E–10	kilowatts
farads	0.000001	microfarads
farad (international of 1948)	0.999505	farad
faraday/second	96,500	ampere (absolute)
faradays	26.8	ampere-hours
faraday (based on carbon-12)	96,486.7	coulomb per mole
faraday (chemical)	96,495.7	coulomb per mole
faraday (physical)	96,521.9	coulomb per mole
fathoms	1.828804	meter
fathoms	6	feet
feet	30.48	centimeters
feet	0.0003048	kilometers
feet	0.3048	meters
feet	0.0001645	miles (naut.)

Unit	Multiplied by	Converts to this unit
feet	0.0001894	miles (stat.)
feet	304.8	millimeters
feet	12,000	mils
feet of water	0.0295	atmospheres
feet of water	0.8826	inch of mercury
feet of water	0.03048	kilograms/square centimeter
feet of water	304.8	kilograms/square meter
feet of water	62.43	pounds/square foot
feet of water	0.4335	pounds/square inch
feet/minute	0.508	centimeters/second
feet/minute	0.01667	feet/second
feet/minute	0.01829	kilometers/hour
feet/minute	0.3048	meters/minute
feet/minute	0.01136	miles/hour
feet/second	30.48	centimeters/second
feet/second	1.097	kilometers/hour
feet/second	0.5921	knots
feet/second	18.29	meters/minute
feet/second	0.6818	miles/hour
feet/second	0.01136	miles/minute
feet/second/second	30.48	centimeters/second/second
feet/second/second	1.097	kms/hour/second
feet/second/second	0.3048	meters/second/second
feet/second/second	0.6818	miles/hour/second
feet/100 feet	1	percent grade
fermi	1.00E–15	meter
foot	0.3048	meter
foot (Cape)	0.3148581	meter
foot (geodetic Cape)	0.31485557516	meter
foot (South African geodetic)	0.3047972654	meter
foot-candle	10.764	lumen/square meter
foot lambert	3.426259	candela/square meter
foot-pounds	0.001286	Btu
foot-pounds	1.36E+07	ergs
foot-pounds	0.3238	gram-calories
foot-pounds	5.05E–07	horsepower-hours
foot-pounds	1.356	joules
foot-pounds	0.000324	kilogram-calories
foot-pounds	0.1383	kilogram-meters
foot-pounds	3.77E–07	kilowatt-hours

Unit	Multiplied by	Converts to this unit
foot-pounds/minute	0.001286	Btu/minute
foot-pounds/minute	0.01667	foot-pounds/second
foot-pounds/minute	0.0000303	horsepower
foot-pounds/minute	0.000324	kilogram-calories/minute
foot-pounds/minute	0.0000226	kilowatts
foot-pounds/second	4.6263	Btu/hour
foot-pounds/second	0.07717	Btu/minute
foot-pounds/second	8.18E-04	horsepower
foot-pounds/second	1.01945	kilogram-calories/minute
foot-pounds/second	0.001356	kilowatts
footE+04 (second moment of area)	8.630975E-03	meter to the fourth power
frigorie	1.162639	watt
furlongs	0.125	miles (US)
furlongs	40	rods
furlongs	660	feet
gal	0.01	meter/second square
gallons	3,785.412	cubic centimeters (cc)
gallons	0.1337	cubic feet
gallons	231	cubic inches
gallons	0.003785	cubic meters
gallons	0.004951	cubic yards
gallons	3.785	liters
gallons (liquid, British Imperial)	1.20095	gallons (US, liquid)
gallons (US)	0.83267	gallons (Imperial)
gallons of water	8.3453	pounds of water
gallons/minute	0.002228	cubic feet/second
gallons/minute	0.6308	liters/second
gallons/minute	8.0208	cubic feet/hour
gamma (magnetic induction)	1.00E-09	tesla (T)
gamma (mass)	1.00E-09	kilogram
gills (British)	142.07	cubic centimeters
gills	0.1183	liters
gills	0.25	pints (liquid)
gon or grade	1.570796E-02	radian (pi/200)
grains	0.03657143	drams (avoirdupois)
grains (troy)	1	grains (avoirdupois)
grains (troy)	0.0648	grams
grains (troy)	0.0020833	ounces (avoirdupois)
grains (troy)	0.04167	pennyweight (troy)
grains/US gallon	17.118	parts/million

Unit	Multiplied by	Converts to this unit
grains/US gallon	142.86	pounds/million
grains/Imperial gallon	14.286	gallon parts/million
grams	5	carat (metric)
grams	0.56438339	dram
grams	980.7	dynes
grams	15.43	grains
grams	9.81E-05	joules/centimeter
grams	9.81E-03	joules/meter (newtons)
grams	0.001	kilograms
grams	1,000	milligrams
grams	0.035273962	ounces (avoirdupois)
grams	0.032150747	ounces (troy)
grams	0.07093	poundals
grams	0.002204623	pounds
grams/centimeter	0.0056	pounds/inch
grams/cubic centimeter	62.43	pounds/cubic foot
grams/cubic centimeter	0.03613	pounds/cubic inch
grams/cubic centimeter	3.41E-07	pounds/mil-foot
grams/liter	58.417	grains/gallon
grams/liter	8.345	pounds/1,000 gallons
grams/liter	0.062427	pounds/cubic foot
grams/liter	1,000	parts/million
grams/square centimeters	2.0481	pounds/square foot
gram-calories	0.0039683	Btu
gram-calories	4.19E-07	ergs
gram-calories	3.088	foot-pounds
gram-calories	1.56E-06	horsepower-hours
gram-calories	1.16E-06	kilowatt-hours
gram-calories	0.001163	watt-hours
gram-calories/second	14.286	Btu/hour
gram-calories	9.30E-08	Btu
gram-centimeters	980.7	ergs
gram-centimeters	980,700	joules
gram-centimeters	2.34E+08	kilogram-calories
gram-centimeters	100,000	kilogram-meters
hand	10.16	centimeters
hectares	2.471	acres
hectares	107,600	square feet
hectograms	100	grams
hectoliters	100	liters
hectometers	100	meters
hectowatts	100	watts

Unit	Multiplied by	Converts to this unit
henries	1,000	millihenries
hogsheads (British)	10.114	cubic feet
hogsheads (US)	8.42184	cubic feet
hogsheads (US)	63	gallons (US)
horsepower	42.44	Btu/minute
horsepower	33,000	foot-pounds/minute
horsepower	550	foot-pounds/second
horsepower (metric)	0.9863	horsepower
horsepower	10.68	kilogram-calories/minute
horsepower	0.7457	kilowatts
horsepower	745.7	watts
horsepower (boiler)	33,479	Btu/hour
horsepower (boiler)	9.803	kilowatts
horsepower-hours	2,547	Btu
horsepower-hours	2.68E+13	ergs
horsepower-hours	1,980,000	foot-pounds
horsepower-hours	641,190	gram-calories
horsepower-hours	2,684,000	joules
horsepower-hours	641.1	kilogram-calories
horsepower-hours	273,700	kilogram-meters
horsepower-hours	0.7457	kilowatt-hours
hours (mean solar)	0.04166667	days
hours (mean solar)	0.005952381	weeks
hundredweights (long)	112	pounds
hundredweights (long)	0.05	tons (long)
hundredweights (short)	1,600	ounces (avoirdupois)
hundredweights (short)	100	pounds
hundredweights (short)	0.0453592	tonnes (metric)
hundredweights (short)	0.0446429	tons (long)
inches	2.54	centimeters
inches	0.08333333	feet
inches	0.0254	meters
inches	0.00001578	miles
inches	25.4	millimeters
inches	1,000	mils
inches	0.027777778	yards
inches of mercury (at 32°F)	3,386.389	pascal
inches of mercury	0.03342	atmospheres
inches of mercury	1.133	feet of water
inches of mercury	0.03453	kilograms/square centimeter
inches of mercury	345.3	kilograms/square meter

Unit	Multiplied by	Converts to this unit
inches of mercury	70.73	pounds/square foot
inches of mercury	0.4912	pounds/square inch
inches of water (at 4°C)	0.002458	atmospheres
inches of water (at 4°C)	0.07355	inches of mercury
inches of water (at 4°C)	0.00254	kilograms/square centimeter
inches of water (at 4°C)	0.5781	ounces/square inch
inches of water (at 4°C)	5.204	pounds/square foot
inches of water (at 4°C)	0.03613	pounds/square inch
international ampere	0.9998	ampere (absolute)
international volt	1.59E−19	joules (absolute)
international volt	96,540	joules
iron (shoes)	5.30E−04	meter
joules	9.48E−04	Btu
joules	10,000,000	ergs
joules	0.7376	foot-pounds
joules	0.0002389	kilogram-calories
joules	0.102	kilogram-meters
joules	0.0002778	watt-hours
joules/centimeter	10,200	grams
joules/centimeter	10,000,000	dynes
joules/centimeter	100	joules/meter (newton)
joules	723.3	poundals
joules	22.48	pounds
kayser	100	waves per meter
kilograms	980,665	dynes
kilograms	1,000	grams
kilograms	0.09807	joules/centimeter
kilograms	9.807	joules/meter (newtons)
kilograms	70.93	poundals
kilograms	2.205	pounds
kilograms	9.84E−04	tons (long)
kilograms	1.10E−03	tons (short)
kilograms/cubic meter	0.001	grams/cubic centimeter
kilograms/cubic meter	0.06243	pound/cubic foot
kilograms/cubic meter	3.61E−05	pounds/cubic inch
kilograms/cubic meter	3.41E−10	pounds/mil-foot
kilograms/meter	0.672	pounds/foot
kilograms/square centimeter	980,665	dynes
kilograms/square centimeter	0.9678	atmospheres

Unit	Multiplied by	Converts to this unit
kilograms/square centimeter	32.81	feet of water
kilograms/square centimeter	28.96	inches of mercury
kilograms/square centimeter	2,048	pounds/square foot
kilograms/square centimeter	14.22	pounds/square inch
kilograms/square meter	9.68E-05	atmospheres
kilograms/square meter	9.81E-05	bars
kilograms/cubic meter	3.28E-03	feet of water
kilograms/cubic meter	2.90E-03	inches of mercury
kilograms/cubic meter	0.2048	pounds/square foot
kilograms/cubic meter	1.42E-03	pounds/square inch
kilograms/square mm	1.00E+06	kilograms/square meter
kilogram-calories	3.968	Btu
kilogram-calories	3,088	foot-pounds
kilogram-calories	1.56E-03	horsepower-hours
kilogram-calories	4,186	joules
kilogram-calories	426.9	kilogram-meters
kilogram-calories	4.186	kilojoules
kilogram-calories	1.16E-03	kilowatt-hours
kilogram-meters	9.29E-03	Btu
kilogram-meters	9.80E+07	ergs
kilogram-meters	7.233	foot-pounds
kilogram-meters	9.804	joules
kilogram-meters	2.34E-03	kilogram-calories
kilogram-meters	2.72E-06	kilowatt-hours
kilolines	1,000	maxwells
kilolitres	1,000	liters
kilometers	6.68E-09	astronomical unit
kilometers	1.00E+05	centimeters
kilometers	3,280.84	feet
kilometers	3.94E+04	inches
kilometers	1.06E-13	light year
kilometers	1,000	meters
kilometers	0.6214	miles
kilometers	1.00E+06	millimeters
kilometers	1,094	yards
kilometers/hour	27.78	centimeters/second
kilometers/hour	54.68	feet/minute
kilometers/hour	0.9113	feet/second

MEASUREMENT AND CONVERSION

Unit	Multiplied by	Converts to this unit
kilometers/hour	0.5396	knots
kilometers/hour	16.67	meters/minute
kilometers/hour	0.6214	miles/hour
kilometers/hour/second	27.78	centimeters/second/second
kilometers/hour/second	0.9113	feet/second/second
kilometers/hour/second	0.2778	meters/second/second
kilometers/hour/second	0.6214	miles/hour/second
kilopond (= kgf)	9.80665	newton
kilowatts	56.92	Btu/minute
kilowatts	4.43E+04	foot-pounds/minute
kilowatts	737.6	foot-pounds/second
kilowatts	1.341	horsepower
kilowatts	14.34	kilogram-calories/minute
kilowatts	1,000	watts
kilowatt-hours	3,413	Btu
kilowatt-hours	3.60E+13	ergs
kilowatt-hours	2.66E+06	foot-pounds
kilowatt-hours	859,850	gram-calories
kilowatt-hours	1.341	horsepower-hours
kilowatt-hours	3.60059E+06	joules
kilowatt-hours	860.5	kilogram-calories
kilowatt-hours	3.67E+05	kilogram-meters
kilowatt-hours	3.53	pounds of water evap. at 212°F
kilowatt-hours	22.75	pounds of water ^ from 62°–212°F
kip	4,448.222	newton
knots	6,080	feet/hour
knots	1.8532	kilometers/hour
knots	1	nautical miles/hour
knots	1.151	statute miles/hour
knots	2,027	yards/hour
knots	1.689	feet/second
lambda	1.00E-09	cubic meter
lambert	3,183.099	candela/square meter
langley	41,840	joule/square meter
league	3	miles (approx.)
leaguer	0.5773534	cubic meter
light-year	63,239.7	astronomical unit
light-year	5.90E+12	miles
light-year	9.46055E+12	kilometers
ligne (buttons)	6.35E-04	meter

Unit	Multiplied by	Converts to this unit
lines/square centimeter	1	gausses
lines/square inch	0.155	gausses
lines/square inch	1.55E−09	webers/square centimeter
lines/square inch	1.00E−08	webers/square inch
lines/square inch	1.55E−05	webers/square meter
links (engineer's)	12	inches
links (surveyor's)	7.92	inches
liters	0.02838	bushels (US, dry)
liters	1,000	cubic centimeters
liters	0.03531	cubic feet
liters	61.02	cubic inches
liters	0.001	cubic meters
liters	1.31E−03	cubic yards
liters	0.2642	gallons (US, liquid)
liters	2.113	pints (US, liquid)
liters	1.057	quarts (US, liquid)
liters/minute	5.89E−04	cubic feet/second
liters/minute	4.40E−03	gallons/second
lumen	0.07958	spherical candle power
lumen	0.001496	watt
lumens/square foot	1	foot-candles
lumens/square foot	10.76	lumen/square meter
lusec	1.333224E−04	pascal cubic meter/ second
lux	0.0929	foot-candles
maxwells	0.001	kilolines
maxwells	1.00E−08	webers
megalines	1.00E+06	maxwells
megohms	1.00E+12	microhms
megohms	1.00E+06	ohms
meters	100	centimeters
meters	3.281	feet
meters	39.37	inches
meters	0.001	kilometers
meters	5.40E−04	miles (nautical)
meters	6.21E−04	miles (statute)
meters	1,000	millimeters
meters	1.094	yards
meters/minute	1.667	centimeters/second
meters/minute	3.281	feet/minute
meters/minute	0.05468	feet/second
meters/minute	0.06	kilometers/hour
meters/minute	0.03238	knots

Unit	Multiplied by	Converts to this unit
meters/minute	0.03728	miles/hour
meters/second	196.8	feet/minute
meters/second	3.281	feet/second
meters/second	3.6	kilometers/hour
meters/second	0.06	kilometers/minute
meters/second	2.237	miles/hour
meters/second	0.03728	miles/minute
meters/second/second	100	centimeters/second/second
meters/second/second	3.281	feet/second/second
meters/second/second	3.6	kilometers/hour/second
meters/second/second	2.237	miles/hour/second
meter-kilograms	9.81E+07	centimeter-dynes
meter-kilograms	1.00E+05	centimeter-grams
meter-kilograms	7.233	pound-feet
microfarad	1.00E−06	farads
micrograms	1.00E−06	grams
microhms	1.00E−12	megohms
microhms	1.00E−06	ohms
misrelates	1.00E−06	liters
microns	1.00E−06	meters
miles (nautical)	6,080.27	feet
miles (nautical)	1,853	kilometers
miles (nautical)	1,853	meters
miles (nautical)	1.1516	miles (statute)
miles (nautical)	2,027	yards
miles (statute)	1.61E+05	centimeters
miles (statute)	5,280	feet
miles (statute)	6.34E+04	inches
miles (statute)	1.609	kilometers
miles (statute)	1,609	meters
miles (statute)	0.8684	miles (nautical)
miles (statute)	1,760	yards
miles/hour	44.7	centimeters/second
miles/hour	88	feet/minute
miles/hour	1.467	feet/second
miles/hour	1.609	kilometers/hour
miles/hour	0.02682	kilometers/minute
miles/hour	0.8684	knots
miles/hour	26.82	meters/minute
miles/hour	0.1667	miles/minute
miles/hour/second	44.7	centimeters/second/second

Unit	Multiplied by	Converts to this unit
miles/hour/second	1.467	feet/second/second
miles/hour/second	1.609	kilometers/hour/second
miles/hour/second	0.447	meters/second/second
miles/minute	2,682	centimeters/second
miles/minute	88	feet/second
miles/minute	1.609	kilometers/minute
miles/minute	0.8684	knots/minute
miles/minute	60	miles/hour
mil-feet	9.43E-06	cubic inches
milliers	1,000	kilograms
millimicrons	1.00E-09	meters
milligrams	0.01543236	grains
milligrams	0.001	grams
milligrams/liter	1	parts/million
millihenries	0.001	henries
milliliters	0.001	liters
millimeters	0.1	centimeters
millimeters	3.28E-03	feet
millimeters	0.03937	inches
millimeters	1.00E-06	kilometers
millimeters	0.001	meters
millimeters	6.21E-07	miles
millimeters	39.37	mils
millimeters	1.09E-03	yards
million gallons/day	1.54723	cubic feet/second
mils	2.54E-03	centimeters
mils	8.33E-05	feet
mils	0.001	inches
mils	2.54E-03	kilometers
mils	2.78E-05	yards
minims (British)	0.059192	cubic centimeters
minims (US, fluid)	0.061612	cubic centimeters
minutes (angles)	0.01667	degrees
minutes (angles)	1.85E-04	quadrants
minutes (angles)	2.91E-04	radians
minutes (angles)	60	seconds
morgen	8,565.32	square meter
nautical mile (international)	1,852	meter
nepers	8.686	decibels
newton	1.00E+05	dynes
oersted	79.57747	ampere/meter
ohm (international)	1.0005	ohm (absolute)

Unit	Multiplied by	Converts to this unit
ohms	1.00E−06	megohms
ohms	1.00E+06	microhms
ounces	16	drams
ounces	437.5	grains
ounces	28.349523	grams
ounces	0.0625	pounds
ounces	0.9115	ounces (troy)
ounces	2.79E−05	tons (long)
ounces	2.84E−05	tonnes (metric)
ounces (fluid)	1.805	cubic inches
ounces (fluid)	0.02957	liters
ounces (troy)	480	grains
ounces (troy)	31.103481	grams
ounces (troy)	1.09714	ounces (avoirdupois)
ounces (troy)	20	pennyweights (troy)
ounces (troy)	0.08333	pounds (troy)
ounces/square inch	4,309	dynes/square centimeters
ounces/square inch	0.0625	pounds/square inch
parsec	1.90E+13	miles
parsec	3.08E+13	kilometers
parts/million	0.0584	grains/US gallon
parts/million	0.07016	grains/Imperial gallon
parts/million	8.345	pounds/million gallon
pecks (British)	554.6	cubic inches
pecks (British)	9.091901	liters
pecks (US)	0.25	bushels
pecks (US)	537.605	cubic inches
pecks (US)	8.809582	liters
pecks (US)	8	quarts (dry)
pennyweights (troy)	24	grains
pennyweights (troy)	0.05	ounces (troy)
pennyweights (troy)	1.55517	grams
pennyweights (troy)	4.17E−03	pounds (troy)
perch (area)	25.2929	square meter
perch (length)	5.0292	meter
perm (0°C)	5.72135E−11	kilogram/newton second
phot	10,000	lux
pica (printing)	4.217518E−03	meter
pieze	1,000	pascal
pints (British)	568.26125	cubic centimeters
pints (British)	34.67743	cubic inches
pints (British)	0.125	gallons (British)
pints (British)	4	gills (British)

Unit	Multiplied by	Converts to this unit
pints (British)	0.56826125	liters
pints (British)	568.26125	milliliters
pints (British)	20	ounces (British, fluid)
pints (British)	1.032057	pints (US, dry)
pints (British)	1.20095	pints (US, liquid)
pints (US, dry)	550.6105	cubic centimeters
pints (US, dry)	33.6003125	cubic inches
pints (US, dry)	0.5506105	liters
pints (US, dry)	550.6105	milliliters
pints (US, dry)	0.0625	peck (US)
pints (US, dry)	0.968939	pint (British, dry)
pints (US, dry)	0.5	quarts (US, dry)
pints (US, liquid)	473.1765	cubic centimeters
pints (US, liquid)	0.01671	cubic feet
pints (US, liquid)	28.875	cubic inches
pints (US, liquid)	4.73E–04	cubic meters
pints (US, liquid)	6.19E–04	cubic yards
pints (US, liquid)	0.125	gallons (US)
pints (US, liquid)	4	gills (US)
pints (US, liquid)	0.4731765	liters
pints (US, liquid)	473.1765	milliliters
pints (US, liquid)	16	ounce (US, liquid)
pints (US, liquid)	0.8326742	pints (British, liquid)
pints (US, liquid)	0.5	quarts (liquid)
Plank's quantum	6.62E–27	erg-second
point (printing)	3.514598E–04	meter
poise	1	gram/centimeters second
poiseuille	1	pascal second
pole (area)	25.2929	meter
pole (length)	5.0292	meter
poundals	13,826	dynes
poundals	14.1	grams
poundals	1.38E–03	joules/centimeter
poundals	0.1383	joules/meter (newtons)
poundals	0.0141	kilograms
poundals	0.03108	pounds
pounds	256	drams
pounds	4.45E+05	dynes
pounds	7,000	grains
pounds	453.5924	grams
pounds	0.04448	joules/centimeter
pounds	4.448	joules/meter (newtons)
pounds	0.4536	kilograms

Unit	Multiplied by	Converts to this unit
pounds	16	ounces
pounds	14.5833	ounces (troy)
pounds	32.17	poundals
pounds	1.21528	pounds (troy)
pounds	0.07142857	stones (British)
pounds	0.0005	tons (short)
pounds (troy)	5,760	grains
pounds (troy)	373.24177	grams
pounds (troy)	13.1657	ounces (avoirdupois)
pounds (troy)	12	ounces (troy)
pounds (troy)	240	pennyweights (troy)
pounds (troy)	0.822857	pounds (avoirdupois)
pounds (troy)	3.67E−04	tons (long)
pounds (troy)	3.73E−04	tonnes (metric)
pounds (troy)	4.11E−04	tons (short)
pounds of water	0.01602	cubic feet
pounds of water	27.68	cubic inches
pounds of water	0.1198	gallons
pounds of water/minute	2.67E−04	cubic feet/second
pound-feet	1.36E+07	centimeter-dynes
pound-feet	13,825	centimeter-grams
pound-feet	0.1383	meter-kilograms
pounds/cubic foot	0.01602	grams/cubic centimeter
pounds/cubic foot	16.02	kilograms/cubic meter
pounds/cubic foot	5.79E−04	pounds/cubic inch
pounds/cubic foot	5.46E−09	pounds/mil-foot
pounds/cubic inch	27.68	grams/cubic centimeter
pounds/cubic inch	2.77E+04	kilograms/cubic meter
pounds/cubic inch	1,728	pounds/cubic foot
pounds/cubic inch	9.43E−06	pounds/mil-foot
pounds/foot	1.488	kilograms/meter
pounds/inch	178.6	grams/centimeter
pounds/mil-foot	2.31E+06	grams/cubic centimeter
pounds/square foot	4.73E−04	atmospheres
pounds/square foot	0.01602	feet of water
pounds/square foot	0.01414	inches of mercury
pounds/square foot	4.882	kilograms/square meter
pounds/square foot	6.94E−03	pounds/square inch
pounds/square inch	0.06804	atmospheres
pounds/square inch	2.307	feet of water
pounds/square inch	2.036	inches of mercury
pounds/square inch	703.1	kilograms/square meter

Unit	Multiplied by	Converts to this unit
pounds/square inch	144	pounds/square foot
quadrants (angle)	90	degrees
quadrants (angle)	5,400	minutes
quadrants (angle)	1.571	radians
quadrants (angle)	3.24E+05	seconds
quarter (2 stone)	12.70059	kilogram
quarts (dry)	67.2	cubic inches
quarts (liquid)	946.4	cubic centimeters
quarts (liquid)	0.03342	cubic feet
quarts (liquid)	57.75	cubic inches
quarts (liquid)	9.46E-04	cubic meters
quarts (liquid)	1.24E-03	cubic yards
quarts (liquid)	0.25	gallons
quarts (liquid)	0.9463	liters
quintal	100	kilogram
rad (ionizing radiation)	0.01	joule/kilogram
radians	57.29578	degrees
radians	3,438	minutes
radians	2.06E+05	seconds
radians/second	57.29578	degrees/second
radians/second	9.549	revolutions/minute
radians/second	0.1592	revolutions/second
radians/second/second	572.9578	revolutions/minute/minute
radians/second/second	9.549	revolutions/minute/second
radians/second/second	0.1592	revolutions/second/second
register ton (shipping)	2.831685	cubic meter
revolutions	360	degrees
revolutions	4	quadrants
revolutions	6.283	radians
revolutions/minute	6	degrees/second
revolutions/minute	0.1047	radians/second
revolutions/minute	0.01667	revolutions/second
revolutions/minute/minute	1.75E-03	radians/second/second
revolutions/minute/minute	0.01667	revolutions/minute/minute
revolutions/minute/minute	2.78E-04	revolutions/second/second
revolutions/second	360	degrees/second
revolutions/second	6.283	radians/second

Unit	Multiplied by	Converts to this unit
revolutions/second	60	revolutions/minute
revolutions/second/ second	6.283	radians/second/second
revolutions/second/ second	3,600	revolutions/minute/ minute
revolutions/second/ second	60	revolutions/minute/ second
rhe	10	per pascal second
rod	0.25	chain (Gunter's)
rod	5.029	meters
rods (surveyor's meas.)	5.5	yards
rods	16.5	feet
roentgen	2.58E-04	coulomb/kilogram
rood (British)	1,011.715	square meter
scruples	20	grains
seconds (angle)	2.78E-04	degrees
seconds (angle)	0.01666667	minutes
seconds (angle)	3.09E-06	quadrants
seconds (angle)	4.85E-06	radians
shake	1.00E-08	seconds
slug	14.59	kilogram
slug	32.17	pounds
span	9	inch
sphere	12.57	steradians
square centimeters	1.97E+05	circular mils
square centimeters	1.08E-03	square feet
square centimeters	0.155	square inches
square centimeters	0.0001	square meters
square centimeters	3.86E-11	square miles
square centimeters	100	square millimeters
square centimeters	1.20E-04	square yards
square feet	2.30E-05	acres
square feet	1.83E+08	circular mils
square feet	929	square centimeters
square feet	144	square inches
square feet	0.0929	square meters
square feet	3.59E-08	square miles
square feet	9.29E+04	square millimeters
square feet	0.1111	square yards
square inches	1.27E+06	circular mils
square inches	6.452	square centimeters
square inches	6.94E-03	square feet
square inches	645.2	square millimeters

Unit	Multiplied by	Converts to this unit
square inches	1.00E+06	square mils
square inches	7.72E-04	square yards
square kilometers	247.1	acres
square kilometers	1.00E+10	square centimeters
square kilometers	1.08E+07	square feet
square kilometers	1.55E+09	square inches
square kilometers	1.00E+06	square meters
square kilometers	0.3861	square miles
square kilometers	1.20E+06	square yards
square meters	2.47E-04	acres
square meters	1.00E+04	square centimeters
square meters	10.763915	square feet
square meters	1,550	square inches
square meters	3.86E-07	square miles
square meters	1.00E+06	square millimeters
square meters	1.196	square yards
square miles	640	acres
square miles	2.79E+07	square feet
square miles	2.59	square kilometers
square miles	2.59E+06	square meters
square miles	3.10E+06	square yards
square millimeters	1,973	circular mils
square millimeters	0.01	square centimeters
square millimeters	1.08E-05	square feet
square millimeters	1.55E-03	square inches
square mils	1.273	circular mils
square mils	6.45E-06	square centimeters
square mils	1.00E-06	square inches
square yards	2.07E-04	acres
square yards	8,361	square centimeters
square yards	9	square feet
square yards	1,296	square inches
square yards	0.8361	square meters
square yards	3.23E-07	square miles
square yards	8.36E+05	square millimeters
statampere	3.33564E-10	ampere
statcoulomb	3.33564E-10	coulomb
statfarad	1.112649E-12	farad
stathenry	8.98755431E+11	henry
statmho	1.112649E-12	siemens (S)
statohm	8.98755431E+11	ohm
statvolt	299.7925	volt
stere	1	cubic meter

Unit	Multiplied by	Converts to this unit
sthene	1,000	newton
stilb	10,000	candela/square meter
stokes	1.00E−04	meter square per second
stone (British)	14	pound (avoirdupois)
tablespoons (metric)	15	milliliter
tablespoons (US)	14.79	milliliter
teaspoons (metric)	5	milliliter
teaspoons (US)	4.93	cubic centimeters
tex	1.00E−06	kilogram/meter
therm	1.05506E+08	joule
thermie	4.1855E+06	joule
thou (mil)	2.54E−05	meter
tons (long)	1,016	kilograms
tons (long)	2,240	pounds
tons (long)	1.12	tons (short)
tons (metric)	1,000	kilograms
tons (metric)	2,205	pounds
tons (metric)	907.1848	kilograms
tons (short)	32,000	ounces
tons (short)	29,166.66	ounces (troy)
tons (short)	2,000	pounds
tons (short)	2,430.56	pounds (troy)
tons (short)	0.89287	tons (long)
tons (short)	0.9078	tonnes (metric)
tons (short)/square foot	9,765	kilograms/square meter
tons (short)/square foot	2,000	pounds/square inch
tons of water/24 hours	83.333	pounds of water/hour
tons of water/24 hours	0.16643	gallons/minute
tons of water/24 hours	1.3349	cubic feet/hour
torr	133.32237	pascal
unit pole	1.256637E−07	weber (Wb)
volt inch	0.3937	volt/centimeters
volt (absolute)	0.003336	statvolts
watts	3.4129	Btu/hour
watts	0.05688	Btu/minute
watts	107	erg/second f
watts	44.27	foot-pounds/minute
watts	0.7378	foot-pounds/second
watts	1.34E−03	horsepower
watts	1.36E−03	horsepower (metric)
watts	0.01433	kilogram-calories/minute
watts	0.001	kilowatts
watts (absolute)	0.056884	Btu (mean)/minute

Unit	Multiplied by	Converts to this unit
watts (absolute)	1	joules/second
watt hour	3,600	joule
watt-hours	3.413	Btu
watt-hours	3.60E+10	ergs
watt-hours	2,656	foot-pounds
watt-hours	859.85	gram-calories
watt-hours	1.34E-03	horsepower-hours
watt-hours	0.8605	kilogram-calories
watt-hours	367.2	kilogram-meters
watt-hours	0.001	kilowatt-hours
watt (international)	1.0002	watt (absolute)
webers	1.00E+08	maxwells
webers	1.00E+05	kilolines
webers/square inch	1.55E+07	gausses
webers/square inch	1.00E+08	lines/square inch
webers/square inch	0.155	webers/square centimeter
webers/square inch	1,550	webers/square meter
webers/square meter	1.00E+04	gausses
webers/square meter	6.45E+04	lines/square inch
webers/square meter	1.00E-04	webers/square centimeter
webers/square meter	6.45E-04	webers/square inch
week	7	days
week	168	hours
week	10,080	minutes (time)
week	0.2299795	months
week	6.05E+05	seconds
yards	91.44	centimeters
yards	0.5	fathoms
yards	3	feet
yards	36	inches
yards	9.14E-04	kilometers
yards	0.9144	meters
yards	4.93E-04	miles (nautical)
yards	5.68E-04	miles (statute)
yards	914.4	millimeters

Area

To convert from	to	multiply by
square foot (ft^2)	square meter (m^2)	0.093
square inch (in^2)	square meter (m^2)	0.00065
square yard (yd^2)	square meter (m^2)	0.836
acre (ac)	hectare (ha)	0.4047

Quantity	From English units	To Metric units	Multiply by
Area	square mile	km^2	2.59
	acre	m^2	4,047
	acre	hectare	0.405
	square yard	m^2	0.836
	square foot	m^2	0.093
	square inch	mm^2	645.2

Length

To convert from	to	multiply by
mile	kilometer (km)	1.61
inch (in)	millimeter (mm)	25.4
inch (in)	centimeter (cm)	2.54
inch (in)	meter (m)	0.025
foot (ft)	meter (m)	0.305
yard (yd)	meter (m)	0.914

Quantity	From English units	To Metric units	Multiply by
Length	mile	km	1.609
	yard	m	0.914
	foot	m	0.305
	inch	mm	25.4

Volume

To convert from	to	multiply by
cubic inch (in³)	cubic meter (m³)	0.0000164
cubic foot (ft³)	cubic meter (m³)	0.028
cubic yard (yd³)	cubic meter (m³)	0.765
gallon (gal)	liter	4.546
gallon (gal)	cubic meter (m³)	0.0038
fluid ounce (fl oz)	milliliters (ml)	29.57
fluid ounce (fl oz)	cubic meter (m³)	0.00003

Quantity	From English units	To Metric units	Multiply by
Volume	acre foot	m³	1.23
	cubic yard	m³	0.765
	cubic foot	m³	0.028
	cubic foot	L (1,000 cm³)	28.32
	gallon	L (1,000 cm³)	3.785

—— DATUM LINE, RANGING WITH TAPE ——

- Range poles are placed at the datum point or a point in line with but beyond the datum point – and the terminal point of the principal meridian line or datum line. They are labeled A and B and the distance between them is measured.
- If they are farther apart than the length of tape, intermediate points must be marked off in increments and measured. If the ground slopes or is rough, the measurements are broken down into shorter horizontal distances. The point farthest from the instrument should be established first.
- The process is repeated to set up the intermediate points. The distance between them is measured and computed for the length of the datum line.
- A third permanent point (C) is usually established along the baseline. It is used as a check on all measurements taken from A, B, and the datum point.

- The dumpy level sits on a tripod and requires a staff on which levels are read.
- The instrument should be set up in the most useful position and leveled.
- It should be tied in to the datum and/or bench mark(s).
- Sight the scope and lock it into position; the dumpy level is adjusted with screws. Set the horizontal line of sight (line of collimation). It is used to take the measurements off the staff.
- The staff can be folding or telescopic and have red and black markings. Stand behind the staff and support it with two hands.
- Take a backsight to the datum. The backsight added to the bench mark value equals collimation.
- Intermediate readings can be taken and these are subtracted from collimation to give the "reduced level," i.e. ground or spot level.
- A final reading should always be taken to the datum to recheck the instrument's position.
- To change to a new station, take a foresight, then set up at the new station. A backsight is then taken.
- In the scope there is a vertical line, horizontal line, and two short horizontal (stadia) lines at the top and bottom. The long lines are for levels, the short lines are for distance. The difference between their readings multiplied by 100 gives the horizontal distance.

EDM, USE OF TO SET UP A GRID

- Permanently set your datum point.
- Use a plumb bob or the EDM's optical plumb, to center the machine over the datum point.
- Select site north and orient the machine in that direction. Make sure you clearly mark your north point.
- Move the staff until the readings show the coordinates of the site grid points you want to establish. Mark each point with a nail or peg.
- Check some of the points with a tape measure to make sure there are no defaults on the EDM that are affecting the measurements.

MEASUREMENT AND CONVERSION

GLOBAL POSITIONING SYSTEM (GPS) INFORMATION

- The known points in GPS use are moving satellites. The measurement of the distances is done by measuring the time taken for a radio signal to pass between the satellites and receiver. The minimum number of measurements in practice is four. The measurements fix the station position in space and by assuming we know the shape of the earth, it is possible to calculate where the station position is on the surface of the earth, and also how far it is above sea level.

- All the information concerning a satellite's orbit is kept up to date and when observations are made from the station position to measure the distance, the current orbit data is supplied. Thus, the receiver at the station position has all the information it needs to work out its position.

- The accuracy of the position obtained by GPS depends on the quality of the timing system and the software. The highest grade consists of a base station and a slave instrument – and it is very costly.

- The lowest grade of GPS is not suitable for detail survey, but it can be useful for establishing the position of monuments in remote or isolated spots. If the GPS gives you the position within 15 m, that will usually be sufficiently accurate for finding the spot in the future. The detail survey can then be done using other field methods, especially using tapes and ranging poles.

- The great advantage of GPS is that it does not depend on optical visibility. It simply requires radio visibility from the GPS to the satellites. That does mean, however, that tall buildings, steep hills, cliff faces, or trees may present problems.

- GPS might be used to establish a series of stations nearby from which the detail can be surveyed using more traditional methods.

MEASUREMENT AND CONVERSION

HORIZONTAL ANGLE MEASUREMENT

Measuring horizontal angles with a compass

- Hold the compass at the point or on a line of a desired bearing and a range pole or leveling rod at the feature to be measured. The compass needle is released and north is pointed along the line to the range pole. The position of the needle is read in relation to the circle. Look along the needle.
- Place the readings in their proper quadrant, i.e. if the north end of the compass is sighted toward the bearing, the north end of the needle should be read.
- Transfer bearings to a chart of the area. Measurement may be made by pacing or taping. Each feature should be plotted on the map, with points measured and survey lines laid out.

Measuring horizontal angles with a tape

- A 2.5 m chord distance is measured down each side of the angle. The chord distance is then measured horizontally between two points, A and B, using the formula

$$\sin {}^1\!/_2 a = \text{chord length divided by AC + BC}$$

- An angle can be measure with the tape alone, using sines and cosines and the formula

$$\cos 60 \text{ degrees} = 10 \text{ divided by Y}$$

- Then Z or the perpendicular to X has to be figured out. Then Y can be determined.

Measuring horizontal angles with optical measuring equipment

- You need to establish a consistent methodology for the routine accurate measurement of horizontal angles. It is suggested that you always measure the angles in a clockwise direction (to the right).
- Set up transit at point B. Loosen the upper and lower clamps.

340

- Set horizontal circle reading to 0°0″ with the telescope in the normal position (Vernier A). Tighten upper clamp. The horizontal circle is now fixed to the upper plate and the Vernier A is reading 0°0″.
- Backsight onto point A and tighten the lower clamp. Align the vertical crosshair with point A using the lower tangent screw.
- Release the upper clamp. The upper plate is now free of the horizontal circle.
- Take a foresight onto point C. Tighten the upper clamp, and align the vertical crosshair using the upper tangent screw. The reading on the Vernier A is approximately equal to the angle θ, although there may be a small error. Say the reading is 30°01″.
- Loosen the lower clamp and take a second backsight onto point A. The Vernier A should still be reading 30°01″ (or whatever it is in your case).
- Tighten the lower clamp, and release the upper clamp. Take a second foresight onto point C. Vernier A should be reading the cumulative angle that has resulted from 2 repetitions, or approximately 60°.
- Repeat steps for a third repetition. The values on Vernier A and B should be approximately 90° and 270°, respectively. It is not necessary to record these interim values, but you probably should initially.
- Plunge the telescope and repeat for an additional three repetitions in the plunged position. Record the final readings from both Verniers.

LEVELS, TAKING IN UNIT

- Taking levels is the method used to locate the relative elevation of a point. This is also called vertical or depth measurement or elevation. One determines this by finding the distance below a level tape line or string.
- The method for taking levels is to pull a string or tape tight and level from the top of the datum point and measure the vertical distance from the string/tape to the point.
- If the field director wishes to have all depth readings adjusted to the datum point, the differences in elevation between the stake and the datum point can be calculated, then the elevation of the object can be adjusted with reference to the datum point.

- You use a line level, making sure the small bubble is centered, that is attached to the string. The string level should always be placed halfway between the datum and the person measuring.
- The tape or string is held horizontal from a measured point (a stake, etc.) to the area just over the object. A plumb bob is dropped over the object's position and a second tape or string is used to measure from the top of the object vertically to the horizontal tape or string. The reading is taken at the intersection of the tapes or strings.
- If the object is difficult to measure from the horizontal tape or string, then taut strings can be held across the unit from two stakes or pins whose elevation is known. A plumb bob is hung from their point of intersection and the measurement is taken. The tape must be absolutely vertical alongside the plumb bob and when the reading is taken against the level lines.
- Note in the record the horizontal measurements with a minus sign.

─── LINES OR TRANSECTS, LAYING OUT ───

- Once the first line is established, AB, there are points of reference established for subsequent lines.
- Occupy a point, C, along line AB, and set up the instrument.
- Sight on either end of AB with the horizontal scale set to 0. This is the point of reference off which you will turn angles to establish new lines.
- Watching the horizontal scale, turn 90 degrees to the left. Measure the appropriate distance from the instrument's position along the 90-degree line. Set a new point D.
- Rotate the instrument back to the 0 sight along the AB line. Now turn 90 degrees to the right, measure that distance along the line and set point E. Now there is one point each set on two new transect lines.
- Occupy E and sight the instrument back to the original C with the horizontal scale set to 0.
- Turn the instrument 90 degrees to the left for one part of the new transect/line. Set a point at the end of the line.
- Turn back to 0 degrees and turn 90 degrees to the right to establish the other end of the new transect/line.
- Repeat this to establish other lines/transects.

- New points can be established along any line by pulling a tape straight and taut between existing points and setting new points at desired intervals. Over uneven ground, you will need to use plumb bobs or pull the tape from the instrument.
- This can also be done with a baseplate compass or compass with rotating housing or dial, but with less accuracy. Stand at A and take the bearing of the line AB, turn 90 degrees left of this bearing (toward D); while still standing at C, turn the dial of the compass so that the index or forward sight is aligned with that last reading; now slowly turn your body until the compass needle aligns with the orienting arrow – the forward sight of the compass will now be pointed at D, having turned 90 degrees off the line AB.

LOCATING A NEWLY SURVEYED SITE ONTO AN ORDNANCE SURVEY MAP

- Set your instrument (such as a theodolite or total station) at the center of your site and align 0 to Ordnance Survey north using a sighting compass. Allow for compass deviation.
- Use your instrument to take bearings to at least three recognizable points on an Ordnance Survey map. Record the bearings for each point.
- On a base map, use a protractor to reconstruct the angles you have taken from each point. Lines from each reference point, on the right angle, will intersect to locate your site.

LOCATING TO THE NATIONAL GRID (UK)

With an EDM

- You must first establish a National Grid point on your site. Take the smallest-scale Ordnance Survey map you can find and measure the distance between a known grid reference to at least three recognizable points on the map.
- In the field, measure that distance from the same three points and the tapes will intersect at the grid point.

- Set up your EDM over the National Grid point. Give the EDM a north point by using an accurate compass or by measurement to a point directly north of your National Grid point.
- Once the EDM knows the coordinates of the National Grid point upon which it is placed and which way is north, it will give all the points for a National Grid reference.

With a programmable EDM

- Take the smallest-scale Ordnance Survey map you can find and determine the National Grid coordinates of at least three easily recognizable features in the field. Program the points into the EDM.
- Take a reading with the EDM on each of the Ordnance Survey points, enabling the EDM to orient itself to the National Grid.

MAP AREA TO FIELD AREA, CONVERTING

- If you are dealing with an area, in which the unit is square feet, or some such unit, you must square the scale of the map to calculate the proper area:

Field Area = Map Area * (Map Scale)^2

- So if the map has a scale of 1 in = 2,000 ft, and you measure a field to have a map area of 7.0 square inches, the total area is:

7.0 * (2,000)^2 = 7.0 * 2,000 * 2,000 = 28,000,000 sq ft

- You have to multiply both the length of the field and the width of the field by the scale to get the actual distance.
- This is equal to 28,000,000 sq ft/43,560 sq ft per acre = 642.8 acres.

MAP SCALE EQUIVALENTS

Map scale	Inches to mile	Statute miles to an inch	Feet to an inch	Kilometers to an inch
1:600	105.6	0.0095	50	0.0153
1:1,200	52.8	0.0189	100	0.0305
1:2,400	26.4	0.0379	200	0.061
1:2,500	25.34	0.0394	208.3	0.0635
1:3,600	17.6	0.0568	300	0.0914
1:4,800	13.2	0.0758	400	0.1219
1:6,000	10.56	0.0947	500	0.1524
1:7,200	8.8	0.1136	600	0.1829
1:7.920	8	0.125 ($^1/_8$ mi)	660	0.2012
1:10,000	6.34	0.1578	833.3	0.254
1:10,560	6	0.167 ($^1/_6$ mi)	880	0.268
1:12,000	5.28	0.1894	1,000	0.305
1:15,840	4	0.250 ($^1/_4$ mi)	1,320	0.402
1:20,000	3.17	0.3156	1,666	0.508
1:21,120	3	0.3333 ($^1/_3$ mi)	1,760	0.536
1:25,000	2.53	0.3945	2,083	0.635
1:31,680	2	0.5 ($^1/_2$ mi)	2,640	0.804
1:62,500	1.01	0.986	5,208	1.587
1:63,360	1	1	5,280	1.609
1:100,000	0.634	1.578	8,333	2.54
1:125,000	0.507	1.972	10,416	3.175
1:316,800	0.2	5	26,400	8.05
1:500,000	0.1267	7.891	41,666	12.7
1:1,000,000	0.063	15.783	83,333.3	25.40

MEASUREMENT AND CONVERSION

Conversion of compass points to degrees

points/angular measure (degree, °)

North to east
North 0 0
N by E 1 11 15
NNE 2 22 30
NE by N 3 33 45
NE 4 45
NE by E 5 56 15
ENE 6 67 30
E by N 7 78 45

East to south
East 8 90 0
E by S 9 101 15
ESE 10 112 30
SE by E 11 123 45
SE 12 135
SE by S 13 146 15
SSE 14 157 30
S by E 15 168 45

South to west
South 16 180
S by W 17 191 15
SSW 18 202 30
SW by S 19 213 45
SW 20 225
SW by W 21 236 15
WSW 22 247 30
W by S 23 258 45

West to north
West 24 270
W by N 25 281 15
WNW 26 292 30
NW by W 27 303 45
NW 28 315
NW by N 29 326 15
NNW 30 337 30
N by W 31 348 45
North 32 360

MEASUREMENT AND CONVERSION

Conversion factors

To change	To	Multiply by
acres	hectares	0.4047
acres	square feet	43,560
acres	square miles	0.001562
atmospheres	cms of mercury	76
Btu/hour	horsepower	0.0003930
Btu	kilowatt-hour	0.0002931
Btu/hour	watts	0.2931
bushels	cubic inches	2,150.4
bushels (US)	hectoliters	0.3524
centimeters	inches	0.3937
centimeters	feet	0.03281
cubic feet	cubic meters	0.0283
cubic meters	cubic feet	35.3145
cubic meters	cubic yards	1.3079
cubic yards	cubic meters	0.7646
degrees	radians	0.01745
dynes	grams	0.00102
fathoms	feet	6.0
feet	meters	0.3048
feet	miles (nautical)	0.0001645
feet	miles (statute)	0.0001894
feet/second	miles/hour	0.6818
furlongs	feet	660.0
furlongs	miles	0.125
gallons (US)	liters	3.7853
grains	grams	0.0648
grams	grains	15.4324
grams	ounces (avdp)	0.0353
grams	pounds	0.002205
hectares	acres	2.4710
hectoliters	bushels (US)	2.8378
horsepower	watts	745.7
horsepower	Btu/hour	2,547
hours	days	0.04167
inches	millimeters	25.4000
inches	centimeters	2.5400
kilograms	pounds (avdp or troy)	2.2046
kilometers	miles	0.6214
kilowatt-hour	Btu	3,412
knots	nautical miles/hour	1.0
knots	statute miles/hour	1.151

To change	To	Multiply by
liters	gallons (US)	0.2642
liters	pecks	0.1135
liters	pints (dry)	1.8162
liters	pints (liquid)	2.1134
liters	quarts (dry)	0.9081
liters	quarts (liquid)	1.0567
meters	feet	3.2808
meters	miles	0.0006214
meters	yards	1.0936
metric tons	tons (long)	0.9842
metric tons	tons (short)	1.1023
miles	kilometers	1.6093
miles	feet	5,280
miles (nautical)	miles (statute)	1.1516
miles (statute)	miles (nautical)	0.8684
miles/hour	feet/minute	88
millimeters	inches	0.0394
ounces (avdp)	grams	28.3495
ounces	pounds	0.0625
ounces (troy)	ounces (avdp)	1.09714
pecks	liters	8.8096
pints (dry)	liters	0.5506
pints (liquid)	liters	0.4732
pounds (ap or troy)	kilograms	0.3782
pounds (avdp)	kilograms	0.4536
pounds	ounces	16
quarts (dry)	liters	1.1012
quarts (liquid)	liters	0.9463
radians	degrees	57.30
rods	meters	5.029
rods	feet	16.5
square feet	square meters	0.0929
square kilometers	square miles	0.3861
square meters	square feet	10.7639
square meters	square yards	1.1960
square miles	square kilometers	2.5900
square yards	square meters	0.8361
tons (long)	metric tons	1.016
tons (short)	metric tons	0.9072
tons (long)	pounds	2,240
tons (short)	pounds	2,000
watts	Btu/hour	3.4121
watts	horsepower	0.001341
yards	meters	0.9144
yards	miles	0.0005682

■ Obstacles can be measured over or around by various means: an equilateral triangle, offsetting, perpendiculars, plumb bobs and range pole or tape, and triangulation.

■ In using an equilateral triangle, a 60-degree angle is established at point A and a distance is taped from A to B to pass the obstacle. A 60-degree angle is then measured at B and points BC are measured equal to AB. Point C should be on the line of the traverse. The distance AC should equal AB and BC.

■ Offsetting: an offset is a horizontal line at a right angle from a line of traverse or grid. These can be established by tape or optical measuring equipment. In taping, you first determine what points are offsets to be used for the measurement. If you want to run a straight line, but there is a feature blocking the measurement, a convenient distance is picked along the line so that the feature can be passed. Offsets may be measured from the line of traverse to or around the feature or from the feature to the line of traverse.

■ A perpendicular, a right angle measured using the Pythagorean principle of the 3–4–5 right triangle, can be measured. AB is a straight line. The distance is measured from C to D on line AB. The tape is held on point C and stretched to D. Then the tape is laid out so a loop or arc is made half that distance from point D, going to point E. What is left of the tape is between points E and C; when line CE is lined up, it will be perpendicular to AB. Alternatively, extend the tape from the object to the right and swing a measured interval of tape down to the point from which the perpendicular is desired. A stake can be placed in the ground on the AB line where the tape and line intersect and a second tape swing can be taken to the left from the object to the AB line. The intersection of the two arcs will position the object perpendicular to line AB.

■ Plumb bobs and range pole or tape: arrange the range pole or tape horizontally over the obstacle and level it with plumb bobs on either side.

■ In triangulation, to obtain the distance from B to D across an obstacle, a distance BC is taped and measured perpendicular to line AB, then the angles at B and C are measured and the BD distance is figured. You can check this from the other side of the obstacle. BC should be at least one-half of the unknown distance BD.

(a) Measuring a horizontal line across an uneven surface

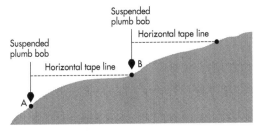

(b) Breaking tape along a slope to reduce it to a horizontal measurement for mapping

Figure 5.2 Measuring distance with tapes over uneven terrain. (R. M. Stewart, Figure 6.32: Methods for taping distance over uneven terrain and slopes, p. 131 from *Archaeology Basic Field Methods*. Dubuque, Iowa: Kendall/Hunt, 2002. Copyright © 2002 by Kendall/Hunt Publishing Company. Reprinted by permission of the publisher)

MEASURING DEPTH OF AN ARTIFACT OR FEATURE

- Measure the location of artifacts and features from the southwest stake.
- Three-dimensional measurement is carried out by orienting a tape north–south from the position at the southwest stake where the coordinates for that stake were recorded.
- The tape is extended north until it intersects at a right angle with another tape oriented east–west over the artifact in situ.
- A plumb bob and string are hung above the object to locate the artifact precisely and a line level is used to obtain an accurate depth below datum.

- A top and bottom measurement might be taken if an artifact or feature is fairly large.
- An alternative method is to employ a measuring triangle which must be properly leveled. It is a right triangle made of wood with one arm 3 feet and the other 4 feet long, each equipped with a fixed spirit level. The short side of the triangle level rests against the nearest stake and the outer edge of the long side of the triangle is positioned vertically over the find. A tape with a plumb bob attached to the zero end is held against the long side over the object and the vertical distance measured (A-S stake to point of triangle along edge, S-T point of triangle along edge to point on triangle directly above artifact or feature, and T-X from point on triangle directly above artifact or feature to the artifact or feature).

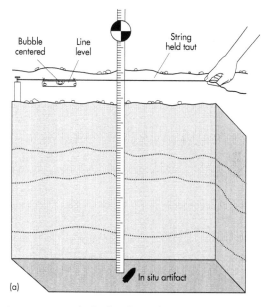

Bubble
centered

Line
level

String
held taut

In situ artifact

(a)

Figure 5.3a Measuring depth of artifact or feature. (Thomas R. Hester, Harry J. Shafer, and Kenneth L. Feder, from *Field Methods in Archaeology*, Seventh Edition. New York: McGraw-Hill, 1997. Copyright © 1997 by Thomas R. Hester, Harry J. Shafer, and Kenneth L. Feder. Reprinted by permission of The McGraw-Hill Companies)

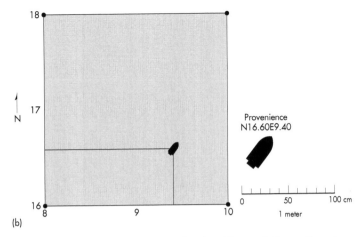

(b)

Figure 5.3b Measuring provenience of artifact. (Thomas R. Hester, Harry J. Shafer, and Kenneth L. Feder, Figure 6.4, from *Field Methods in Archaeology*, Seventh Edition. New York: McGraw-Hill, 1997. Copyright © 1997 by Thomas R. Hester, Harry J. Shafer, and Kenneth L. Feder. Reprinted by permission of The McGraw-Hill Companies)

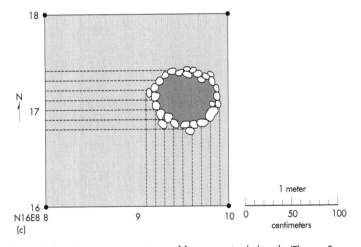

(c)

Figure 5.3c Measuring provenience of feature: a simple hearth. (Thomas R. Hester, Harry J. Shafer, and Kenneth L. Feder, Figure 6.5: Measuring provenience of a feature, from *Field Methods in Archaeology*, Seventh Edition. New York: McGraw-Hill, 1997. Copyright © 1997 by Thomas R. Hester, Harry J. Shafer, and Kenneth L. Feder. Reprinted by permission of The McGraw-Hill Companies)

352

- Measured pace is fine for rough estimates when making sketch maps of sites. You must first walk a long tape repeatedly to count your normal pace and determine its average.
- Over long distances on fairly level terrain, you can roughly estimate distance covered by elapsed time if you know your average coverage per mile.
- Distance can also be measured by the odometer of a vehicle, but it is approximate.
- Using tapes is more accurate for measuring distance. To measure a horizontal line across an uneven surface, suspend a plumb bob on either end and pull the tape taut.
- Breaking tape is the same approach for a slope, done in increments, preferably proceeding downhill. If the terrain slopes more than 4 degrees, measurements should be reduced to the horizontal. Only one end needs a suspended plumb bob and the other end is held at ground level. This is repeated until the whole slope has been measured. Surveying pins or nails to mark point B before establishing point C (etc.) is recommended.
- Slope reduction employs an Abney level or clinometer and tape to measure the distance on a slope. The Abney level or clinometer figures the angle of the slope, which is used in a trigonometric formula, for which you will also need a scientific notation calculator. A, B, and C are angles of the right triangle and a, b, and c are the sides/lengths of the right triangle. To solve for b (length/distance), use the trigonometric formula: COS A = b divided by c (or COS A × c = b) with b being the slope reduction of c.
- Another method of measuring distance employs an alidade, transit, or theodolite with a stadia rod. The instrument is set up and leveled on or over a point from which measurements are to be taken. Looking through the scope to the stadia rod, you will see 3 horizontal crosshairs and a single vertical crosshair. First, read the stadia rod where the topmost crosshair intersects the graduations of the rod. Then read the lowest crosshair where it intersects the rod. Subtract the lower reading from the upper reading, multiply by 100 or move the decimal point two places to the right. The formula for measuring distance from a level scope is Distance = stadia factor K (usually 100) × stadia interval s (top stadia hair minus bottom stadia hair) + (C) distance from the center of the instrument to its principal focus – Distance = (100 × stadia interval) + 0.

MEASUREMENT AND CONVERSION

- To measure distance with an instrument and stadia rod when the scope is not level is calculated as: Distance = stadia factor K (usually 100) × stadia interval s (top stadia hair minus bottom stadia hair) $\cos^2$ (cosine of the angle at which the instrument scope is inclined from the horizontal, squared) + (C) distance from the center of the scope to its principal focus − Distance = (100 × stadia interval) × (cosine of angle squared) + 0.

- Theodolites with electronic distance measurement give even greater accuracy and are most efficient.

- GPS units can also do distance measurement. Multiple GPS readings that are averaged will increase the accuracy of the measurement. Post-field correction of data using GPS software will also reduce errors.

- Distance measurement can also be done with a dumpy level and stadia rod.

MEASURING HEIGHTS/ELEVATION

- The instrument (transit, theodolite, etc.) is set up on a fixed point of known height. The instrument height is measured to a marked central point on the scope. The instrument's scope is leveled and sighted to the stadia rod positioned over the elevation datum. Using the middle horizontal crosshair of the scope, read the height on a stadia rod placed on the datum point. The reading tells you that the level of the instrument's scope is X above the datum. Since you also know the height of the instrument, the elevation of point A can be calculated by subtraction. Total station in combination with reflective prisms can also be used for this.

- The elevation of additional points can be determined from the instrument setup at A. If the position of A is marked, it can be used as a reference point for calculating elevations because you have determined its elevation relative to the datum.

- Always work from a known elevation to an unknown point. Every time the instrument is put in a new position, record the height of the instrument.

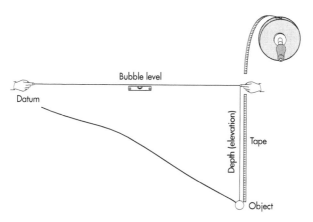

Figure 5.4 Taking an elevation with tapes. (Martha Joukowsky, Figure 9.23: Elevation with hand held tapes, p. 224 from *A Complete Manual of Field Archaeology*. Englewood Cliffs, NJ: Prentice Hall, 1980. Copyright © 1980 by Martha Joukowsky. Reprinted by permission of Simon & Schuster Adult Publishing Group)

OFFSETTING

- Offsetting is a method for measuring a feature to make a plan of it.
- An offset is a horizontal line at a right angle from a line of traverse or grid. These can be established by tape or optical measuring equipment.
- In taping, you first determine what points are offsets to be used for the measurement.
- A baseline is set out running along the major axis of the feature and a series of straight lines or "offsets" are run out from the baseline to points along the edges of the feature, such as where the edge of the feature changes direction.
- One person stands holding the tape (point A) and the other stands at the baseline (point B) and moves that end of the tape until it forms a right angle with the baseline (at point C). The measurement is the shortest distance between A and the baseline. When the tape is perpendicular to the baseline, the distances along and out from that line can be recorded.
- Offsets are taken until there are enough points to produce an accurate outline of the feature.

- This technique works best when one person is drawing and another is measuring.
- A single person can do this using a plumb bob and hand tape set at right angles to a tape, noting the two measurements and then plotting the point. The tape must be perpendicular to the baseline to be accurate.

ORIENTEERING COMPASS, USING WITH A MAP

- First, you need to determine your bearing (the direction you need to travel). The procedure will work if the magnetic north–south lines are drawn on the map.
- Place the compass on the map so that the long edge connects the starting point with the desired destination.
- Make sure that the direction arrows are pointing from the starting point to the place of destination (and not the opposite way).
- At this point, you may want to use the scales on your compass (if available) to determine the distance you need to travel.
- Hold the compass firm on the map in order to keep the base plate steady.
- Turn the rotating capsule until the north–south lines on the bottom of the capsule are parallel with the north–south lines on the map.
- Be sure that the north–south arrow on the bottom of the capsule points to the same direction as north on the map. It is here you will make adjustments for declination, if necessary.
- Hold the compass in your hand in front of you. Make sure that the base plate is in horizontal position, and that the direction arrows are pointing straight ahead.
- Rotate your body until the north–south arrow on the bottom of the capsule lines up with the magnetic needle, and the red end of the needle points in the same direction as the arrow.
- The directional arrows on the baseplate now show your desired travel direction.
- Now that you have determined your necessary bearing, you need to make sure you maintain an accurate bearing. First, you should find a suitable target in the terrain (e.g., a tree, boulder, or bush) toward which the direction arrows point. Walk toward the chosen object without looking at your compass. When you

reach your target, find a new object that is aligned with your bearing, and repeat the process.

■ Note that sometimes the compass capsule may get turned accidentally while you are walking. Remember to check from time to time that the capsule has not deviated from the direction that had been set on the compass.

■ Remember the difference between the magnetic needle that always points to the magnetic North Pole and the direction arrows that show the travel direction.

——— OVERALL SITE GRID, ESTABLISHING AN ———

■ The datum line and datum point are established.

■ Decide the grid's orientation, its extent, and its scale.

■ Decide on the naming/numbering system for the grid.

■ The grid should be oriented to true north, the direction of the datum line.

■ Each of its intersections should be marked with a permanent stake labeled with its bearing and position in relation to the site datum point and the coordinate system, using the cardinal points of the compass.

■ The size of the site determines the scale of the grid.

■ After the datum line is set, the bearings and distances of each grid point are taken in order around the site. These intersections are tied to permanent landmarks. Each point is measured and each measurement checked.

■ Use a transit or theodolite and stadia or tape to grid the site. The grid is set up by creating lines at right angles or 90 degrees off the baseline.

■ Create the baseline AB with the fixed points at A and B.

■ Set up the instrument over A and sight to B, setting the horizontal scale to 0.

■ Record the magnetic bearing of the line AB. It is the point of reference to which all other lines of the grid will be oriented.

■ Using the instrument, tape the distance between A and B, setting points at specific intervals.

■ Turn 90 degrees to the right of line AB and set point C, establishing line AC.

■ Using the instrument, tape the distance between A and C, setting points at specific intervals.

- Now occupy the individual points along line AC to set up the rest of the grid. Move the instrument to the first grid point D to the west of A. Sight the instrument on C with the horizontal scale set to 0. Rotate the scope vertically so you are looking back to A (or turn 180 degrees to back-sight). Make sure the alignment is precise. Use the horizontal scale, turn 90 degrees to establish DE. Use the instrument, tap between D and E, setting points at specific intervals. You can complete the grid system by repeating this operation.
- Recheck every measurement.

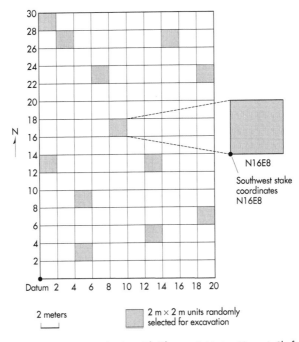

Figure 5.5 Drawing a simple site grid. (Thomas R. Hester, Harry J. Shafer, and Kenneth L. Feder, Figure 6.2, p. 117 from *Field Methods in Archaeology*, Seventh Edition. New York: McGraw-Hill, 1997. Copyright © 1997 by Thomas R. Hester, Harry J. Shafer, and Kenneth L. Feder. Reprinted by permission of The McGraw-Hill Companies)

PERCENT GRADE TO DEGREES

- % grade is the tangent of the angle measured from the horizontal.
- Tangent [Slope Degrees] = Vertical Rise Distance divided by Horizontal Distance.
- Gradient = 1 unit in Horizontal Distance divided by Vertical Rise Distance units or 1:H/V.
- % Grade is 100 × Tangent [Slope] or 100 × Vertical Rise divided by Horizontal Distance.
- Grade = Rise divided by Run.
- % Grade = Rise divided by Run times 100.

Example:

Slope degrees	gradient 1:X	% Grade
4.0	14.3	7.0
5.0	11.4	8.7
6.0	9.5	10.5
7.0	8.1	12.3
8.0	7.1	14.1
9.0	6.3	15.8
10.0	5.7	17.6
11.0	5.1	19.4
12.0	4.7	21.3
13.0	4.3	23.1
14.0	4.0	24.9
15.0	3.7	26.8
16.0	3.5	28.7
17.0	3.3	30.6
18.0	3.1	32.5
19.0	2.9	34.4
20.0	2.7	36.4
21.0	2.6	38.4
22.0	2.5	40.4
23.0	2.4	42.4
24.0	2.2	44.5
25.0	2.1	46.6
26.0	2.1	48.8
27.0	2.0	51.0
28.0	1.9	53.2
20.0	1.8	55.4
30.0	1.7	57.7

Slope degrees	gradient 1:X	% Grade
31.0	1.7	60.1
32.0	1.6	62.5
33.0	1.5	64.9
34.0	1.5	64.9
35.0	1.4	70.0
36.0	1.4	72.7
37.0	1.3	75.4
38.0	1.3	78.1
39.0	1.2	81.0
40.0	1.2	83.9
41.0	1.2	86.9
42.0	1.1	90.0
43.0	1.1	93.3
44.0	1.0	96.6
45.0	1.0	100.0
46.0	1.0	103.6
47.0	0.9	107.2
48.0	0.9	111.1
49.0	0.9	115.0
50.0	0.8	119.2
51.0	0.8	123.5
52.0	0.8	128.0
53.0	0.8	132.7
54.0	0.7	137.6
55.0	0.7	142.8
56.0	0.7	148.3
57.0	0.6	154.0
58.0	0.6	160.0
59.0	0.6	166.4
60.0	0.6	173.2
61.0	0.6	180.4
62.0	0.5	188.1
63.0	0.5	196.2
64.0	0.5	205.0
65.0	0.5	214.5
66.0	0.4	224.6
67.0	0.4	235.6
68.0	0.4	247.5
69.0	0.4	260.5
70.0	0.4	274.7
71.0	0.3	290.4
72.0	0.3	307.8

Slope degrees	gradient 1:X	% Grade
73.0	0.3	327.1
74.0	0.3	348.7
75.0	0.3	373.2
76.0	0.2	401.1
77.0	0.2	433.1
78.0	0.2	470.5
79.0	0.2	514.5
80.0	0.2	567.1
81.0	0.2	631.4
82.0	0.1	711.5
83.0	0.1	814.4
84.0	0.1	951.4
85.0	0.1	1,143.0
86.0	0.1	1,430.1
87.0	0.1	1,908.1
88.0	0.0	2,863.6
89.0	0.0	5,729.0
90.0	0.0	–

PERPENDICULARS

- A perpendicular, a right angle measured using the Pythagorean principle of the 3–4–5 right triangle, can be measured using a 20-meter (+) tape.
- AB is a straight line. The distance is measured from C to D on line AB. The tape is held on point C and stretched to D.
- Then the tape is laid out so a loop or arc is made half that distance from point D, going to point E.
- What is left of the tape is between points E and C; when line CE is lined up, it will be perpendicular to AB.
- Alternatively, extend the tape from the object to the right and swing a measured interval of tape down to the point from which the perpendicular is desired. A stake can be placed in the ground on the AB line where the tape and line intersect and a second tape swing can be taken to the left from the object to the AB line. The intersection of the two arcs will position the object perpendicular to line AB.

- Given: Point P is on a given line.
- Task: Construct a line through P perpendicular to the given line.
- Directions:
- Place your compass point on P and sweep an arc of any size that crosses the line twice (below the line). You will be creating (at least) a semicircle. (Actually, you may draw this arc above *or* below the line.)
- Place the compass point where the arc crossed the line on one side and make a small arc below the line. (The small arc could be above the line if you prefer.)
- Without changing the span on the compass, place the compass point where the arc crossed the line on the *other* side and make another arc. Your two small arcs should be crossing.
- With your straightedge, connect the intersection of the two small arcs to point P.
- This new line is perpendicular to the given line.

─────────────── **PLANE TABLE USE** ───────────────

- The plane table is a drawing board mounted on a tripod from which the bearings of points are plotted and recorded. The table needs to be leveled.
- You may use radiation, traversing, and intersection on a plane table.
- Select the points to be plotted. The surveyor sights the alidade on the ranging pole held by the assistant on each point and plots each point to scale.
- To change station, select a new station and plot its position. Then set up the table over the new point.

To level and orient the plane table

- Set the tripod up with its legs inclined about 30 degrees from vertical, loosen both set screws of the Johnson head, and move the upper/main part of the head until it is upright.
- Tighten both set screws and screw the plane table down so that it fits firmly against the head.
- Place the assembly over the station occupied such that the map is oriented approximately and the ground marker of the station lies under the corresponding point on the map.

- Level the board approximately by moving the tripod legs; on steep slopes, place two of the legs downhill.
- Press the tripod feet into the ground or brace them with chunks of rock so they stay in place.
- Place the alidade without its striding level in the center of the board, parallel to the board's length.
- Grip the far side of the board with one hand, hold the blade down under that arm, and press the near edge of the board firmly against the waist.
- Loosen both set screws of the Johnson head with the free hand and level the board by referring to the level on the blade. Tighten the upper set screw of the Johnson head.

To orient the table for mapping

- Place the fiducial edge (zero reference) so that it bisects the map point of the station occupied and also the map point of the station that will be sighted.
- Rotate the board on its vertical axis until the alidade is pointing at the station to be sighted; look through the telescope in order to bring the station sighted exactly on the vertical crosshair.
- Tighten the lower set screw of the Johnson head, making sure that the crosshair remains on the station sighted.
- Check the parallax and make sure the board and tripod are set firmly enough so that they will not be disoriented during mapping.

PLANIMETER USE

- The first step is to calculate the planimeter constant. This constant may be printed inside the planimeter case and is usually around 10.0, but it is always more accurate to calculate it again for each user.
- To calculate the constant, plot out a square of known area; say 2 in^2 and a circle of known area, say a diameter of 2 in. Set the anchor base outside of your plotted area and place the anchor arm into the drum assembly.
- Place the tracing point at one corner of your square and write down the initial planimeter reading.

- The next two readings are a bit more difficult. The drum and the Vernier are next to each other. The Vernier has markings from 0 to 10. The drum also has markings from 0 to 10 with intermediate markings at each 0.1 interval. Use the 0 mark from the Vernier to read the drum reading. The Vernier reading is taken by matching up marks from the Vernier and drum.
- Trace around the outline of the square with the tracing point directly on top of the lines. Do not worry if the planimeter reading seems to be going backwards at times. Once you have traced around the square, note the final planimeter reading. If you traced in a clockwise motion, the number of revolutions equals the final reading minus the initial reading.

—— PLUMBING THE LINE/TAPING A SLOPE ——

- A level can be held along the tape line or on the tape to determine the horizontal position of the tape.
- Some prefer to hold the zero end of the tape at the high point. If the lower point is being set, then the zero end of the tape with a plumb bob is held over the desired position.
- Each end of the tape is held above the points.
- A string with the plumb bob is hung directly over the point to be measured.
- If there are obstacles, both people may have to measure using plumb bobs.
- Once the tape is horizontal, the plumb bob is allowed to fall to a point just above the ground, holding the plumb bob and tape over the point until they are aligned.
- The tape is pulled taut and the plumb bob string aligned from the tape while holding a level on the tape – while another person puts the pin in the ground directly under the plumb bob.
- Remeasure after the pin is in position.

RADIAL MEASUREMENT

- Radial measurement involves locating a series of points in relation to a plotted position.
- This is useful for small sites where the measuring instrument can be placed on the datum point and each point to be measured is visible. Radiation is also useful for surveys made with a plane table and for checking other methods of measurement, such as the traverse.
- The measurements should be checked and the total of the measured angles should equal 360 degrees.

RADIOCARBON SAMPLE SIZE

(Beta Analytic, radiocarbon dating company)

Radiometric technique

Material	Recommended sample size	Minimum sample size
Charcoal	30 g	1.7 g*
Shell	100 g	7 g*
Wood	100 g	7 g*
Peat	100 g	15 g*
Organic sediment	1–2 kg	n/a
Bone	500 g	200 g*
Dung	30 g	7 g*
Water BaCO3 SrCO3	50 g	7 g*
Water (as liquid)	call laboratory	

* Extended counting required/recommended.

Quantities assume the material is dry and free associated matrix. Wet and/or dirty samples require sending as much as is available.

Accelerator Mass Spectrometry technique (AMS)

Material	Recommended sample size	Minimum sample size
Charcoal	50 mg	5 mg
Shell	100 mg	30 mg
Forams	100 mg**	15 mg**
Wood and seeds	100 mg	10 mg
Peat	100 mg	15 mg
Organic sediment	10 g	(*)
Bone	30 g	2 g
Plant material	50 mg	10 mg
Water BaCO3 SrCO3	50 mg	15 mg
Water (as liquid)	1 L	1 L

* Variable, requires examination.
** Laboratory pretreatments are not possible.

Material	Minimum weight	Optimum weight
Antler	100 g	
Bone (apatite)	500 g	1,000 g
Bone (charred)	200–500 g	1,500–3,000 g
Bone (collagen)	100–300 g	800–3,000 g
Bone (uncharred)	20–100 g	1,000 g
Charcoal	2–5 g	10–50 g
Charred organic material	10 g	
Cloth and paper	3–5 g	30–100 g
Grass and leaves	5 g	35–50 g
Hide	10 g	
Iron (cast)	30 g	100–150 g
Iron (steel)	150 g	
Ivory	50 g	
Limestone and plaster	5 g	50–100 g
Peat	10–70 g	100–200 g
Seeds	10 g	10 g or more
Shell	5–40 g	100–200 g
Skin and hair	5 g	45 g
Soil	500 g	1,500–2,000 g
Wood	3–5 g	30–100 g

Right triangle

- In any right triangle, the hypotenuse h is the longest side. The three sides are related in such a way that if you square the length of the hypotenuse, you will get the same answer as you do when you square each of the other two sides, and add the values together:

$$h^2 = a^2 + b^2$$

- For example, consider a triangle with a 90-degree angle and when you measure its sides, the lengths are 3, 4, and 5 cm. The Pythagorean Theorem says that the three sides must follow this rule – 5 squared = 3 squared + 4 squared – which works out to 25 = 9 + 16.
- This is equivalent to stating that the area of the square on the hypotenuse is equal to the areas of the squares on the other two sides, added together.
- There are other whole numbers that also work: 3,4,5 or 6,8,10 or 9,12,15 or 12,16,20 . . . etc.; or these: 5,12,13 or 10,24,26 or 15,36,39 or 20,48,52 . . . etc.; or these: 7,24,25 or 14,48,50 or 21,72,75 or 28,96,100.
- The formulas for a right triangle are:

longest side = hypotenuse = c

shortest side = shorter leg = b

middle length side = longer leg = a

Pythagorean theorem = c squared = a squared + b squared

angle A and angle B = acute angles

angle C = 90-degree angle

angle A + angle B + angle C = 180 degrees

angle A + angle B = 90 degrees (complementary)

sine angle = (opposite leg)/(hypotenuse) . . . sin A = a/c

cosine angle = (adjacent leg)/(hypotenuse) . . . cos A = b/c

tangent angle = (opposite leg)/(adjacent leg) . . . tan A = a/b

sin = opp/hypot

cos = adj/hypot

tan = opp/adj

sin A = a divided by c

cos A = b divided by c

tan A = a divided by b

cot A = b divided by a

sec A = c divided by b

cosec A = c divided by a

area = (a times b) divided by 2

Sine

■ Sine is truly the basis of trigonometry. With this function, you can calculate values for any other trigonometric function. It is simply the ratio between the side opposite the given angle over the hypotenuse of any right triangle. If you needed to find sin A in the triangle given, it would be a/c. In this case, sin 70° = 0.939693, or the ratio between side a and side c.

Cosine

■ Cosine is usually the second trigonometric function taught, often in the same lesson as sine. Cosine is the adjacent side over the hypotenuse. It can also be calculated as sin (90° − angle). In the triangle here, cos A = cos 70° = b/c = 0.34202. Note that cos 20° = sin 70°.

Tangent

- Tangent is often the next trigonometric function. It is the ratio of the side opposite over the side adjacent. In our triangle, tan A = tan 70° = a/b = 2.74748. Another way of defining tangent is as the sine of an angle over its cosine (0.939693/0.34202 = 2.74748). One can then define tan A as sin A/(sin 90° − A). The usage of these first three trig functions can be remembered by recalling the mnemonic SOHCAHTOA – Sine: Opposite Hypotenuse; Cosine: Adjacent Hypotenuse; Tangent: Opposite Adjacent.

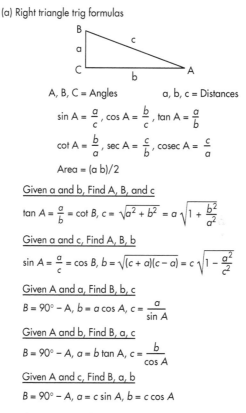

(a) Right triangle trig formulas

A, B, C = Angles   a, b, c = Distances

$$\sin A = \frac{a}{c}, \ \cos A = \frac{b}{c}, \ \tan A = \frac{a}{b}$$

$$\cot A = \frac{b}{a}, \ \sec A = \frac{c}{b}, \ \operatorname{cosec} A = \frac{c}{a}$$

$$\text{Area} = (a\,b)/2$$

Given a and b, Find A, B, and c

$$\tan A = \frac{a}{b} = \cot B, \ c = \sqrt{a^2 + b^2} = a\sqrt{1 + \frac{b^2}{a^2}}$$

Given a and c, Find A, B, b

$$\sin A = \frac{a}{c} = \cos B, \ b = \sqrt{(c + a)(c - a)} = c\sqrt{1 - \frac{a^2}{c^2}}$$

Given A and a, Find B, b, c

$$B = 90° - A, \ b = a\cos A, \ c = \frac{a}{\sin A}$$

Given A and b, Find B, a, c

$$B = 90° - A, \ a = b\tan A, \ c = \frac{b}{\cos A}$$

Given A and c, Find B, a, b

$$B = 90° - A, \ a = c\sin A, \ b = c\cos A$$

Figure 5.6a Right triangle trig formulas

(b) Oblique triangle formulas

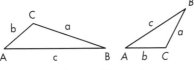

Given A, B and a,   Find b, C and c

$$b = \frac{a \sin B}{\sin A} \, , C = 180° - (A + B), c = \frac{a \sin C}{\sin A}$$

Given A, a and b,   Find B, C and c

$$\sin B = \frac{b \sin A}{a} \, , C = 180° - (A + B), c = \frac{a \sin C}{\sin A}$$

Given a, b and C,   Find A, B and c

$$\tan A = \frac{a \sin C}{b - (a \cos C)} \, , B = 180° - (A + C)$$

$$c = \frac{a \sin C}{\sin A}$$

Given a, b and c,   Find A, B and C

$$\cos A = \frac{b^2 + c^2 - a^2}{2 \, bc} \, , \cos B = \frac{a^2 + c^2 - b^2}{2 \, ac}$$

$$C = 180° - (A + B)$$

Given a, b, c, A, B and C,   Find Area

$$s = \frac{a + b + c}{2} \, , \text{Area} = \sqrt{s(s - a)(s - b)(s - c)}$$

$$\text{Area} = \frac{bc \sin A}{2} \, , \text{Area} = \frac{a^2 \sin B \sin C}{2 \sin A}$$

Figure 5.6b   Oblique triangle trig formulas

(c) Plane figure formulas

Rectangle

If square, a = b

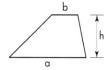

Area = ab
Perimeter = $2(a + b)$, Diagonal = $\sqrt{a^2 + b^2}$

Parallelogram

All sides are
parallel
θ = degrees

Area = $ah = ab \sin \theta$, Perimeter = $2(a + b)$

Trapezoid

Area = $\dfrac{(a + b)}{2} h$

Perimeter = Sum of lengths of sides

Quadrilateral

θ = degrees

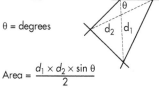

Area = $\dfrac{d_1 \times d_2 \times \sin \theta}{2}$

Figure 5.6c Plane figure formulas

(c) Plane figure formulas

Trapezium

a to g
= lengths

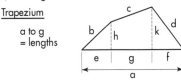

Perimeter = $a + b + c + d$

$$Area = \frac{(h + k)\,g + e\,h + f\,k}{2}$$

Equilateral triangle

a = all sides equal

Perimeter = $3a$, $h = \dfrac{a}{2}\sqrt{3} = 0.866\,a$

$$Area = a^2\,\frac{\sqrt{3}}{4} = 0.433\,a^2$$

Annulus

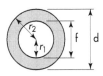

$Area = 0.7854\,(d^2 - f^2)$

$Area = \pi(r_1 + r_2)(r_2 - r_1)$

Figure 5.6c Continued

RIM MEASURING SCALE

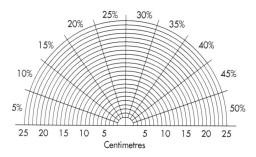

Figure 5.7 Ceramics rim diameter measurement. (Mark Q. Sutton and Brooke S. Arkush, Figure 57: A rim diameter-measurement template, which determines rim sherd radius and estimates the percentage of the total vessel rim circumference present, p. 122 from *Archaeological Laboratory Methods: An Introduction*, Third Edition. Dubuque, IA: Kendall/Hunt Publishing, 2002. Copyright © 2002 by Kendall/Hunt Publishing Company. Reprinted by permission of the publisher)

SITES AND FEATURES, TAKING LEVELS OF

- Levels are used to establish the height of sites and features above sea level.
- Site the level or machine at a spot from which you can see the temporary bench mark and the place where you want to take a level. Make sure the level or machine are level.
- Have someone place the base of the staff on the temporary bench mark. Make sure the staff is vertical.
- Take a reading to the bench mark, i.e. backsight.
- Turn the level and take the other readings, i.e. foresights.
- Find out the height above sea level of your temporary bench mark. Add the backsight figure to this number to get the instrument height.
- Subtract each of the foresight readings from the instrument height to get the height of each point you took, i.e. reduced levels.

Using an EDM

- Site the EDM on the point and level it with the plumb bob. Measure the staff height or locate the prism on the staff to the EDM level symbol on the machine.
- Have someone place the base of the staff on the temporary bench mark. Make sure the staff is vertical.
- Take a reading to the bench mark, i.e. backsight.
- Turn the machine and take the other readings, i.e. foresights.
- Add your backsight measurement to the height of your temporary bench mark above sea level. If your backsight is a minus figure, take it away and you will get the height of the ground under the EDM.
- Subtract each of the foresight readings from this figure to get the height above sea level for each point you took, i.e. reduced levels.

SLOPE, TAPING A

- A taped distance along a slope is greater than the horizontal distance. Instead of plumbing, a tape can be positioned on the ground and the slope distance can be converted to a horizontal measurement. Slopes with less than 20-degree grade can be measured with a transit or Abney level.
- The Pythagorean theorem is used. You measure the length of the slope (s), the length of the horizontal level line from the high end of the slope to the low end of the slope (h), to find the slope's vertical elevation (v). The formula is: s squared = h squared + v squared *or* h squared = s squared − v squared.
- Another method is to determine the angle of the slope. The formula is: h divided by s = cos × (the ratio between the side adjacent to the angle, or the horizontal distance when part of a right triangle).
- On gentle slopes, hold the tape horizontal and use a plumb at one or both ends.
- On a steep slope, a method of finding horizontal distance is breaking tape, which is as follows:

  - Measure shorter distances one at a time to allow the tape to be held horizontal at or below chest height.
  - The forward tapeperson places a pin at a tape mark.

- The rear tapeperson moves ahead and holds the tape mark at the pin while the forward tapeperson proceeds.
- This is repeated until the full distance is marked.
- Taping downhill is preferable and easier to taping uphill.

STADIA FORMULA

- Most theodolites have internal crosshairs that, when used with a stadia rod, allow the calculation of slope distance. Magnification is normally 100. Slope distance = 100 × stadia rod vertical intercept.
- If there are angles, then the formula is:

  $D = HI + [\text{Slope distance} \times Sin\ (2V)/2] - M$
  D = elevation difference between survey points
  HI = instrument height above survey point
  V = vertical angle (degrees) at the theodolite
  M = midpoint crosshair reading on stadia rod

STADIA REDUCTION TABLES

Assume stadia slope distance of 100

Slope angle in degrees	Vertical distance (difference in angle)	Horizontal distance	Horizontal elevation
0.0	0.00	100.00	–
0.5	0.87	99.99	–
1.0	1.74	99.97	–
1.5	2.62	99.93	–
2.0	3.49	99.88	0.1
2.5	4.36	99.81	–
3.0	5.23	99.73	0.3
3.5	6.09	99.63	–
4.0	6.96	99.51	0.5
4.5	7.82	99.38	–
5.0	8.68	99.24	0.8
5.5	9.54	99.08	–
6.0	10.40	98.91	1.1
6.5	11.25	98.72	–
7.0	12.10	98.51	1.5
7.5	12.94	98.30	–
8.0	13.78	98.06	1.9
8.5	14.62	97.82	–
9.0	15.45	97.55	2.5
9.5	16.28	97.28	–
10.0	17.10	96.98	3.0
10.5	17.92	96.68	3.3
11.0	18.73	96.36	3.6
11.5	18.73	96.36	4.0
12.0	20.34	95.68	4.3
12.5	21.13	95.32	4.7
13.0	21.92	94.94	5.1
13.5	22.70	94.55	5.5
14.0	23.47	94.15	5.9
14.5	24.24	93.73	6.3
15.0	25.00	93.30	6.7
15.5	25.75	92.86	7.2
16.0	26.50	92.40	7.6
16.5	27.23	91.93	8.1
17.0	27.96	91.45	8.5
17.5	28.68	90.96	9.0
18.0	29.39	90.45	9.5
18.5	30.09	89.93	10.1
19.0	30.78	89.40	10.6

Slope angle in degrees	Vertical distance (difference in angle)	Horizontal distance	Horizontal elevation
19.5	31.47	88.86	11.2
20.0	32.14	88.30	11.7
20.5	32.14	88.30	12.3
21.0	33.46	87.16	12.8
21.5	34.10	86.57	13.4
22.0	34.73	85.97	14.0
22.5	35.36	85.36	14.7
23.0	35.97	84.73	15.3
23.5	36.57	84.10	15.9
24.0	37.16	83.46	16.5
24.5	37.74	82.80	17.2
25.0	38.30	82.14	17.9
25.5	38.86	81.47	18.6
26.0	39.40	80.78	19.2
26.5	39.93	80.09	19.9
27.0	40.45	79.39	20.6
27.5	40.96	78.68	21.3
28.0	41.45	77.96	22.0
28.5	41.93	77.23	22.8
29.0	42.40	76.50	23.5
29.5	42.86	75.75	24.3
30.0	43.30	75.00	25.0
35.0	46.98	67.10	–
40.0	49.24	58.68	–
45.0	50.00	50.00	–
50.0	49.24	41.32	–
55.0	46.98	32.90	–
60.0	43.30	25.00	–

SUBDATUM POINTS

■ Subdatum points are established for mapping purposes. All subdatums are triangulated and/or backshot to the site datum.
■ The elevation of each unit datum is measured with respect to the elevational datum through use of a transit or similar instrument.
■ Once excavation begins, three-dimensional recordation within individual units is done by measuring horizontally from the unit datum and associated reference lines, and vertically from the unit datum with the aid of a line level.

MEASUREMENT AND CONVERSION

Slope angle (°)	Assumed stadia slope distance of 100	
	Vertical distance	Horizontal distance
0.0	0.00	100.0
0.5	0.87	99.99
1.0	1.74	99.97
1.5	2.62	99.93
2.0	3.49	99.88
2.5	4.36	99.81
3.0	5.23	99.73
3.5	6.09	99.63
4.0	6.96	99.51
4.5	7.82	99.38
5.0	8.68	99.24
5.5	9.54	99.08
6.0	10.40	98.91
6.5	11.25	98.72
7.0	12.10	98.51
7.5	12.94	98.30
8.0	13.78	98.06
8.5	14.62	97.82
9.0	15.45	97.55
9.5	16.28	97.28
10.0	17.10	96.98
10.5	17.92	96.68
11.0	18.73	96.36
11.5	19.54	96.03
12.0	20.34	95.68
12.5	21.13	95.32
13.0	21.92	94.94
13.5	22.70	94.55
14.0	23.47	94.15
14.5	24.24	93.73
15.0	25.00	93.30
15.5	25.75	92.86
16.0	26.50	92.40
16.5	27.23	91.93
17.0	27.96	91.45
17.5	28.68	90.96
18.0	29.39	90.45
18.5	30.09	89.93
19.0	30.78	89.40
19.5	31.47	89.86
20.0	32.14	88.30
20.5	32.80	87.74
21.0	33.46	87.16
21.5	34.10	86.57
22.0	34.73	85.97
22.5	35.36	85.36
23.0	35.97	84.73
23.5	36.57	84.10
24.0	37.16	83.46
24.5	37.74	82.80
25.0	38.30	82.14
25.5	38.86	81.47
26.0	39.40	80.78
26.5	39.93	80.09
27.0	40.45	79.39
27.5	40.96	78.68
28.0	41.45	77.96
28.5	41.93	77.23
29.0	42.40	76.60
29.5	42.86	75.75
30.0	43.30	75.00
30.5	43.73	74.24

Table 5.1
Stadia table, mapping scales and areas. (T. J. Glover, Surveying tables, pp. 376–80 from *Pocket Ref*, Second Edition. Littleton, CO: Sequoia Publishing, 1999. Copyright © 1999 by T. J. Glover. Reprinted by permission of Sequoia Publishing, Inc.)

Table 5.1
Continued

Slope angle (°)	Assumed stadia slope distance of 100	
	Vertical distance	Horizontal distance
31.0	44.15	73.47
31.5	44.55	72.70
32.0	44.94	71.92
32.5	45.32	71.13
33.0	45.68	70.34
33.5	46.03	69.54
34.0	46.36	68.73
34.5	46.68	67.92
35.0	46.98	67.10
35.5	47.28	66.28
36.0	47.55	65.45
36.5	47.82	64.62
37.0	48.06	63.78
37.5	48.30	62.94
38.0	48.51	62.10
38.5	48.72	61.25
39.0	48.91	60.40
39.5	49.08	59.54
40.0	49.24	58.68
40.5	49.38	57.82
41.0	49.51	56.96
41.5	49.63	56.09
42.0	49.73	55.23
42.5	49.81	54.36
43.0	49.88	53.49
43.5	49.93	52.62
44.0	49.97	51.74
44.5	49.99	50.87
45.0	50.00	50.00
45.5	49.99	49.13
46.0	49.97	48.26
46.5	49.93	47.38
47.0	49.88	46.51
47.5	49.81	45.64
48.0	49.73	44.77
48.5	49.63	43.91
49.0	49.51	43.04
49.5	49.38	42.18
50.0	49.24	41.32
50.5	49.08	40.46
51.0	48.91	39.60
51.5	48.72	38.75
52.0	48.51	37.90
52.5	48.30	37.06
53.0	48.06	36.22
53.5	47.82	35.38
54.0	47.55	34.55
54.5	47.28	33.72
55.0	46.98	32.90
55.5	46.68	32.08
56.0	46.36	31.27
56.5	46.03	30.46
57.0	45.68	29.66
57.5	45.32	28.87
58.0	44.94	28.08
58.5	44.55	27.30
59.0	44.15	26.53
59.5	43.73	25.76
60.0	43.30	25.00

Horizontal Distance = Slope Distance × Cos^2 (Slope Degrees)
Vertical Distance = (Slope Distance/2) × Sin (2 × Slope Degrees)

MEASUREMENT AND CONVERSION

Mapping scales & areas					**Table 5.1** Continued
Scale 1:X	Feet/ inch	Inch/ mile	Acres/ sq inch	Sq miles/ sq inch
100	8.3	633.60	0.0016	0.000002
120	10.0	528.00	0.0023	0.000004
200	16.7	316.80	0.0064	0.000010
240	20.0	264.00	0.0092	0.000014
250	20.8	253.44	0.0100	0.000016
300	25.0	211.20	0.0143	0.000022
400	33.0	158.40	0.0255	0.000040
480	40.0	132.00	0.0367	0.000057
500	41.7	126.72	0.0399	0.000062
600	50.0	105.60	0.0574	0.000090
1,000	83.3	63.36	0.1594	0.000249
1,200	100.0	52.80	0.2296	0.000359
1,500	125.0	42.24	0.3587	0.000560
2,000	166.7	31.68	0.6377	0.000996
2,400	200.0	26.40	0.9183	0.001435
2,500	208.3	25.34	0.9964	0.001557
3,000	250.0	21.12	1.4348	0.002242
3,600	300.0	17.60	2.0661	0.003228
4,000	333.3	15.84	2.5508	0.003986
4,800	400.0	13.20	3.6731	0.005739
5,000	416.7	12.67	3.9856	0.006227
6,000	500.0	10.56	5.7392	0.008968
7,000	583.3	9.05	7.8117	0.012206
7,200	600.0	8.80	8.2645	0.012913
7,920	660.0	8.00	10.0000	0.015625
8,000	666.7	7.92	10.2030	0.015942
8,400	700.0	7.54	11.2489	0.017576
9,000	750.0	7.04	12.9132	0.020177
9,600	800.0	6.60	14.6924	0.022957
10,000	833.3	6.34	15.9423	0.024910
10,800	900.0	5.87	18.5950	0.029055
12,000	1,000.0	5.28	22.9568	0.035870
13,200	1,100.0	4.80	27.7778	0.043403
14,400	1,200.0	4.40	33.0579	0.051653
15,000	1,250.0	4.22	35.8701	0.056047
15,600	1,300.0	4.06	38.7971	0.060620
15,840	1,320.0	4.00	40.0000	0.062500
16,000	1,333.3	3.96	40.8122	0.063769
16,800	1,400.0	3.77	44.9954	0.070305
18,000	1,500.0	3.52	51.6529	0.080708
19,200	1,600.0	3.30	58.7695	0.091827
20,000	1,666.7	3.17	63.7690	0.099639
20,400	1,700.0	3.11	66.3453	0.103664

SURVEYING WITH A HAND LEVEL

- A hand level (also called Locke level) is a device that allows you to determine a line of equal elevation (a line on a distant object that is of the same elevation as your eyeball). It is a small, simple, hand-held surveying instrument for establishing horizontal lines-of-sight over short distances.
- To use the level, peer through the scope and notice three things: the distant terrain, the level bubble, and the centerline (crosshair). Line up the bubble with the centerline. Anything you see behind that line in the field of view is perfectly level with your eye.
- Common errors are to look right at the highpoint forgetting the bubble, or to forget that your eye is 5 feet above the ground. To be more accurate, lie on your belly so that your eyes are nearly the same elevation as the ground.
- Back sighting usually confirms or conflicts with an original sighting.
- The Abney hand level has a clinometer for measuring the vertical angle and the percent of grade. The clinometer has a reversible graduated arc assembly mounted on one side. The lower side of the arc is graduated in degrees, and the upper side is graduated in percent of slope. The level vial is attached to the axis of rotation at the index arm. When the index arm is set at zero, the clinometer is used like a plain hand level. The bubble is centered by moving the arc, and not the sighting tube as is the case in the plain hand level. Thus, the difference between the line of sight and the level bubble axis can be read in degrees or percent of slope from the position of the index arm of the arc. The 45 degree reflector and the sighting principle with its view of the landscape, bubble, and index line are the same as in the plain hand level.

MEASUREMENT AND CONVERSION

SURVEYING, COMMON ERRORS IN

- Always check for error; take readings twice to reduce the chance of error.
- Instruments should be tested at regular intervals as they can be the source of errors.
- Read both sides of a tape to reduce human error.
- Repeat all number values out loud.

- Recheck a tape's straightness and alignment.
- Recheck an instrument to make sure it is properly centered or sighted, etc.
- Carry out independent checks.
- Systematically record all detail.
- Note that forgetting a backsight is a common error.

TAPE MEASUREMENTS

- At the beginning of field season, measuring tapes should be checked for accuracy. Weather/temperature can affect them.
- If a measuring tape is not as long as the distance to be measure, it must be used to measure to intermediate points which are in alignment. Intermediate points can be marked with pins or flags.
- Generally, one person holds the reel end of the tape over the point from which the measurements are to be taken and the other person holds the zero end of the tape over the object. The person holding the reel calls out the measurement.
- All measurements should be called out, checked, and rechecked. Then record!
- Many vertical and horizontal measurements are necessary because most units and features are uneven. In relation to a unit, layer, feature, or artifact, these include the opening measurement of the top of the layer, the closing elevation (the bottom measurement), and measurement of the sides.
- It is important that the horizontal/lateral extent of a feature is accurately measured.

TAPING, COMMON ERRORS IN

Many things may affect the tape – temperature, a slope, too loose or taut tension, sagging, poor alignment, tape not horizontal, improper plumbing, faulty marking, or incorrect reading or interpretation.

Temperature other than standard

- Steel tapes are standardized at 68°F (20°C).
- A temperature higher or lower will change the length of the tape.

MEASUREMENT AND CONVERSION

- Coefficient of thermal expansion for steel:

  0.0000065 per unit length per °F
  0.0000116 per unit length per °C

- Temperature of the tape can be quite different from the air temperature measured.
- This error can be accounted for by correcting the value of measured lengths.

Tension other than standard

- If tension is greater than standard the tape will stretch.
- If less than standard tension is applied the tape will be shorter than standard. Modulus of Elasticity for steel:

  $29,000,000$ lb/in^2
  $2,000,000$ kg/cm^2

- This error can be accounted for by correcting the value of measured lengths.

Sag

- A steel tape not supported along its entire length will sag.
- The tape length stays the same, so the sag reduces the horizontal distance between the end graduations of the tape.
- Sag may be reduced by increasing the tension, but not eliminated.
- This error can be accounted for by correcting the value of measured lengths.

Poor alignment

- This error occurs when one end of the tape is off-line or there is an obstruction in-line.
- The actual distance will be less than the measured distance.
- These errors may be reduced by carefully following correct field procedures.
- This error can be accounted for by correcting the value of measured lengths.

Tape not horizontal

- This error occurs when the tape is inclined in a vertical plane.
- The actual distance will be less than the measured distance.
- These errors may be reduced by using a hand level or by differential leveling to account for differences in elevation.
- This error can be accounted for by correcting the value of measured lengths.

Improper plumbing

- This error is random in that it may make the measured distance too long or too short.
- Touching the plumb bob on the ground or steadying it with one foot can decrease the swinging motion.
- Practice in plumbing will reduce errors.
- This error cannot be accounted for by correcting the value of measured lengths.

Incorrect reading or interpolation

- This error is random as the result of incorrect interpolation while reading the tape.
- Careful reading and using a small scale to determine the last figure will reduce errors.
- This error cannot be accounted for by correcting the value of measured lengths.

TAPING PROCEDURES

Taping crew

Head/forward tapeperson
- Leads with zero end of tape, heading directly toward desired point.
- Sets chaining pins or keel marks when at end of tape or when "breaking tape."
- Reads graduations on tape to determine fractions of a foot.
- Applies correct tension as suggested by tape manufacturer.
- Ten pounds on a flat tape suspended along its length.
- Twenty pounds suspended (a suspended tape needs more pull due to sag from effect of gravity).
- Records distances in survey notebook.

Rear tapeperson

- Follows with 100-ft-end of tape, notifying first person when end is being reached.
- Maintains alignment by guiding forward tapeperson towards desired point.
- Maintains level by eyeballing or by using hand level or other instrument.
- Picks up chaining pins and notes total full tape lengths measured.

THEODOLITE USE

- A theodolite is somewhat more accurate than a dumpy level. Its main advantage is that it can take readings above and below the instrument by moving the scope; the dumpy level only reads on the horizontal line of collimation.
- Set up the theodolite's tripod with the legs as wide as possible; level the instrument.
- The horizontal scale should be adjusted to read "0."
- Take readings for levels along the center line, for distance from the stadia, and also the horizontal bearing. The vertical angle is also needed, which introduces a need for trigonometry. This is important as it is equivalent to the dumpy level's line of collimation. You can figure the axis level by knowing the theodolite's level, then measure and add the height from that to the axis of the scope.
- You can use a trigonometric formula or tacheometric tables. The formula involves V, the difference between the observed vertical angle and the horizontal (90 degrees), the three staff readings (S1, S2 the stadii, h on the center line). Distance and height can now be figured:

> distance = 100 to the eighth power cos squared V
> height = 100 to the eighth power cos V sin V

- To establish the reduced level (ground or spot level) the center line reading h is used: R/L = Axis+H−h or R/L = Axis+(H−h), or R/L = Axis−(h+H)

MEASUREMENT AND CONVERSION

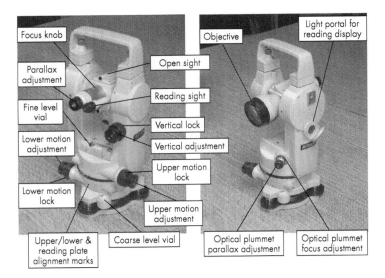

Figure 5.8 Parts of a Theodolite. (Theodolite microscope parts, from www.surv.ufl.edu/courses/wwwusers/sur2101fall04/Lab3 Horizontal Angles.pdf. Reprinted with permission of The Geomatics Program, University of Florida)

—— THEODOLITE, USE OF TO SET UP A GRID ——

- Set up the theodolite directly over the datum, using a plumb bob.
- Align north, zero degrees, to site north, and then turn the machine 90 degrees so it faces east.
- Stretch a tape from this point along the easterly line and have someone stand at each 10-meter point with a ranging rod or level staff.
- Check that each grid point is aligned with your 90-degree east-facing line.
- Turn back to north, zero, and stretch the tape in that direction and repeat the procedure.
- Move the theodolite over the next grid point east of the datum and align it 90 degrees along the east line. Have someone with a ranging rod or level staff on the line. Then turn the machine to zero degrees north to set out your next line of grid points. Repeat for each line.
- Double-check the distances on the diagonal with a tape.

NOTES:

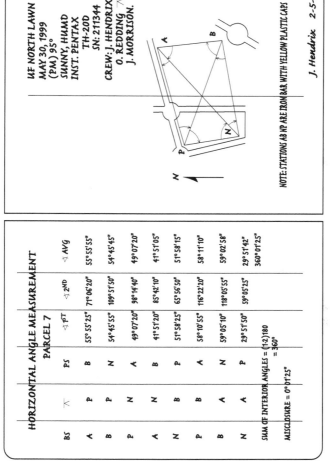

HORIZONTAL ANGLE MEASUREMENT
PARCEL 7

BS	⋋	FS	⊲ 1ST	⊲ 2ND	⊲ AVG
A	P	B	55°55'25"	71°06'20"	55°55'55"
B	P	N	54°45'55"	109°51'50"	54°45'45"
P	N	A	49°07'20"	98°14'40"	49°07'20"
A	N	B	41°51'20"	85°42'10"	41°51'05"
N	B	P	51°58'25"	65°56'50"	51°58'15"
P	B	A	58°10'55"	116°22'20"	58°11'10"
B	A	N	59°05'10"	118°05'55"	59°02'58"
N	A	P	29°51'50"	59°05'25"	29°51'42"

SUM OF INTERIOR ANGLES = (n-2)180
= 360°
360°01'25"

MISCLOSURE = 0°01'25"

UF NORTH LAWN
MAY 30, 1999
(PM) 95°
SUNNY, HUMID
INST. PENTAX
TH-20D
SN: 211344
CREW: J. HENDRIX. N
O. REDDING
J. MORRISON.

NOTE: STATIONS AB N P ARE IRON BAR WITH YELLOW PLASTIC CAPS

J. Hendrix 2-5-99

Figure 5.9 Notes from a Theodolite. (Notebook notation from Theodolite, from www.surv.ufl.edu/courses/wwwusers/sur2101fall04/Lab3 Horizontal Angles.pdf. Reprinted with permission of The Geomatics Program, University of Florida)

THREE-POINT PROBLEM

- A three-point problem requires three points, of known location and elevation, which lie *on the same plane.* The accuracy of the method requires that great care be taken to ensure that they lie on the same plane. The emphasis on plane underlines the assumption that the surface is planar, that is, that it is not folded. This means that the technique should only be applied over short distances, unless the major geological structures are clearly planar. This is also used in surveying to determine the strike/bearing of a topographic surface, etc. when the location and elevation of three points on the surface are known.

- The elevation and location of points A, B, and C are known. The elevation of point B is between the elevations of points A (the highest point) and C (the lowest point), then the strike/bearing of the plane defined by ABC is determined by locating point D, on the line between A and C, and then drawing a strike/bearing line between B and D. Since this is defined as the bearing of a horizontal line on the plane of ABC, the elevations of point B and D must be the same. The exact location of point D can be calculated from the following equation:

  length CD = length AC × BC elevation difference divided by AC elevation difference

- Note that the true dip must always be at a right angle to the strike/bearing. The value of the true dip can be calculated with this equation:

  Dip angle (in degrees) = Arc tan ([elev D–C] divided by length true dip line)

TOTAL STATION USE

There are various brands and models; these are general guidelines.

- A total station is a combination electronic transit and electronic distance measuring device (EDM). With this device, as with a transit and tape, one may determine angles and distances from

388

the instrument to points to be surveyed. With the aid of trigonometry, the angles and distances may be used to calculate the actual positions (x, y, and z, or northing, easting, and elevation) of surveyed points in absolute terms. Many total stations also include data recorders. The raw data (angles and distances) and/or the coordinates of points sighted are recorded, along with some additional information (usually codes to aid in relating the coordinates to the points surveyed). The data thus recorded can be directly downloaded to a computer at a later time. The use of a data recorder further reduces the potential for error and eliminates the need for a person to record the data in the field.

■ The total station is mounted on a tripod and leveled before use. Meanwhile, the prism is mounted on a pole of known height; the mounting bracket includes aids for aiming the instrument. The prism is mounted so that its reflection point is aligned with the center of the pole on which it has been mounted. Although the tip of the pole is placed on the point to be surveyed, the instrument must be aimed at the prism, so it will calculate the position of the prism, not the point to be surveyed. Since the prism is directly above the tip, the height of the pole may be subtracted to determine the location of the point. That may be done automatically. (The pole must be held upright, and a bubble level is attached to give the worker holding the pole a check.)

■ When the instrument is set up and turned on, it sets itself to be pointing to zero degrees (north) when power is first supplied. The user must then re-set the instrument to zero degrees when it is actually pointing north. When the battery dies, the instrument must be re-set for zero degrees.

Setting up the total station

Leveling the instrument

■ Center the instrument above the datum point using the optical plumb bob, moving two legs of the tripod to maneuver the total station.

■ Press the tripod feet into ground.

■ Center the bull's eye level, first using tripod leg adjustments, then using the three knuckle screws for finer adjustment. After centering the bull's eye, center the line level, first using two knuckle screws concurrently; then turn the total station 90 degrees, and use the third knuckle screw to finally center the line level.

Preparing instrument
- Connect the data collector to the total station.
- Turn on the total station (with data collector off).
- Break plane by moving the scope up and down.
- Measure the height of the instrument with tape measure, to center mark on side of scope.
- Prepare the data collector.

Putting total station away

- Replace the lens cap on the total station and prism pole.
- Lock the vertical and horizontal axes by gently snugging the friction brakes.
- Place the total station in the carrying case so that the horizontal and vertical axis controls are facing down and the telescope eyepiece is up.
- Securely fasten the outer latches of the case.

TRANSFERRING HEIGHT FROM BENCH MARK TO TEMPORARY BENCH MARK (UK)

- Bench marks are marked on Ordnance Survey maps. If you have one on your site, you can use it as your site bench mark. Otherwise, you will have to transfer an absolute height above sea level to a temporary bench mark on your site. The temporary bench mark should be securely marked.
- Set up a level so you can see the bench mark. (If you are lucky, you will be able to transfer it directly to your site.)
- Take a backsight measurement to the staff, with its base resting on the bench mark.
- Move the staff as far toward the site as possible and take a foresight measurement.
- Keeping the staff in the same place, move the machine as far toward the site as possible and take another backsight.
- If you can see the new temporary bench mark, you can move on to the next step. If not, you must keep repeating the above steps until you can.
- Place the staff on the new temporary bench mark and take a foresight. Add your first backsight to the height of the bench mark. Subtract the next foresight from this figure. Add the next

backsight. If this was the final measurement you took before the foresight to the temporary bench mark, you can move on to the next step. If not, once repeat the subtraction of the next foresight and next backsight until you get to that measurement.

■ Subtract your final foresight. This is the height above sea level of your temporary bench mark.

TRANSIT, THEODOLITE, DUMPY LEVEL, SETTING UP OF

■ Place the instrument on the ground near or on the point from which measurements are to be taken.
■ Spread the legs and extend them so they are level.
■ Gently pick up the instrument without disturbing the relative position of the legs and scope.
■ Set up the plumb bob from the base of the instrument. Position the plumb bob 0.30 m over the point.
■ Level the scope by gently adjusting the legs, trying not to change the position of the plumb bob.
■ Push each leg firmly into the ground while watching the plumb bob so it stays over the point.
■ Adjust the plumb bob to hang 0.01 m over the point.
■ Additional fine leveling is needed once the instrument is in position. This is done by turning knobs on the instrument itself.

TRANSIT-STADIA TRAVERSE MEASUREMENT

■ The transit-stadia method is often used to measure distances. One person looks through the telescope of a transit or theodolite and reads the stadia crosshairs on the leveling rod.
■ When the stadia rod is positioned at different distances, different graduations are focused on and observed in the line of sight. The graduations that intercept the stadia measure the distance from the rod. The crosshairs read one-hundredth of the distance, which is calculated with the formula:

$$distance = 100 \times stadia\ interval$$

- The traverse is run from an established mark. The transit is set up over the point and sighted to another known point. You note the direction, take the angle, and measure the distance.
- This is repeated from the known point to all the points on the site whose locations are desired.
- The angles and distances are then plotted to make up a traverse. The coordinates make forced closures between the points. The traverse is complete when the points are correctly located and interrelated.
- The step-by-step below is for an open traverse, when only one end point of the traverse has a fixed or known horizontal location. A closed traverse is when both ends of the traverse are known points or it starts at known point and loops around to end at the same point.

Step-by-step:
- Establish a traverse point A.
- Choose a traverse point B and set the instrument up over this point and level it.
- Determine the magnetic bearing of line BA. Free the compass needle on the instrument and allow it to settle on north, then adjust the horizontal scale of the instrument so that "0" is aligned with the compass needle.
- Turn the instrument to sight on point A and read the angle on the horizontal scale. This is the azimuth of line BA relative to true north. (With a theodolite with no mounted compass, you will have to use a compass and stadia rod.)
- Sight the instrument on point A with the horizontal scale set to "0."
- Turn the instrument clockwise (right) till you can sight the point selected to be C.
- Read the angle on the horizontal scale.
- Set up the instrument over point C and sight back to point B with the horizontal scale set to "0." Turn the angle to the right until you sight point D and read the measured angle.
- Record the magnetic bearing for line CB and measure the distance between the points.
- Occupy point D and determine the bearing for line DC.
- The azimuth for lines CB and DC can be calculated if you know the bearing/azimuth of line BA. This can be used as a cross-check with the magnetic bearings/azimuths taken at each traverse point.

MEASUREMENT AND CONVERSION

- A traverse consists of a series of lines, whose lengths and directions are measured, connecting points whose positions are to be determined. The route of the traverse line can be adjusted for obstacles such as rough or timbered terrain, swampy land, buildings, and areas of heavy traffic.

- Traversing is normally associated with the field work of measuring angles and distances between points on the ground. Closed traverses provide the primary method used in checking surveying fieldwork. Almost all site surveying starts with either an open or closed traverse.

- A traverse is essentially a series of established stations tied together by distances and angles. They may be open (route survey) or closed (geometric figures).

- An open traverse begins at a point of known position and ends at a station whose relative position is unknown. This type of traverse is frequently used for preliminary surveys for highways. A closed traverse begins and ends at the same point whose position is known.

- An example of this type of traverse is a perimeter survey of a tract of land.

- They are used as control surveys to locate topographic detail for the preparation of plans, to lay out or locate fieldwork, and for the collection of measurements needed for the determination of fieldwork.

- An open traverse originates at a starting station, proceeds to its destination, and ends at a station with an unknown relative position. The open traverse is the least desirable traverse type, because it does not provide the opportunity for checking the accuracy of the fieldwork. All measurements must be carefully collected, and every procedure for checking position and direction must be used. Therefore, the planning of a traverse should always provide for closure of the traverse.

- A closed traverse either begins and ends on the same point or begins and ends at points with previously determined (and verified) coordinates. In both cases, the angles can be closed and closure accuracy can be mathematically determined.

- A traverse that starts at a given point, proceeds to its destination, and returns to the starting point without crossing itself in the process is referred to as a loop traverse. Surveyors use this type of traverse to provide control if there is little existing control in the area and only the relative position of the points is required. While the loop traverse provides some check of the fieldwork and computations, it does not ensure the detection of all the systematic errors that may occur in a survey.

- A traverse that is closed on a second known point begins at a point of known coordinates, moves through the required point(s), and terminates at a second point of known coordinates. Surveyors prefer this type of traverse because it provides a check on the fieldwork, computations, and starting data. It also provides a basis for comparing data to determine the overall accuracy of the work.

- In a traverse, three stations are considered to be of immediate significance. These stations are the rear, the occupied, and the forward. The rear station is the station that the surveyors who are performing the traverse have just moved from, or it is a point to which the azimuth is known. The occupied station is the station at which the party is located and over which the instrument is set. The forward station is the immediate destination of the party or the next station in succession.

- At each point, the length and direction from the previous initial point are measured and a stake or rod driven into the ground to indicate the point's position.

- Always measure horizontal angles at the occupied station by sighting the instrument at the rear station and measuring the clockwise angles to the forward station. Make instrument observations to the clearest and most defined and repeatable point of the target that marks the rear and forward stations. Measurements are repeated according to the required specifications.

- Measure the distance in a straight line between the occupied and the forward stations. Measurements are repeated according to the required specifications.

- Select sites for traverse stations as the traverse progresses. Locate the stations in such a way that at any one station both the rear and forward stations are visible. The number of stations in a traverse should be kept to a minimum to reduce the accumulation of instrument errors and the amount of computing required. Short traverse legs (sections) require the establishment and use of a greater number of stations and may cause excessive errors in the azimuth. Small errors in centering the instrument, in station-marking equipment, and in instrument pointings are magnified and absorbed in the azimuth closure as errors in angle measurement.

- The transit and instrument person are generally one station behind the other members of the surveying team. After the backsight of the first station is taken and recorded, the first angle is measured and recorded. While that is happening, others measure by tape the distance between stations and the process is repeated until the traverse is closed.
- After the traverse has been established, then the location of features can be determined by offsets or radial measurement.

TRIANGULATION

- Triangulation consists of a series of connected triangles which adjoin or overlap each other, angles being measured from determined fixed stations. Triangulation reduces the number of measures that need to be taped and for this reason is often a preferred method of survey. A known baseline measurement is required, i.e. if one side and two angles of any triangle are known, the other calculations such as lengths of the other two sides, can be determined. If the length of three sides of a triangle are known and the angles are known, the vertex of each triangle will then be a point related to the baseline and therefore related to the survey site as a whole.
- A system of triangles usually affords superior horizontal control. All of the angles and at least one side (the base) of the triangulation system are measured. Though several arrangements can be used, one of the best is the quadrangle or a chain of quadrangles. Each quadrangle, with its four sides and two diagonals, provides eight angles that are measured. To be geometrically consistent, the angles must satisfy three so-called angle equations and one side equation. That is to say the three angles of each triangle, which add to 180 degrees, must be of such sizes that computation through any set of adjacent triangles within the quadrangles will give the same values for any side. Ideally, the quadrangles should be parallelograms. If the system is connected with previously determined stations, the new system must fit the established measurements.
- Trigonometric leveling often is necessary where accurate elevations are not available or when the elevations of inaccessible points must be determined. From two points of known position and elevation, the horizontal position of the unknown point is

found by triangulation, and the vertical angles from the known points are measured. The differences in elevation from each of the known points to the unknown point can be computed trigonometrically.

- In archaeology, a site is measured with a series of triangles with angles of 30 to 120 degrees. A traverse is set up on level ground with the measurement of two points and the distance between them – the first side of the triangle.

Triangulation to determine an object's horizontal position

- First record the diameter/length/height/width of the object and make notes about at which point(s) on its surface the measurements were taken.
- Then measure from stake/spike/nail/pin 1 (datum or subdatum point) to the object and then stake/spike/nail/pin 2 (datum or subdatum point) to the object. (If the artifact or feature is below the control points, the line will have to be plumbed.) The zero end of the tape is on the stake/spike/nail/pin. Be sure to note the corner from which each measurement is taken, along with the measurement.

Triangulation to create a site plan

- A taped line is chosen which provides easy access to the greatest number of natural and cultural features to be included in the plan.
- Reference points are established along the taped line.
- The features are measured using two reference points for triangulation.

Triangulation to set up a grid (with 1 m × 1 m squares)

- (If each side of the square is 1 m and the potential sides are a, b, c, d, the formula would be the square root of $a \times a + b \times b$ = hypotenuse (diagonal) of the square. The hypotenuse of a 1-meter square is 1.414 meters, based on the Pythagorean Theorem.)
- Set the baseline and intervals along it.
- Person #1 stands at one of the two measured stakes along the baseline, holding one end of the tape measure.
- Person #2 stands at the second of the two measured stakes along the baseline, holding one end of a second tape measure.

MEASUREMENT AND CONVERSION

- Person #3 extends the other end of person #1's tape measure to 1.4 meters and person #2's tape to 1 meter.
- Person #3 takes the two ends of the tape measures and moves them from side to side until the two points on the tapes meet exactly. Person #4 can put in the stake where they intersect. This provides the third side of a 1 m × 1 m square.
- Reversing the two tapes, person #3 repeats the intersection to get the fourth corner of the square.
- Each of the sides is measured to make sure it is 1 meter.

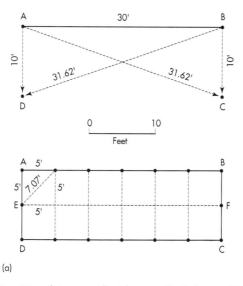

Figure 5.10a Triangulating a small grid system. (R. M. Stewart, Figure 6.50: Triangulating a small grid system, p. 150 from *Archaeology Basic Field Methods*. Dubuque, Iowa: Kendall/Hunt, 2002. Copyright © 2002 by Kendall/Hunt Publishing Company. Reprinted by permission of the publisher)

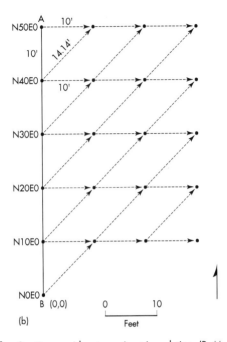

Figure 5.10b Creating a grid system using triangulation. (R. M. Stewart, Figure 6.51: Another method for creating a grid system using triangulation, p. 151 from *Archaeology Basic Field Methods*. Dubuque, Iowa: Kendall/Hunt, 2002. Copyright © 2002 by Kendall/Hunt Publishing Company. Reprinted by permission of the publisher)

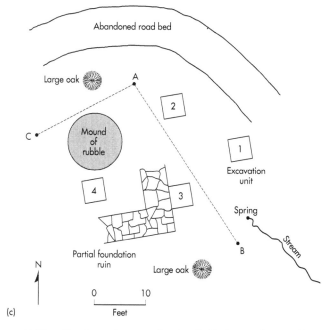

Figure 5.10c Creating a plan map of a site. (R. M. Stewart, Figure 6.52: Creating a plan map of a site area, p. 151 from *Archaeology Basic Field Methods*. Dubuque, Iowa: Kendall/Hunt, 2002. Copyright © 2002 by Kendall/Hunt Publishing Company. Reprinted by permission of the publisher)

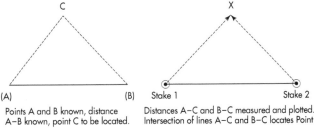

(A) Points A and B known, distance A–B known, point C to be located.

(B) Distances A–C and B–C measured and plotted. Intersection of lines A–C and B–C locates Point C.

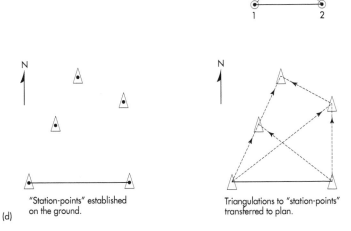

(d) "Station-points" established on the ground.

Triangulations to "station-points" transferred to plan.

Figure 5.10d Preparing a triangulation grid. (Philip C. Hammond, Preparing triangulation grid, from *Archaeological Techniques for Amateurs*. New York: Van Nostrand, 1963. Copyright © 1963 by Philip C. Hammond. Reprinted by permission of the author)

UTM GRID LOCATION OF ARCHAEOLOGICAL SITE, DETERMINING

The simplest method of determining a UTM reference is based on drawing part of the UTM grid on the map, and measuring from the grid lines to the point. It requires the following:

a flat work surface on which the map may be spread out in full
a straightedge (ordinary rulers may not be accurate enough) long
enough to reach completely across the map – generally 28″ to 36″
a very sharp pencil and a worksheet
a UTM coordinate counter

To measure each point, follow these steps:

1. Draw a line from the top of the map to the bottom (north to south), connecting the UTM ticks of the same value directly west of the point, that is the ticks with the highest easting value west of the point.
2. Draw a line from the left to the right side of the map (west to east), connecting the grid ticks of the same value directly south of the point, that is the ticks with the highest northing value south of the point. This line will intersect the north–south line somewhere to the southwest of the point.
3. Record the zone number on a worksheet. This number appears in the lower left corner of the map.
4. Record on a worksheet the numbers given by the map ticks through which the lines have been drawn. These are the first three digits of the easting value and the first four digits of the northing value.
5. Locate the scale on the coordinate counter matching that of the map, e.g. 1:24,000.
6. Align the counter on the map (check the alignment to be sure that it is precise) so that:

    the side of the scale that reads from right to left lies along the east–west line;
    the side of the scale that reads from left to right passes directly through the point.

7. Read the coordinate counter scales, right to left for the easting and upward for the northing to get a measured value in three decimal places. In each case, enter the measured value on the worksheet after the number recorded in step 4.
8. Check the readings – are all figures in the correct decimal place? The easting will have six digits and the northing seven.
9. Check the figures for accuracy by remeasuring.
10. Be sure the following are given: zone number, easting, and northing (Z,E,N).

VERTICAL ANGLE MEASUREMENT

- Level the plane table as precisely as possible and set the tripod firmly.
- Record the vertical distance from the station marker to the horizontal axis of the alidade (HI) and enter the height of the station signal being sighted (HF).
- Place the alidade in the center of the plane table.
- Align the telescope on the station and bring the horizontal crosshair onto the top of the signal. Make the final adjustment by turning the tangent screw clockwise. Check to be sure that the crosshair rather than a stadia hair has been used in the sighting. Do not touch the plane table or walk around it until the measurement is finished.
- Read the vertical-angle Vernier with the help of a magnifying glass and estimate the reading to the nearest half or quarter minute if possible; record the measurement.
- Level the telescope with a clockwise turn of the tangent screw.
- Read the vertical-angle Vernier and record the reading, then reverse the striding level, center the bubble by turning the tangent screw, and take a second reading. The average of the two readings compensates for an unadjusted striding level.
- Repeat after shifting the Vernier a few degrees by turning the Vernier tangent screw.
- Subtract each set of readings and repeat if the results do not agree within acceptable limits. The difference is computed from the trigonometric formula: vertical distance = horizontal distance × tangent of vertical angle.

VERTICAL DISTANCE MEASUREMENT

- The difference in elevation between two points is the vertical distance between them. Elevation is the distance above or below the datum point. Vertical distance may be measured by plumbing the line, by using an Abney hand level, transit, theodolite, dumpy level, or plane table.
- **Abney level**: sight an object through the telescope and move the level bubble to the center position. A control screw changes the Vernier and bubble level. When the bubble level is bisected by the crosshair, the angle can be read on the vertical arc. This

angle is equal to the angle of the line of sight with the horizontal. The number on the scale is the correct reading. For leveling, the Vernier is set to "0" and when the bubble is horizontal, the leveling rod can be read.

- **Leveling rod**: A leveling rod is graduated rod used in measuring the vertical distance between a point on the ground and the line of sight of a surveyor's level.

- The difference in elevation between two points is determined by holding the bottom of a leveling rod at the point of desired measurement.

- The optical measuring instrument is set up on a point of known elevation and its telescope is focused until the leveling rod is clearly seen to be bisected by the horizontal crosshair of the telescope.

- The reading is the distance between the bottom of the leveling rod and the telescope line of sight. The instrument height has to be measured and subtracted from the reading to get the difference in elevation. From this the elevation of the line of sight has to be subtracted to get the vertical distance.

Calculating vertical distance with a clinometer

- Open the lid and sighting arm about 45 degrees, but hold the compass so that the box is on edge and the clinometer is upright. The sighting tip should be about one foot from the eye.

- Move the compass until the point to be sighted is visible through the window in the lid and coincides with the axial line and the sighting tip.

- Holding the compass in this position, rotate the clinometer by the lever on the base of the compass box until the tube bubble, as observed in the mirror, is centered.

- Recheck the alignment, and bring the compass down in order to read the angle indicated by the vertical angle index. Record it at once and repeat the entire procedure as a check.

6

Planning Help

This chapter offers some guidelines for planning and designing archaeological fieldwork projects and for organizing administrative matters. Planning is extremely important; part of this is research design and choosing sampling techniques, which are touched on lightly here but are not really within the scope of this book. This chapter provides some lists that may be helpful to archaeologists heading out into the field.

Fieldwork manuals and textbooks go into pre-excavation planning in more detail. Before an excavation is physically undertaken, much reading must be done. An extensive review of written references, maps, illustrations, and reports is particularly important. Research design for the archaeologist involves defining the problems that need to be solved and determining the questions that need to be answered. Legal restrictions and implications have to be studied and these vary from place to place, state to state, and country to country. The level of finance available will determine the number of staff who can be employed and this then determines the number of volunteers needed. Finally, permit applications will need to be made, and the site will need to be surveyed.

CONTENTS

———— ADMINISTRATIVE MATTERS ————

budget (payroll, supplies)
curation (conservation, storage, transport)
media
other (food, transportation, medical, housing)
permits, contracts, and forms
pre-excavation research
staffing (paid, volunteer, specialists)
survey

———— BUDGET, SAMPLE ————

communications (computers, email, mail, etc.)
conservation and storage
laboratory, cataloging, and analysis
logistical and related field costs, including actual data collection;
supplies, tools, and equipment
report preparation and delivery, including illustrations
salaries for labor in the field
start-up, research design, preparation (including permits, applications)
travel and lodging
use of specialists and outside analysis

PLANNING HELP

DAILY SCHEDULE

(generic, to be fashioned as needed)

breakfast	transport
break	artifact processing
lunch	artifact conservation
dinner	drawing
fieldwork	database entry
recordation	report writing
packing	

DIG PREPARATION

Archaeological fieldwork is not the romantic treasure hunt some-times seen in the movies. On the contrary, archaeology is a blend of scientific disciplines requiring methodological attention to pro-cedure and detail. Most expeditions are staffed by skilled individuals with specialized knowledge. You can learn a great deal from the experienced excavators and specialists you will be working with, and as part of an expedition you will have an opportunity to con-tribute personally to the recovery and preservation of our past.

Before an excavation starts, many countries require that foreign workers receive permission and clearance, which is usually gained through an antiquities services government agency. Unless the option is clearly stated, appearing at a site unannounced would be personally irresponsible and might place the project director in an uncomfortable situation. Once advance contact has been established with a representative of the expedition team, find out what equip-ment is necessary, what clothes are the most sensible for work and leisure time, the general schedule of operations, and what sightseeing opportunities will be available.

Read about the local culture and climate, and plan your pack-ing accordingly. It is strongly recommended to pack as lightly as possible, since space is often limited and transportation may be less than efficient. As with most travel, you must be able to carry your own luggage. A good test is to limit yourself to what you can com-fortably carry for a brisk quarter-mile walk.

Check into necessary vaccinations and have thorough physical and dental examinations. Identify your need for health and travel insurance. Some expeditions provide the former; you should know, however, what facilities will be available in the event that you require medical treatment.

Bring a small medical kit with an assortment of bandages, disinfectants, and ointments. Additional items – on any experienced traveler's list – include an alarm clock, flashlight and extra batteries, sunglasses, scarf or work hat, sunscreen, a regional guidebook, reading material, notebooks, pens and pencils, measuring tape marked in inches and centimeters, and a water bottle. Of course, this is a general checklist; check with your project director to see if more specific equipment will be needed.

The success of an archaeological expedition depends, to a great extent, on the excavation team. Organization is a key factor in the smooth management of the work schedule, and the field director must be able to depend upon a responsive and responsible staff. If you have never worked on an excavation before, do some homework and keep a flexible and cooperative attitude. The former will ensure that you will have some familiarity with professional archaeology, the material under investigation, the local culture, and the climate. The latter will certainly make you a better worker and a more pleasant person to live with under what can sometimes be less-than-ideal circumstances. You, personally, will find the experience a great deal richer for your efforts.

The director and supervisors will appreciate your questions and your attention to detail and procedure, and there are a number of "dig life" lessons to learn by word of mouth from others who have had the experience. If you find that you have time on your hands and wish to make the most of the season, staff members are usually more than willing to give informal instruction in the different skills required on an expedition (drafting, recording, etc.).

Try to set up a personal schedule outside of work hours, which will enable you maintain a comfortable working/sleeping/leisure schedule, as well as a stock of clean clothes. Take the opportunity to keep a daily journal describing the work you are doing, camp life, your impressions of the local culture, etc. Months or years later, you will be able to recall the sense of the excavation.

EXCAVATION CREW

field director	conservator
principal investigator	dating specialist
administrative assistant	draftsperson/cartographer
site supervisor(s)	ethnobotanist/palynologist
foreman or crew chief	geologist/geoarchaeologist
field technicians	laboratory staff
unit supervisors	laboratory supervisor
staff members	other specialists
volunteers	photographer
architect	small-finds specialist
artifact analyst	support crew (cook, etc.)
cataloger	surveyor
computer specialist	zooarchaeologist

GROUND-SEARCH SURVEY CONSIDERATIONS

- Consider the suitability of the proposed methods in solving problems and answering questions.
- Consider the expense and manageability of the proposed methods.
- Prepare a list of objectives for the ground-search survey and a proposed time schedule.
- Study maps of the area, e.g. stratigraphic, topographic, geological, and economic.
- Study photographs and drawings of the site.
- Read any publications about the area, especially regarding previous studies of the site or its environs.
- Research ethnographic data, especially any oral traditions, demography, linguistics, and cultural activities.
- Do a complete literature search (archives, published archaeological reports, contract archaeology reports, historic documents, museum collections).
- File for the proper permits before the survey is undertaken.
- Investigate the type of vegetation and its growth patterns, the source of a water supply, the location of the site for defense purposes, landforms and features, climate, etc., especially in relation to the topography and geology of the site.

PLANNING HELP

- Look at study collections for the area and carry out comparisons with related sites.
- Take overall and panoramic photos.
- Besides looking for artifacts on the ground, the ground-search survey might also collect flora and fauna samples as well as soil samples.

— INDICATORS OF ARCHAEOLOGICAL SITES —

conspicuous surface features, earthworks, or ruins
literature search (site files, journal articles, contract reports)
soil discolorations
surface finds of artifacts, bones, etc.
vegetational cover, especially lush areas where subsoil has been disturbed or nitrogen content of soil is greater *or* stunted vegetation caused by artifact-filled alkaline soil

—————— LANDLORD/PROPERTY —————— OWNER QUESTIONNAIRE

Survey organization _____ Address _____ Telephone, fax, email _____

Please check the appropriate line, sign below, and return in the enclosed self-addressed, stamped envelope.

_____ I grant permission to the survey organization to conduct an archaeological survey on my property.

_____ Please talk to me personally before conducting an archaeological survey on my property. Please contact me at _____.

_____ I am aware that this site is archaeologically significant and would like to discuss this with the survey organization's archaeologist.

Signature _____

Name _____

Address _____

Telephone, fax, email _____

federal government (US Bureau of Land Management, US Forest
   Service)
landowner and/or tenant
local government
Native American groups in the area or which claim ancestry to the
   site
state government

PLACEMENT OF DUMP/SIFTING AREA

- The position of the sifting area/dump depends on the terrain and
  proximity to the excavation area. It must be an area that will
  never be excavated. It would be a waste to dump matrix and
  then have to move it prior to using it for backfill.
- The position of the sifting area/dump should not interfere with
  access to the site or units. Those doing the sifting should not
  have to cross areas being excavated.
- The dump must be far enough away from excavation so that
  the screened matrix will not fall back into units or collapse the
  edge of excavation. Materials should not be piled closer than 2
  feet from the edge of an open excavation. Also, the dump should
  be far enough away so that rain does not carry the material back
  into the excavated units.
- The sifting area/dump should not be on a slope since this would
  mean material would have to be carried uphill.
- The sifting area/dump should be far enough from the datum point
  and datum line so as to not interfere with measurements.
- However, if the material is to be used for backfill, it must be
  close enough to the excavation so that this may be carried out
  reasonably well upon completion of the excavation.
- Topsoil and humus should be kept separate if they are to be put
  back on top when the site is restored.
- If possible, place plastic sheeting in the dump area(s) to separate
  excavated matrix from the surface.

PLANNING HELP

410

RESEARCH DESIGN

- Identify goals, problems, and/or issues – outline current knowledge, basic assumptions, and the implications of previous research.
- Decide areas of interest and both general and specific problems to be worked on as the basis for specific hypotheses.
- Develop specific hypotheses (research questions) to be tested in relation to the goals, problems, issues.
- Determine the types of data you will need to complete the research design.
- Determine how you will find the data, the standards of the data required, and how to maintain the quality of the data.
- Determine what survey plans are required and at what scale.
- Develop the specific operating procedures and schedule for fieldwork (survey, excavation, sampling) and lab work up to completion of the final report (i.e. scope or plan of work).
- Create a budget for the project.
- Collect data.
- Analyze collected data with methods appropriate to the project's goals, problems, issues, and hypotheses.
- Address the project's goals with analyzed and evaluated data.
- Disseminate information and plan for the curation and storage of data.

SURVEY PREPARATION

- Study the site before starting work. Identify important features, possible problems, and datums that may be needed.
- Do the background research involving literature review, local informants, historical and ethnohistorical sources, and environmental considerations.
- Do the survey outline before deciding on the details. Plan the two phases: reconnaissance survey and intensive survey. You are looking for site constituents: artifacts, features, anthropic soil horizons, chemical anomalies, and instrument anomalies.
- Research the three factors in survey design: visibility (the extent to which archaeological materials can be detected at the place); obtrusiveness (the ease with which the materials produced by a people can be discerned by an archaeologist); and accessibility

(the practicality of working at the particular site, especially, as far as climate, terrain, other environmental concerns, presence or absence of roads, political issues, etc.).

- Decide on the survey methods, e.g. pedestrian survey, subsurface survey, chemical survey, remote sensing survey.
- Plan the land survey, the topographic survey, and the ongoing excavation survey.
- Plot your survey notes on a map if possible.
- Decide on the measurement system for your survey.
- Gather the equipment and materials to do the survey.
- Prepare the survey forms.
- Get permits.
- Establish the site datum point, the datum line, the baseline, bench marks, and the position of the overall site grid. Determine longitude, latitude, sea level, legal boundaries, natural boundaries, and archaeological boundaries.
- Prepare a topographic survey of the contours and natural features of the area so that interpretation of the site includes an understanding of the environment.
- Locate utility lines, pipes, etc.
- Plan, plot, and lay out the overall site grid – and map it.
- Decide on the sifting/dump area(s).
- Establish the excavation grid and units.
- Complete survey descriptions for each level of excavation.
- Interpret and publish findings.

SURVEY TEAM RESPONSIBILITIES

- Take the time to plan the work.
- Do the right things in the right order.
- Locate, with high precision, horizontal points to which the work will be referenced.
- Determine the terrain accurately.
- Put in stakes for site control points and lines.
- Cross-reference the detailed surveys within an overall site survey.
- Ensure accuracy of field notes.
- Check and double-check the accuracy of instruments.
- Accurately adjust and read instruments.
- Be responsible for vertical positioning of points to be measured. Master the proper handling of the survey target or prism rod.

7

Resources

This chapter provides useful resources, particularly for reading within the field of archaeology. It offers some guidelines for ethics that have been drawn up by various organizations. The chapter also describes some current legislation covering archaeological fieldwork as well as links to websites which offer more about international legislation. There are website links to US state and federal offices overseeing archaeological projects and links to websites about volunteer opportunities. There is also a complete bibliography for the information provided in this book.

———————— CONTENTS ————————

RESOURCES

ARCHAEOLOGICAL ASSOCIATIONS

American Anthropological Association (AAA): www.aaanet.org
American Cultural Resources Association (ACRA):
  www.acra-crm.org
Archaeological Institute of America (AIA):
  www.archaeological.org
European Association of Archaeologists (EAA): www.e-a-a.org
Society for American Archaeology (SAA): www.saa.org
Society for Historical Archaeology (SHA): www.sha.org
World Archaeological Congress (WAC): www.wac.uct.ac.za

ARCHAEOLOGICAL JOURNALS

Adumatu: www.adumatu.com/
American Anthropologist: www.ameranthassn.org/
American Antiquity: www.saa.org/Publications/
American Journal of Archaeology: www.ajaonline.org/
Ancient Mesoamerica: uk.cambridge.org/journals/atm/
Andean Past: www2.umaine.edu/anthropology/AndeanP.html
Antiquity: antiquity.ac.uk/
Archaeological Dialogues:
  www.archaeologicaldialogues.com/content/ad.htm
Archaeology magazine: www.archaeological.org/
Athena Review: www.athenapub.com/
Current Anthropology: www.journals.uchicago.edu/CA/
Current Archaeology: www.archaeology.co.uk/cahome.htm
Discovering Archaeology: www.discoveringarchaeology.com/
Environmental Archaeology:
  www.shef.ac.uk/uni/academic/A_C/ap/envarch/
European Journal of Archaeology: www.e-a-a.org/journal.htm
Geoarchaeology: www.interscience.wiley.com/jpages/0883-6353/
Heritage Archaeology Journal: www.heritagearchaeology.com.au/
Historical Archaeology: www.sha.org/
International Journal of Historical Archaeology:
  www.kluweronline.com/issn/1092-7697/current
International Journal of Nautical Archaeology:
  www.elsevier.com/locate/issn/1057-2414
Internet Archaeology: intarch.ac.uk/

Journal of Archaeological Method and Theory:
  www.kluweronline.com/issn/1072-5369/contents
Journal of Archaeological Research:
  www.kluweronline.com/issn/1059-0161/contents
Journal of Archaeological Science:
  www.elsevier.com/locate/issn/0305-4403
Journal of Field Archaeology: www.bu.edu/jfa/
Journal of Near Eastern Studies:
  www.journals.uchicago.edu/JNES/
Journal of Roman Archaeology: www.journalofromanarch.com/
Journal of World Prehistory: www.kluweronline.com/issn/
  0892-7537/current
KMT: Journal of Ancient Egypt: www.egyptology.com/kmt/
Latin American Antiquity: www.saa.org/Publications/
London Museum of Archaeology Publications:
  www.uwo.ca/museum/publications.html
Near Eastern Archaeology: www.bu.edu/asor/pubs/nea/index.html
Nordic Archaeological Abstracts: www.naa.dk/
Public Archaeology: www.jxj.com/parch/index.php
Society for American Archaeology Bulletin:
  www.saa.org/publications/saabulletin/
World Archaeology:
  www.tandf.co.uk/journals/titles/00438243.asp

--------------------- **BIBLIOGRAPHY** ---------------------

Abbot, R. T. and Morris, P. A. (1995) *Peterson Field Guides: Shells of the Atlantic and Gulf Coasts and West Indies.* Houghton Mifflin, Boston.

Alexander, J. (1970) *The Directing of Archaeological Excavations.* Humanities Press, New York.

American National Red Cross (1973) *Standard First Aid and Personal Safety.* Doubleday, New York.

Ashmore, W. and Sharer, R. J. (1999) *Discovering our Past: A Brief Introduction to Archaeology*, Third Edition. McGraw-Hill, New York.

Banning, E. B. (2002) *Archaeological Survey.* Kluwer Academic/Plenum Publishers, New York.

Banning, E. B. (2000) *The Archaeologist's Laboratory.* Kluwer Academic/ Plenum Publishers, New York.

Barber, R. J. (1994) *Doing Historical Archaeology.* Prentice-Hall, Englewood Cliffs, NJ.

Barker, P. (2002) *Techniques of Archaeological Excavation, Third Edition.* Routledge, New York.

Barraclough, A. (1992) Quaternary sediment analysis: a deductive approach at A-level. Powers' scale of roundness, *Teaching Geography*, 17(1), 15–18.

Bettess, F. (1998) *Surveying for Archaeologists, Third Edition*. Durham, UK.

Brothwell, D. R. (1981) *Digging Up Bones, Third Edition*. Oxford University Press, Oxford, UK.

Collins, J. M. and Molyneaux, B. L. (2003) *Archaeological Survey*. AltaMira Press, New York.

Compton, R. R. (1985) *Geology in the Field*. John Wiley & Sons, New York.

Crow Canyon Archaeological Center (2001a) *The Crow Canyon Archaeological Center Field Manual* (HTML title). Available at http://www.crowcanyon.org/fieldmanual.

Crow Canyon Archaeological Center (2001b) *The Castle Rock Pueblo Database* (HTML title). Available at http://www.crowcanyon.org/castlerockdatabase.

Dancey, W. S. (1981) *Archaeological Field Methods: An Introduction*. Burgess Publishing Company, Minneapolis.

Dibble, H. L., McPheron, S. P., and Roth, B. J. (2003) *Virtual Dig*. McGraw-Hill Mayfield, New York.

Dillon, B. D. (1993) *Practical Archaeology*. Institute of Archaeology, University of California at Los Angeles, Los Angeles.

Fagan, B. (2000) *Ancient Lives*. Prentice-Hall, Upper Saddle River, NJ.

Fagan, B. (1994) *In the Beginning, Eighth Edition*. HarperCollins, New York.

Feldman, M. (1977) *Archaeology for Everyone*. Demeter Press, New York.

Glover, T. J. (1999) *Pocket Ref, Second Edition*. Sequoia Publishing, Littleton, CO.

Grant, J., Gorin, S., and Fleming, N. (2002) *The Archaeology Coursebook*. Routledge, New York.

Greene, K. (1983) *Archaeology, An Introduction*. University of Pennsylvania Press, Philadelphia.

Hammond, P. C. (1963) *Archaeological Techniques for Amateurs*. Van Nostrand, New York.

Hawker, J. M. (2001) *A Manual of Archaeological Field Drawing*. RESCUE, The British Archaeological Trust, Hertford, UK.

Heizer, R. F. (1959) *A Guide to Archaeological Field Methods*. National Press, Palo Alto, CA.

Hester, T. R., Shafer, H. J., and Feder, K. L. (1997) *Field Methods in Archaeology, Seventh Edition*. Mayfield Publishing, Mountain View, CA.

Hodges, H. (1988) *Artifacts*. Ronald P. Frye, Kingston, Canada.

Hume, I. N. (1970) *A Guide to Artifacts of Colonial America*. Knopf, New York.

Joukowsky, M. (1980) *A Complete Manual of Field Archaeology*. Prentice-Hall, Englewood Cliffs, NJ.

Kipfer, B. A. (2001) *The Order of Things, Second Edition*. Random House, New York.

Leach, P. (1994) *The Surveying of Archaeological Sites.* Archetype Publications, London.

McDowell-Loudan, E. E. (2002) *Archaeology: Introductory Guide for Classroom and Field.* Prentice-Hall, Upper Saddle River, NJ.

McIntosh, J. (1999) *The Practical Archaeologist, Second Edition.* Checkmark Books, New York.

McMillon, B. (1991) *The Archaeology Handbook: A Field Manual and Resource Guide.* John Wiley and Sons, New York.

Meighan, C. W. (1961) *The Archaeologist's Note Book.* Chandler Publishing, San Francisco.

Neumann, T. W. and Sanford, R. M. (2001) *Practicing Archaeology: A Training Manual for Cultural Resources Archaeology.* AltaMira Press, New York.

Oakley, K. P. (1956) *Man the Tool-maker.* British Museum, London.

Orton, C. (2000) *Sampling in Archaeology.* Cambridge University Press, New York.

Orton, C., Tyers, P., and Vince, A. (1997) *Pottery in Archaeology.* Cambridge University Press, New York.

Peregrine, P. N. (2001) *Archaeological Research.* Prentice-Hall, Upper Saddle River, NJ.

Purdy, B. A. (1996) *How to Do Archaeology the Right Way.* University Press of Florida, Gainesville.

Renfrew, C. and Bahn, P. (2000) *Archaeology: Theories Methods and Practices, Third Edition.* Thames and Hudson, New York.

Rice, P. C. (1998) *Doing Archaeology: A Hands On Laboratory Manual.* Mayfield Publishing, Mountain View, CA.

Rice, P. M. (1987) *Pottery Analysis: A Sourcebook.* University of Chicago Press, Chicago.

Robbins, M. and Irving, M. B. (1965) *The Amateur Archaeologist's Handbook.* Thomas Y. Crowell, New York.

Roskams, S. (2001) *Excavation.* Cambridge University Press, New York.

Sease, C. (1994) *A Conservation Manual for the Field Archaeologist, Third Edition.* Institute of Archaeology, University of California at Los Angeles, Los Angeles.

Sharer, R. J. and Ashmore, W. (2003) *Archaeology: Discovering Our Past, Third Edition.* McGraw-Hill, New York.

Shopland, N. (2005) *Archaeological Finds.* Tempus Publishing, Stroud.

Staeck, J. P. (2001) *Back to the Earth: An Introduction to Archaeology.* Mayfield Publishing, Mountain View, CA.

Stewart, R. M. (2002) *Archaeology Basic Field Methods.* Kendall/Hunt Publishing, Dubuque, IA.

Sullivan, G. (1980) *Discover Archaeology.* Doubleday, New York.

Sutton, M. Q. and Arkush, B. S. (2002) *Archaeological Laboratory Methods: An Introduction, Third Edition.* Kendall/Hunt Publishing, Dubuque, IA.

Thomas, D. H. (1989) *Archaeology, Second Edition.* Holt, Rinehart and Winston, New York.

ETHICS IN FIELD ARCHAEOLOGY

Code of Conduct (Register of Professional Archaeologists) (www.rpanet.org/)

Archaeology is a profession, and the privilege of professional practice requires professional morality and professional responsibility, as well as professional competence, on the part of each practitioner.

I. The Archaeologist's Responsibility to the Public

1.1 An archaeologist shall:

a. Recognize a commitment to represent Archaeology and its research results to the public in a responsible manner;
b. Actively support conservation of the archaeological resource base;
c. Be sensitive to, and respect the legitimate concerns of, groups whose culture histories are the subjects of archaeological investigations;
d. Avoid and discourage exaggerated, misleading, or unwarranted statements about archaeological matters that might induce others to engage in unethical or illegal activity;
e. Support and comply with the terms of the UNESCO Convention on the means of prohibiting and preventing the illicit import, export, and transfer of ownership of cultural property, as adopted by the General Conference, 14 November 1970, Paris.

1.2 An archaeologist shall not:

f. Engage in any illegal or unethical conduct involving archaeological matters or knowingly permit the use of his/her name in support of any illegal or unethical activity involving archaeological matters;
g. Give a professional opinion, make a public report, or give legal testimony involving archaeological matters without being as thoroughly informed as might reasonably be expected;
h. Engage in conduct involving dishonesty, fraud, deceit or misrepresentation about archaeological matters;
i. Undertake any research that affects the archaeological resource base for which she/he is not qualified.

II. The Archaeologist's Responsibility to Colleagues, Employees, and Students

2.1 An archaeologist shall:

a. Give appropriate credit for work done by others;
b. Stay informed and knowledgeable about developments in her/his field or fields of specialization;
c. Accurately, and without undue delay, prepare and properly disseminate a description of research done and its results;
d. Communicate and cooperate with colleagues having common professional interests;
e. Give due respect to colleagues' interests in, and rights to, information about sites, areas, collections, or data where there is a mutual active or potentially active research concern;
f. Know and comply with all federal, state, and local laws, ordinances, and regulations applicable to her/his archaeological research and activities;
g. Report knowledge of violations of this Code to proper authorities.
h. Honor and comply with the spirit and letter of the Register of Professional Archaeologist's Disciplinary Procedures.

2.2 An archaeologist shall not:

i. Falsely or maliciously attempt to injure the reputation of another archaeologist;
j. Commit plagiarism in oral or written communication;
k. Undertake research that affects the archaeological resource base unless reasonably prompt, appropriate analysis and reporting can be expected;
l. Refuse a reasonable request from a qualified colleague for research data;
m. Submit a false or misleading application for registration by the Register of Professional Archaeologists.

III. The Archaeologist's Responsibility to Employers and Clients

3.1 An archaeologist shall:

a. Respect the interests of her/his employer or client, so far as is consistent with the public welfare and this Code and Standards;
b. Refuse to comply with any request or demand of an employer or client which conflicts with the Code and Standards;

c. Recommend to employers or clients the employment of other archaeologists or other expert consultants upon encountering archaeological problems beyond her/his own competence;

d. Exercise reasonable care to prevent her/his employees, colleagues, associates and others whose services are utilized by her/him from revealing or using confidential information. Confidential information means information of a non-archaeological nature gained in the course of employment which the employer or client has requested be held inviolate, or the disclosure of which would be embarrassing or would be likely to be detrimental to the employer or client. Information ceases to be confidential when the employer or client so indicates or when such information becomes publicly known.

3.2 An archaeologist shall not:

e. Reveal confidential information, unless required by law;

f. Use confidential information to the disadvantage of the client or employer;

g. Use confidential information for the advantage of herself/himself or a third person, unless the client consents after full disclosure;

h. Accept compensation or anything of value for recommending the employment of another archaeologist or other person, unless such compensation or thing of value is fully disclosed to the potential employer or client;

i. Recommend or participate in any research which does not comply with the requirements of the Standards of Research Performance.

Standards of Research Performance

The research archaeologist has a responsibility to attempt to design and conduct projects that will add to our understanding of past cultures and/or that will develop better theories, methods, or techniques for interpreting the archaeological record, while causing minimal attrition of the archaeological resource base. In the conduct of a research project, the following minimum standards should be followed:

I. The archaeologist has a responsibility to prepare adequately for any research project, whether or not in the field. The archaeologist must:

1.1 Assess the adequacy of her/his qualifications for the demands of the project, and minimize inadequacies by acquiring additional expertise, by bringing in associates with the needed qualifications, or by modifying the scope of the project;

1.2 Inform herself/himself of relevant previous research;

1.3 Develop a scientific plan of research which specifies the objectives of the project, takes into account previous relevant research, employs a suitable methodology, and provides for economical use of the resource base (whether such base consists of an excavation site or of specimens) consistent with the objectives of the project;

1.4 Ensure the availability of adequate and competent staff and support facilities to carry the project to completion, and of adequate curatorial facilities for specimens and records;

1.5 Comply with all legal requirements, including, without limitation, obtaining all necessary governmental permits and necessary permission from landowners or other persons;

1.6 Determine whether the project is likely to interfere with the program or projects of other scholars and, if there is such a likelihood, initiate negotiations to minimize such interference.

II. In conducting research, the archaeologist must follow her/his scientific plan of research, except to the extent that unforeseen circumstances warrant its modification.

III. Procedures for field survey or excavation must meet the following minimal standards:

3.1 If specimens are collected, a system for identifying and recording their proveniences must be maintained.

3.2 Uncollected entities such as environmental or cultural features, depositional strata, and the like, must be fully and accurately recorded by appropriate means, and their location recorded.

3.3 The methods employed in data collection must be fully and accurately described. Significant stratigraphic and/or associational relationships among artifacts, other specimens, and cultural and environmental features must also be fully and accurately recorded.

3.4 All records should be intelligible to other archaeologists. If terms lacking commonly held referents are used, they should be clearly defined.

3.5 Insofar as possible, the interests of other researchers should be considered. For example, upper levels of a site should be scientifically excavated and recorded whenever feasible, even if the focus of the project is on underlying levels.

IV. During accessioning, analysis, and storage of specimens and records in the laboratory, the archaeologist must take precautions to ensure that correlations between the specimens and the field records

RESOURCES

are maintained, so that provenience contextual relationships and the like are not confused or obscured.

V. Specimens and research records resulting from a project must be deposited at an institution with permanent curatorial facilities, unless otherwise required by law.

VI. The archaeologist has responsibility for appropriate dissemination of the results of her/his research to the appropriate constituencies with reasonable dispatch.

6.1 Results reviewed as significant contributions to substantive knowledge of the past or to advancements in theory, method or technique should be disseminated to colleagues and other interested persons by appropriate means such as publications, reports at professional meetings, or letters to colleagues.

6.2 Requests from qualified colleagues for information on research results directly should be honored, if consistent with the researcher's prior rights to publication and with her/his other professional responsibilities.

6.3 Failure to complete a full scholarly report within 10 years after completion of a field project shall be construed as a waiver of an archaeologist's right of primacy with respect to analysis and publication of the data. Upon expiration of such 10-year period, or at such earlier time as the archaeologist shall determine not to publish the results, such data should be made fully accessible to other archaeologists for analysis and publication.

6.4 While contractual obligations in reporting must be respected, archaeologists should not enter into a contract which prohibits the archaeologist from including her or his own interpretations or conclusions in the contractual reports, or from a continuing right to use the data after completion of the project.

6.5 Archaeologists have an obligation to accede to reasonable requests for information from the news media.

Code of Ethics and Professional Conduct (American Cultural Resources Association) (www.acra-crm.org/Ethics.html)

Preamble
This Code of Ethics and Professional Conduct is a guide to the ethical conduct of members of the American Cultural Resources

Association (ACRA). The Code also aims at informing the public of the principles to which ACRA members subscribe. The Code further signifies that ACRA members shall abide by proper and legal business practices, and perform under a standard of professional behavior that adheres to high principles of ethical conduct on behalf of the public, clients, employees, and professional colleagues.

The ACRA member's responsibilities to the public

A primary obligation of an ACRA member is to serve the public interest. While the definition of the public interest changes through ongoing debate, an ACRA member owes allegiance to a responsibly derived concept of the public interest. An ACRA member shall:

1) Have concern for the long-range consequences of that member's professional actions.
2) Be cognizant of the relevance to the public of that member's professional decisions.
3) Strive to present the results of significant research to the public in a responsible manner.
4) Strive to actively support conservation of the cultural resource base.
5) Strive to respect the concerns of people whose histories and/or resources are the subject of cultural resources investigation.
6) Not make exaggerated, misleading, or unwarranted statements about the nature of that member's work.

The ACRA member's responsibilities to clients

An ACRA member is obligated to provide diligent, creative, honest, and competent services and professional advice to its clients. Such performance must be consistent with the ACRA member's responsibilities to the public interest. An ACRA member shall:

1) Exercise independent professional judgment on behalf of clients.
2) Accept the decisions of a client concerning the objectives and nature of the professional services provided unless the decisions involve conduct that is illegal or inconsistent with the ACRA member's obligations to the public interest.
3) Fulfill the spirit, as well as the letter, of contractual agreements.
4) Not provide professional services if there is an actual, apparent, or perceived conflict of interest, or an appearance of impropriety, without full written disclosure and agreement by all concerned parties.

RESOURCES

5) Not disclose information gained from the provision of professional services for private benefit without prior client approval.

6) Not solicit prospective clients through the use of false or misleading claims.

7) Not sell or offer to sell services by stating or implying an ability to influence decisions by improper means.

8) Not solicit or provide services beyond the level or breadth of the professional competence of its staff or project team.

9) Solicit or provide services only if they can responsibly be performed with the timeliness required by its clients.

10) Not solicit or accept improper compensation for the provision of judgments or recommendations favorable to its clients.

11) Not offer or provide improper compensation as a material consideration in obtaining or sustaining client or prospective client favor.

12) Disclose information identified as confidential by its client only if required by law, required to prevent violation of the law, or required to prevent injury to the public interest.

The ACRA member's responsibilities to employees
As an employer, an ACRA member firm has certain responsibilities to its employees, and shall strive to:

1) Comply with all applicable employment/labor laws and regulations.

2) Provide a safe work environment in compliance with all applicable laws and regulations.

3) Appropriately acknowledge work performed by employees.

4) Provide opportunities for the professional growth and development of employees.

5) Develop clear lines of communication between employer and employee, and provide employees with a clear understanding of their responsibilities.

6) Consistently maintain fair, equitable, and professional conduct toward its employees.

The ACRA member's responsibilities to professional colleagues
An ACRA member shall strive to contribute to the development of the profession by improving methods and techniques, and contributing knowledge. An ACRA member shall also fairly treat the views and contributions of professional colleagues and members of other professions. Accordingly, an ACRA member shall:

1) Act to protect and enhance the integrity of the cultural resources profession.
2) Accurately and fairly represent the qualifications, views, and findings of colleagues.
3) Review the work of other professionals in a fair, professional, and equitable manner.
4) Strive to communicate, cooperate, and share knowledge with colleagues having common professional interests.
5) Not knowingly attempt to injure the professional reputation of a colleague.

First Code of Ethics (World Archaeological Congress) (www.wac.uct.ac.za/)

Principles to Abide By:

Members agree that they have obligations to indigenous peoples and that they shall abide by the following principles:

To acknowledge the importance of indigenous cultural heritage, including sites, places, objects, artefacts, human remains, to the survival of indigenous cultures.
To acknowledge the importance of protecting indigenous cultural heritage to the well-being of indigenous peoples.
To acknowledge the special importance of indigenous ancestral human remains, and sites containing and/or associated with such remains, to indigenous peoples.
To acknowledge that the important relationship between indigenous peoples and their cultural heritage exists irrespective of legal ownership.
To acknowledge that the indigenous cultural heritage rightfully belongs to the indigenous descendants of that heritage.
To acknowledge and recognise indigenous methodologies for interpreting, curating, managing and protecting indigenous cultural heritage.
To establish equitable partnerships and relationships between Members and indigenous peoples whose cultural heritage is being investigated.
To seek, whenever possible, representation of indigenous peoples in agencies funding or authorising research to be certain their view is considered as critically important in setting research standards, questions, priorities and goals.

Generally accepted principles of ethics in field archaeology

- Those who participate in fieldwork should be aware of ethical standards and codes of performance, as well as federal, state, and local laws regarding fieldwork, the collection and ownership of artifacts, and the treatment of human remains. Permits are required to excavate in most places.
- Abide by the rules of the project.
- Abide by the rules of the project regarding project photos taken for personal use, as in a presentation.
- Adhere to the work schedule. Follow through and complete your part of the project.
- Admit mistakes and accept good advice.
- Be concerned about worker safety and education.
- Be considerate and respectful of fellow team members.
- Communicate ideas to benefit the project.
- Confidential information should not be revealed without the consent of the field director.
- Do not become involved with poorly organized projects.
- Do not review the work of a fellow archaeologist without the consent of the field director.
- Fieldwork should be organized according to a research design or scientific plan.
- Fieldworkers should not do anything to harm the project or be involved with conflict-of-interest activities.
- Follow prescribed procedures.
- In cultural resource work, keep information confidential.
- In cultural resource work, know employment and labor laws and regulations.
- In cultural resource work, understand and acknowledge the needs of your clients.
- Keep up-to-date with advances in archaeological methods and techniques.
- Maintain high level of project skills, care, and judgment.
- Never degrade fellow workers; follow prescribed procedures to clear up problems.
- Never excavate on a site previously excavated by other archaeologists or institutions without the consent of those archaeologists or institutions.
- Never write articles about discoveries of other projects in progress without the explicit approval of the responsible project director.

- No business on behalf of the project should be conducted without prior consultation with the project director.
- No tools and records should be borrowed without the consent of the field director.
- Offer public tours of excavations and provide volunteer opportunities for fieldwork.
- Practice an impartial approach to research and public needs.
- Recognize personal limitations and seek the contributions of specialists when needed.
- Remain sensitive to the customs, needs, and views of the local population.
- Team members are responsible for the accurate completion and safety of research and records.
- The archaeologist or institution in charge of a project is responsible for the long-term preservation and storage of artifacts and records.
- The archaeologist or institution in charge of a project is responsible for reporting and disseminating the results of the project.
- Those who do fieldwork should have adequate training, supervision, and access to needed resources.
- Uphold legislation and policies.

Websites with a wealth of information on ethics:

www.aaanet.org/committees/ethics/ethics.htm
www.archaeological.org/pdfs/AIA_Code_of_EthicsA5S.pdf
www.archaeologists.net/code.html
www.arizonaarchcouncil.org/ethics-links.html
www.cast.uark.edu/other/nps/nagpra/nagpra.html
www.saa.org/Aboutsaa/Ethics/prethic.html
www.wac.uct.ac.za/archive/content/ethics.html

Principles of Archaeological Ethics (SAA) (http://www.saa.org)

Principle No. 1: Stewardship
The archaeological record, that is, in situ archaeological material and sites, archaeological collections, records and reports, is irreplaceable. It is the responsibility of all archaeologists to work for the long-term conservation and protection of the archaeological record by practicing and promoting stewardship of the archaeological record. Stewards are both caretakers of and advocates for the archaeological record for the benefit of all people; as they investigate and

RESOURCES

interpret the record, they should use the specialized knowledge they gain to promote public understanding and support for its long-term preservation.

Principle No. 2: Accountability
Responsible archaeological research, including all levels of professional activity, requires an acknowledgment of public accountability and a commitment to make every reasonable effort, in good faith, to consult actively with affected group(s), with the goal of establishing a working relationship that can be beneficial to all parties involved.

Principle No. 3: Commercialization
The Society for American Archaeology has long recognized that the buying and selling of objects out of archaeological context is contributing to the destruction of the archaeological record on the American continents and around the world. The commercialization of archaeological objects – their use as commodities to be exploited for personal enjoyment or profit – results in the destruction of archaeological sites and of contextual information that is essential to understanding the archaeological record. Archaeologists should therefore carefully weigh the benefits to scholarship of a project against the costs of potentially enhancing the commercial value of archaeological objects. Whenever possible they should discourage, and should themselves avoid, activities that enhance the commercial value of archaeological objects, especially objects that are not curated in public institutions, or readily available for scientific study, public interpretation, and display.

Principle No. 4: Public Education and Outreach
Archaeologists should reach out to, and participate in cooperative efforts with others interested in the archaeological record with the aim of improving the preservation, protection, and interpretation of the record. In particular, archaeologists should undertake to: 1) enlist public support for the stewardship of the archaeological record; 2) explain and promote the use of archaeological methods and techniques in understanding human behavior and culture; and 3) communicate archaeological interpretations of the past. Many publics exist for archaeology including students and teachers; Native Americans and other ethnic, religious, and cultural groups who find in the archaeological record important aspects of their cultural heritage; lawmakers and government officials; reporters, journalists, and others involved in the media; and the general public. Archaeologists who are unable to undertake public education and outreach

directly should encourage and support the efforts of others in these activities.

Principle No. 5: Intellectual Property
Intellectual property, as contained in the knowledge and documents created through the study of archaeological resources, is part of the archaeological record. As such it should be treated in accord with the principles of stewardship rather than as a matter of personal possession. If there is a compelling reason, and no legal restrictions or strong countervailing interests, a researcher may have primary access to original materials and documents for a limited and reasonable time, after which these materials and documents must be made available to others.

Principle No. 6: Public Reporting and Publication
Within a reasonable time, the knowledge archaeologists gain from investigation of the archaeological record must be presented in accessible form (through publication or other means) to as wide a range of interested publics as possible. The documents and materials on which publication and other forms of public reporting are based should be deposited in a suitable place for permanent safekeeping. An interest in preserving and protecting in situ archaeological sites must be taken into account when publishing and distributing information about their nature and location.

Principle No. 7: Records and Preservation
Archaeologists should work actively for the preservation of, and long-term access to, archaeological collections, records, and reports. To this end, they should encourage colleagues, students, and others to make responsible use of collections, records, and reports in their research as one means of preserving the in situ archaeological record, and of increasing the care and attention given to that portion of the archaeological record which has been removed and incorporated into archaeological collections, records, and reports.

Principle No. 8: Training and Resources
Given the destructive nature of most archaeological investigations, archaeologists must ensure that they have adequate training, experience, facilities, and other support necessary to conduct any program of research they initiate in a manner consistent with the foregoing principles and contemporary standards of professional practice.

Underwater archaeology ethics (Nautical Archaeological Society) (www.nasportsmouth.org.uk/)

1. Adhere to the highest standards of ethical and responsible behavior in the conduct of archaeological affairs.
2. Have a responsibility for the conservation of the archaeological heritage.
3. Conduct archaeological work in such a way that reliable information about the past may be acquired, and shall ensure that the results are properly recorded.
4. Have a responsibility for making available the results of archaeological work with reasonable dispatch.

FEDERAL (UNITED STATES) LEGISLATION REGARDING ARCHAEOLOGY

Americans with Disabilities Act of 1990 (42 U.S.C. §§12101–12213, known as ADA)

ADA was designed to prevent discrimination in housing, employment and public accommodations and other areas. It is not a historic preservation statute but has already had a far-reaching effect on historic properties because it requires that historic buildings that are places of public accommodation conform to certain standards of accessibility. This may mean physical alterations, and such alterations may affect the building's historic or architectural character. In effect, any proposal to alter or restore a historic structure for a public purpose or with public support will mean a review by the state or local entity that enforces the ADA, and a negotiation to achieve the alteration without damaging the historic or architectural significance of the building.

Archaeological Resources Protection Act of 1979 (16 U.S.C. §§470aa through 470 mm, usually referred to as ARPA)

ARPA protects archaeological resources on federal and Indian lands. The law prohibits the removal, excavation, or alteration of any archaeological resource from federal or Indian lands except by a permit issued by the Department of the Interior.

Department of Transportation Act of 1966 (49 U.S.C. §§1651 et. seq.)

Unlike Section 106, this provides substantive protection. By §1753(f), formerly §4(f), Congress prohibits the destruction or adverse use of historic sites (as well as parklands) by transportation projects unless there is no feasible and prudent alternative.

Intermodal Surface Transportation Efficiency Act of 1991 (23 U.S.C. §133, known as ISTEA)

ISTEA establishes as national policy an "intermodal transportation system" that is "economically efficient and environmentally sound" and is also "energy efficient." Under this statute, the Department of Transportation makes grants to states, which in turn make grants to localities and public agencies to develop intermodal transportation plans and to convert railroad stations (in particular those listed on the National Register of Historic Places), into "intermodal transportation terminals" and civic and cultural activity centers.

National Environmental Policy Act (42 U.S.C. §§4321–4347 usually referred to as NEPA)

NEPA obligates federal agencies to prepare an environmental impact statement for every major federal action affecting the human environment, which is defined to include cultural resources. Accordingly, an environmental impact statement must include the comments of the Advisory Council on Historic Preservation and must also carry out the other requirements of the NHPA.

Native American Graves Protection and Repatriation Act (P.L. 101–601, known as NAGPRA)

NAGPRA gives ownership of Native American cultural items – human remains, associated funerary objects, unassociated funerary objects, sacred objects, and items of cultural patrimony – to lineal descendants of the deceased, tribes on whose lands the cultural items are discovered, or to culturally affiliated tribes. The law requires federal agencies and museums that receive federal funds to inventory archaeological and ethnological collection from their lands or in their collection for such cultural items and to arrange to repatriate these items on the request of the appropriate tribe. The law further requires that, on federal or tribal lands, any intentional excavation of Native American burials and other cultural items and any inadvertent discoveries of such cultural items be carried out according to specific provisions and in consultation with the appropriate tribe or tribes.

Surface Mining Control and Reclamation Act of 1977 (30 U.S.C. §1272(e))

The Surface Mining Control and Reclamation Act governs surface mining activities in the United States. The Office of Surface Mining (OSM) issues permits for surface mining of coal and monitors state regulatory programs that operate by the delegated authority of the federal agency. The Act prohibits surface coal mining activities that would adversely affect any site entered in The National Register of Historic Places, unless approved by the regulatory authority and the federal, state, or local agency with jurisdiction over the site.

Tax Reform Act of 1986 (Public Law 99–514)

The Tax Reform Act of 1986 comprehensively amended the Internal Revenue code to provide valuable tax credits for substantial rehabilitation of historic buildings and a favorable depreciation formula for rehabilitated buildings.

The Advisory Council on Historic Preservation

Created by NHPA (16 U.S.C. §470; 36 C.F.R. Part 800), this council comments on proposed federal actions that will affect significant historic and prehistoric properties. This authority is a procedural, not a substantive, safeguard, but can be effective, particularly when backed by state preservation agencies and the courts.

The National Historic Preservation Act of 1966 (16 U.S.C. §470–470w-6, known as NHPA)

NHPA creates the National Register of Historic Places, which identifies and evaluates properties of national, state, and local historic significance. This act also creates the matching grants-in-aid program designed to assist state and local support of historic preservation and the application of federal programs in each state. Grants support survey and inventory of historic and archaeological resources and other preservation activities, and give assistance to local governments that establish their own historic preservation programs. The

NHPA requires that a state that accepts funding create its own historic preservation activities, and give assistance to local governments that establish their own historic preservation programs. The NHPA requires that a state that accepts funding create its own historic preservation office, designate a director (State Historic Preservation Officer, or SHPO), hire a professional staff, and participate in federal programs including the review of federal actions (NHPA, 16 U.S.C. §470f, commonly referred to as Section 106). The NHPA was the basis for most of the existing state historic preservation programs, since it made money available for restoration projects, surveys and staff.

See also:

ADA Accessibility Guidelines for Buildings and Facilities (ADAAG):
   www.access-board.gov/adaag/html/adaag.htm
American Antiquities Act of 1906:
   www.cr.nps.gov/local-law/anti1906.htm
American Indian Religious Freedom Act of 1978:
   www2.cr.nps.gov/laws/religious.htm
Archaeological and Historic Preservation Act of 1974:
   www2.cr.nps.gov/laws/archpreserv.htm
Archaeological Resources Protection Act of 1979:
   www2.cr.nps.gov/laws/archprotect.htm
Executive Order 13007: Protection and Accommodation of Access
   to Indian Sacred Sites: hydra.gsa.gov/pbs/pt/call-in/eo13007.htm
Federal Laws and Archaeology:
   www.arch.dcr.state.nc.us/fedlaws.htm
Historic Sites Act of 1935:
   www4.law.cornell.edu/uscode/16/ch1AschI.html
National Environmental Policy Act:
   ceq.eh.doe.gov/nepa/regs/nepa/nepaqia.htm
National Historic Preservation Act of 1966:
   www2.cr.nps.gov/laws/NHPA1966.htm
Section 106 Regulations of the National Historic Preservation Act:
   www.achp.gov/regs.html
State Historic Preservation Legislation Database:
   www.ncsl.org/programs/arts/statehist.htm
World Heritage Properties Act:
   whc.unesco.org/nwhc/pages/home/pages/homepage.htm

RESOURCES

FIELDWORK INFORMATION SOURCES

One of the best sources is the annually published *Archaeological Fieldwork Opportunities Bulletin* of the Archaeological Institute of America.

See also:

About.com Current Digs: archaeology.about.com/cs/currentdigs/
Archaeological fieldwork opportunities:
   www.cincpac.com/afos/testpit.html
Archaeological Institute of America:
   www.archaeological.org/webinfo.php?page=10016
ArchaeologyFieldwork.com: www.archaeologyfieldwork.com/
Dig's State-by-State Guide to Archaeology:
   www.digonsite.com/guide/index.html
National Association of State Archaeologists:
   www.uiowa.edu/~osa/nasa/index.html
National Park Service page for volunteer opportunities:
   www.cr.nps.gov/aad/public/archvol.htm
Shovelbums: groups.yahoo.com/group/shovelbums/

INTERNATIONAL ARCHAEOLOGY ETHICS, LAWS, POLICIES

International Centre for the Study of the Preservation and Restoration of Cultural Property: www.iccrom.org
International Council on Monuments and Sites: www.icomos.org, www.icomos.org/unesco/delhi56.html
UNESCO: www.unesco.org/culture/laws/archaeological/html_eng/page1.shtml
World Heritage Center: www.whc.unesco.org

LABEL RIGHTS FOR PAID WORKERS IN ARCHAEOLOGY

OSHA rights

Your right to a safe and healthful workplace including:

A posted safety plan, regular safety meetings
Adequate drinking water or toilet facilities
Adequate access to emergency responders
Adequate protection in deep excavations
Adequate shelter from severe weather
Safe transportation to remote job sites

Wage and hour rights

Your right to legal compensation for your work:

Prevailing wage for work on federal contracts, the national average is $15/hour for this work
Holiday pay on all federal contracts
Mandatory benefits on federal contracts
Time-and-a-half for all overtime hours on all jobs

STATE HISTORIC PRESERVATION OFFICERS (SHPO)

The current SHPOs and Deputy SHPOs are listed at www.ncshpo.org/stateinfolist/

UNITED STATES FEDERAL ARCHAEOLOGY INFORMATION

See www.cr.nps.gov/archeology.htm
and www.cr.nps.gov/aad/SITES/Fedarch.htm

RESOURCES

UNITED STATES PROTECTION OF ARCHAEOLOGICAL RESOURCES (INCLUDING PERMIT REQUIREMENTS)

See www.cr.nps.gov/local-law/43cfr7.htm

—— WHERE TO BUY EQUIPMENT, SUPPLIES ——

(representative)

Archaeology Store: www.archaeologystore.com/
ASC Scientific: www.ascscientific.com/
Ben Meadows Company: www.benmeadows.com/
Duluth Trading Company: www.duluthtrading.com/
Fisher Scientific: www1.fishersci.com/index.jsp
Forestry Supplies: www.forestry-suppliers.com/
Ingalls Archaeological Supply: www.patiche.com/
Stoney Knoll Archaeological Supplies: www.stoneyknoll.com/
   archsupplies.html

Appendix: Abbreviations and Codes

The lists of abbreviations in this chapter are examples and samples of coding that may be used for various topics, especially on forms and records and in field notebooks. These may be adapted by the archaeologist for use in a specific project. The use of computers has somewhat lessened the need for abbreviations in some activities.

CONTENTS

ANIMAL TAXON CODES

This is a sample of a coding system for animal taxa. The taxon is the name applied to an animal group in a formal system of classification. Some numbers are unused so other animals may be added.

Mammal taxon codes

Small/medium mammal

001	opossum
002	shrew
003	bat
004	pika/mouse hare
005	cottontail rabbit
010	blacktail jackrabbit
014	unidentified rabbit
015	unidentified hare
016	unidentified lagomorph
024	unidentified small/medium mammal
025	unidentified vertebrate

Small mammal

026	chipmunk
027	marmot
028	antelope squirrel
029	ground squirrel
030	prairie dog
031	gopher
032	pocket mouse
033	kangaroo rat
034	beaver
035	house mouse
036	harvest mouse
037	white-footed mouse
038	woodrat

APPENDIX: ABBREVIATIONS AND CODES

039	vole
040	porcupine
049	unidentified rodent
050	unidentified small mammal

Carnivore

051	coyote
052	wolf
053	red fox
054	kit fox
055	gray fox
056	black bear
057	grizzly bear
058	ringtail/cacomistle
059	raccoon
060	marten
061	weasel
062	badger
063	little spotted skunk
064	striped skunk
065	otter
066	mountain lion
067	lynx
069	walrus
070	sea lion
071	seal
073	unidentified carnivore
074	unidentified medium mammal
075	unidentified medium/large mammal

Large mammal

076	horse
077	burro
078	nonruminant ungulate
079	peccary
080	wild boar
081	elk
082	deer
083	moose
084	caribou
085	pronghorn
086	bison
087	mountain goat

088	musk ox
089	bighorn sheep
090	domestic cow
091	unidentified hooved placental mammal
092	armadillo
093	manatee
096	whale
098	dolphin, porpoise
100	unidentified large mammal

Amphibian/reptile taxon codes

Frog, toad, turtle, tortoise

201	toad
202	frog
203	unidentified toad
204	unidentified frog
206	snapping turtle
207	western pond turtle
208	western box turtle
209	desert tortoise
210	green turtle
211	leatherback
212	softshell turtle
219	unidentified turtle
220	unidentified tortoise
221	unidentified chelonian
225	unidentified amphibian

Lizard

226	desert iguana
227	chuckwalla
228	zebra-tailed lizard
229	leopard lizard, collared lizard
230	horned lizard
231	whiptail lizard
238	gila monster
250	unidentified lizard

Snake

| 251 | racer |
| 252 | corn snake |

253	gopher snake
254	king snake
255	garter snake
256	coral snake
257	rattlesnake
275	unidentified snake

Other

300	unidentified reptile

Avian taxon codes

401	California gull
403	sandhill crane
404	American coot
406	roadrunner
407	mourning dove
408	pigeon
410	bald eagle
411	golden eagle
412	falcon
413	red-tailed hawk
415	osprey
418	prairie chicken
420	sage grouse
421	gray partridge
423	ring-necked pheasant
426	ptarmigan
428	scaled quail
430	California quail
433	grebe
435	common egret
437	great blue heron
442	common loon
446	barn owl
447	great horned owl
448	burrowing owl
451	cormorant
455	pelican
460	Brewer's blackbird
462	eastern bluebird
464	common crow

467	blue jay
470	oriole
472	common raven
476	redhead
479	mallard
482	Canada goose
484	swan
495	willow woodpecker
500	unidentified bird

Fish taxon codes

Marine species

601	leopard shark
621	lamprey
624	sturgeon

Riverine species

626	catfish
627	sucker
628	squawfish
632	pupfish
639	salmon
640	trout
641	smelt
642	striped mullet
643	sea bass
644	tule perch
645	black bass
646	yellow perch

Lake species

651	razorback sucker, humpback sucker
663	unidentified sucker

Other

676	carp
677	hitch
681	hardhead
682	split-tail perch
684	blackfish
694	unidentified minnow

Invertebrate taxon codes

Freshwater shellfish, other freshwater animals

901	freshwater mussel
908	freshwater gastropod
912	crayfish
914	brine shrimp
915	horseshoe shrimp

Marine shellfish

927	mussel
930	scallop
932	oyster
934	pismo clam
935	butter clam
936	softshell clam
937	hardshell clam
939	red abalone
940	green abalone
941	black abalone
943	limpet
945	cowrie
946	olive shell
948	chiton
950	cusk/tusk

Insect

951	blackfly
952	termite
953	Mormon cricket
954	field cricket
955	grasshopper
958	lice
959	cicada
961	crane fly
962	flea
963	pandor moth
964	sphinx moth
965	beetle
966	black ant
967	carpenter ant
968	honey ant
969	wasp
970	bee

Other terrestrial invertebrate

976	land snail
983	scorpion

BONE AND ANTLER
ARTIFACT CODES

This is an example of a coding system for bone and antler artifacts.

AAW	antler awl
ACH	antler chisel
ACO	antler comb
AFT	antler flaking tool
AHA	antler harpoon
AHN	antler handle
AKN	antler knife
APK	antler pick
APP	antler projectile point
APU	antler punch
ASC	antler scraper
BAF	bone/antler fragment
BAW	bone awl
BBD	bone band
BBE	bone bead
BBM	bone or antler beamer
BBS	bone bead stock
BCO	bone comb
BDE	bone detritus
BFH	bone fish hook
BFT	bone flaking tool
BHA	bone harpoon
BHP	bone hairpin
BHR	bone bait holder
BNE	bone needle
BOH	bone handle
BPD	bone pendant
BPI	bone pipe
BPO	bipointed bone object
BPP	bone projectile point
BPU	bone punch
BSR	bone scraper

BST	bone spatula
BTU	bone tube
DAN	domestic animal bone
HSG	human skull gorget
MAA	miscellaneous antler artifact
MAF	modified antler fragment
MBA	miscellaneous bone artifact
MBF	modified bone fragment
MBH	modified human bone
MBN	miscellaneous bone fragment
MDP	modified deer phalange
MML	modified mandible
MTS	modified turtle shell
PMK	bone pottery marker
TBB	toe bone bead

BONE CODES

This is an example of a coding system for bones.

General and mammal

001	skull, parietal
002	skull, frontal
003	skull, occipital
004	skull, temporal
005	skull, sphenoid
006	skull, zygomatic
007	unidentified skull
008	maxilla
009	mandible
010	molar
011	premolar
012	canine
013	incisor
014	axis vertebra
015	atlas vertebra
016	cervical vertebra
017	thoracic vertebra
018	lumbar vertebra
019	clavicle

020	sternum
021	rib
022	scapula
023	humerus
024	radius
025	ulna
026	carpal
027	metacarpal
028	phalange
029	scarum
030	pelvis
031	femur
032	patella
033	tibia
034	fibula
035	tarsal
036	metatarsal
037	metapodial
039	calcaneous
040	astragalus/talus
043	caudal/tail vertebra
044	precaudal vertebra

Reptile-specific

048	plastron
049	carapace

Bird-specific

081	furcula
082	coracoid
083	carpometacarpus
084	tibiotarsus
085	tarsometatarsus
086	premaxilla/beak

Fish-specific

123	parapophysis
124	haemal spine
125	scale
126	otolith

127	pharyngeal
128	basioccipital
129	fin ray
130	brachiostegal
131	ceratohyal
132	pterygiophore
134	pleural rib
136	quadrate
138	dentary
140	opercular
142	epilyal

CERAMICS BURNISH AND LUSTER CODES

This is an example of a coding system for a representative selection of burnishes and lusters on ceramics.

B	hand-burnished to an uneven medium glossy surface luster
D	possible combination of hand and wheel burnishing
F	uncertain method with medium glossy surface luster
H	hand-burnished to a very glossy surface luster
I	combination of hand and wheel burnishing with low semi-matte surface
J	combination of hand and wheel burnishing with high or medium glossy surface
W	wheel-burnished to a very glossy luster
X	wheel-burnished to a medium glossy luster
Z	wheel-burnished to a semi-matte low-surface luster

Direction of burnish

1	vertical
2	horizontal
3	pattern
4	lattice
5	spiral
6	oblique
7	sloppy
8	vertical and horizontal
9	other

This is an example of a coding system for ceramic artifacts.

Vessel part codes (#1)

B	base
D	disk
H	handle
M	miscellaneous
N	neck
O	other
R	rim
S	spout
T	construction tile
X	sherd, unrecognizable
Z	untypeable fragment

Vessel part codes (#2)

APQ	appliqué
BAS	basal sherd
BSH	body sherd
CBA	ceramic ball/sphere
CBE	clay bead
CFI	ceramic figurine
CFO	ceramic foot
DBS	decorated body sherd
EFF	ceramic effigy
EMM	ceramic with maker's mark
FRS	fragmentary rim sherd
FSH	fragmentary sherd
GDI	gaming disk
HDL	handle
JPT	juvenile pottery fragment
JVE	juvenile vessel
LOC	lump of clay
MCO	miscellaneous ceramic object
MFS	modified ceramic sherd
MPO	miscellaneous pottery
NSS	neck/shoulder sherd

RSH	rim sherd
VES	reconstructed vessel > 50%

Type-function codes

New combinations can be created to denote groups within the same function or to add types.

B	base
BC	clay ball, unfired
BE	bead
BS	body sherd
BT	baking tray
CB	clay ball, fired
CC	crescentic ceramic
CD	ceramic disk
CP	cooking pot
CS	cup and saucer
H	handle
ID	idol
J	jar, jug
L	lid
LW	loom weight
O	no function can be ascertained
PC	carinated body sherd
PF	perforated fragment
PL	plaque
S	spout
SS	stamp seal
SW	spindle whorl
U	urn
W	weight
WP	work pot
X	bowl

CERAMICS CONSTRUCTION AND SURFACE TREATMENT CODES

This is an example of a coding system for construction and surface treatments on ceramic artifacts.

b	burnished
d	tin-glazed
f	salt-glazed
g	copper-stained glaze
k	other glaze
m	mica-slipped or -dusted
n	slipped "white" (high Munsell value)
o	other slipped
t	knife-trimmed
w	wheel-made, whole or part
x	molded
y	not wheel-made or doubtful wheel-made
z	other treatments

CERAMICS EXCISION AND INCISION CODES

This is an example of a coding system using representative types of simple and multiple incision and excision traits.

1	diagonal hatching or slashing on neck
2	combing and pinpricks
3	concentric circles
4	diagonally grooved
5	ribbed squared-off ribs
6	random slashing
7	ribbed rounded ribs
8	wavy line over grooves

A	arc
B	wave grooves
C	combing
D	dots
F	carved
G	groove
H	herringbone
J	slashing between excised band
K	zoned
L	linear vertical
M	linear horizontal

N	linear oblique
O	other
P	plain pinpricks
R	square pinpricks
S	shaving
T	triangular pinpricks
U	rouletting
V	turning
W	wavy lines above or below grooves
Z	zigzag

CERAMICS FABRIC CODES

This is an example of a coding system for fabrics used in making ceramics.

C	organic
F	flint
G	grog
H	shell
I	ironstone
L	limestone
M	mica
N	wares without obvious inclusions
S	sand (quartz or quartzite)
W	volcanic igneous
X	other or unknown

CERAMICS FRAGMENT SIZE CODES

Ceramic fragments may be coded in a system such as this.

L	12 cm–20 cm
M	7 cm–12 cm
S	2.5 cm–7 cm
T	smaller than 2.5 cm
X	20 cm and larger

CERAMICS PAINTED MOTIF CODES

This is an example of a coding system for painted motifs on ceramic artifacts.

01	arc
02	basket
03	chessboard
04	circular
05	concentric circles
06	crisscross
07	crosses
08	cross-hatching
09	diagonal
10	zoomorphic
11	anthropomorphic
12	geometric
13	horizontal bands 5 mm or less
14	linear
15	meanders between bands
16	net
17	oval
18	spiral
19	spruce twig
20	trellis
21	square
22	triangle
23	vertical bands
24	wave
25	zigzag
26	zoned
27	other
28	horizontal bands 5 mm or more
29	band in groove of handle
30	combination horizontal and linear
31	multiple horizontal bands
32	multiple horizontal bands with waves
33	free-form designs
34	crisscross between horizontal bands
35	horizontal bands with dots in between
36	zigzags between bands
37	line with angled lines descending

38	palm branch
39	encircled sun rays
40	vertical bands in circles
41	scallops
42	flat-topped pyramid
43	overlapping
44	trickle
45	drops
46	two parallel lines with two legs
47	rainbow shape

CERAMICS WARE COLOR CODES/MUNSELL CODES

(Based on Munsell Color Chart.)

01	white (5Y8/1, 10YR8/1, 7.5YRN8/, 2.5YN8/, 5YR8/1)
02	light gray (7.5RN/, 2.5YN7/, 5Y7/1.6/1)
03	light brown-gray (5YR7/1, 2.5YRN/, 10YR5/1)
04	reddish-gray (10R6/1)
05	gray (2.5YRN6/N5, 7.5RN6/N5, 2.5YN6, 5Y5/1)
06	brown gray (5YR6/1,5/1)
07	dark reddish-gray (10R4/1, 5YR4/1,5/1)
08	pinkish-gray (5YR6/2, 7.5YR7/2,6/2)
09	light brownish-gray (10YR6/2,5/2,6/3,6/4)
10	light brownish-gray (2.5Y6/2,7/2)
11	redish-gray brown (5YR5/2,5/3,5/4)
12	dark reddish-gray brown (5YR4/2,4/3,4/4, 2.5YR5/2,4/2)
13	dark gray (2.5YR N4/, 7.5YR N4/, 2.5Y N4/, 10YR4/1)
14	very dark gray (2.5YR N3/, 7.5YR N3/, 2.5Y N3/, 10YR3/1, 5YR3/1, 10R3/1)
15	black (10R2.5/1, 2.5YR N/2.5, 5YR2.5/1, 7.5YR N/2.5, 10YR2.5/1, 2.5YN/2.5, 5Y2.5/1,5/2, 10YR3/1)
16	dark brown (2.5YR3/2,2.5/2, 5YR2.5/2, 7.5YR3/2, 10YR4/3,3/3)
17	dark reddish-brown (2.5YR3/4,2.5/4, 10R2.5/2,3/2,3/3,3/4,3/6, 5YR3/2,3/3,3/4)
18	dark red (2.5YR5/4,4/4)
19	red-brown (2.5YR5/4,4/4)
20	red (2.5YR5/6)

21	reddish-yellow (5YR7/8,6/8)
22	reddish-yellow (5YR7/6,6/6)
23	light reddish-brown (2.5YR6/4)
24	brown (7.5YR5/2,5/4, 10YR5/3, 10R4/2,3/2,5/3,5/4)
25	strong brown (7.5YR5/6,5/8, 10YR5/6,5/8)
26	brownish-yellow (10YR6/6,6/8,7/8)
27	dark yellowish-brown (10YR4/4)
28	yellow (10YR8/6,8/8,7/6, 2.5Y8/6,8/8,7/6,7/8)
29	pale brown (10YR8/2,8/3,8/4,7/1,7/2,7/3,7/4)
30	pale yellow (2.5Y8/4,7/4,8/2)
31	grayish brown (2.5Y5/2,4/2,3/2)
32	olive-yellow (2.5Y6/6,6/8)
33	light yellowish-brown (2.5Y6/4)
34	light olive-brown (2.5Y5/4,5/6,4/4)
35	pinkish-white (7.5YR8/2, 5YR8/2)
36	pink (7.5YR8/4,7/4, 5YR8/3,8/4,7/3,7/4)
37	light brown (7.5YR6/4)
38	reddish-yellow (7.5YR8/6,7/6,7/8,6/6,6/8)
39	yellowish-red (5YR5/6,5/8,4/6,4/8)
40	light red (2.5YR6/6,6/8, 10R6/4,6/6,6/8)
41	pale red (2.5YR6/2, 10R6/2,6/3)
42	red (10R4/6,5/6,5/8,4/8)
43	weak red (10R5/2,5/3,5/4,4/3,4/4)
44	pale yellow (5Y8/2,8/3,8/4,7/2,7/4,7/2)
45	dark gray/very dark gray (5Y4/1,4/2,3/1)
46	light olive-gray (5Y6/2)
47	dark olive-gray (5Y3/2)
48	olive (5Y5/3,5/4,5/6,4/3,4/4)
49	yellow (5Y8/6,8/8,7/6,7/8)
50	pale olive (5Y6/3,6/4)
51	olive-yellow 5Y6/6,6/8)

Other ware colors/important single colors

52	gold
53	mottled red and black
54	mottled black and brown
55	yellow discoloration
56	mottled red and reddish-yellow
57	mottled black, brown, and red
58	mottled red and brown
59	light gray (10YR7/1)

60	white (7.5YRN8/)
61	light gray (5Y7/1)
62	reddish-gray (10R5/1)
63	gray (2.5YRN/5)
64	gray (5Y5/1)
65	gray (5YR5/1)
66	light red (10R6/6)
67	reddish-gray (10R6/1)
68	pale red (10R6/4)
69	pinkish-gray (5YR7/2)
70	pinkish-gray (7.5YR6/2)
71	pinkish-gray (7.5YR7/2)
72	light brownish-gray (10YR6/2)
73	pale brown (10YR6/3)
74	light gray (2.5Y7/2)
75	reddish-brown (5YR5/3)
76	reddish-brown (5YR5/4)
77	reddish-brown (5YR4/3)
78	reddish-brown (5YR4/4)
79	weak red (2.5YR5/2)
80	reddish-yellow (5YR6/8)
81	reddish-yellow (5YR6/6)
82	light reddish-brown (5YR6/3)
83	light reddish-brown (5YR6/4)
84	reddish-yellow (7.5YR7/6)
85	reddish-yellow (7.5YR7/8)
86	reddish-yellow (7.5YR6/6)
87	reddish-yellow (7.5YR6/8)
88	pink (7.5YR8/4)
89	pink (5YR8/3)
90	pink (5YR7/3)
91	weak red (2.5YR4/2)
92	red (2.5YR4/6)
93	red (2.5YR5/8)
94	red (2.5YR4/8)
95	light reddish-brown (5YR6/3)
96	red (10R4/8)
97	red (10R5/6)
98	unable to type color
99	miscellaneous colors

CHIPPED-STONE ARTIFACT CODES

The following are two examples of coding systems for chipped-stone artifacts.

(#1)

AD	adze
AE	aeolith
AR	arrowhead
AW	awl
AX	axe
BA	battle-ax
BB	backed blade
BC	blade core
BI	biface
BL	blade
BU	burin/graver
CE	celt
CH	chisel
CL	cleaver
CM	composite multipurpose tool
CO	chopper
CT	chopping tool
DA	dagger
DC	disk core
DI	disk
ES	end-scraper/graver
FO	foliate point
FT	flake tool
HA	hand-ax
HO	hoe
LL	laurel-leaf point
LP	lanciolate point
MB	microburin
ML	microlith
OC	core
OF	flake
PC	prepared core
PI	pick
PP	projectile point
PT	pebble tool

SC	scraper
SI	sickle
SP	spearhead
SS	side-scraper/racloir
UN	uniface

(#2)

BIF	biface
BSP	burin spall
BUR	burin
CDE	chipping detritus
COR	core
DRI	drill
FCR	fire-cracked rock
FHO	fish hook
GRA	graver
KNI	knife
MCS	miscellaneous chipped stone
NOD	nodule
PPF	projectile point fragment
PPO	projectile point
PPP	preform projectile point
PRF	perforator
SCR	scraper
SPS	spokeshave
UFL	utilized flake
UNI	uniface
WED	wedge

CLAY PIPE CODES

This is an example of a coding system for clay pipe artifacts.

JPF	juvenile pipe fragment
JPI	juvenile pipe bowl fragment
PBF	pipe bowl fragment
PBL	complete pipe bowl
PCN	pipe contents
PEL	pipe elbow fragment
PRE	pipe residue

PSF	juvenile pipe stem fragment
PST	pipe stem fragment
WPP	whole pipe

FIELD REPORT ABBREVIATIONS

This is an example of a coding system that may be adopted or adapted for field reports.

ALC	alcove
APE	aperture
ARB	arbitrary unit
ARCH	archaeology
ARP	architectural petroglyph
ASP	ashpit
AUGR	auger
BEG	beginning
BKHO	heavy equipment
BNC	corner bin
BNO	bench surface
BNS	bin
BRF	bedrock feature
BSC	bell-shaped cist
BSP	burned spot
BUP	burial pit
CA	about
CAT	catalog
CERM	ceramics
CIS	cist
DEF	deflector
DOR	doorway
E	east
ELEV	elevation
EST	estimate
EXT	exterior
FIP	firepit
FLV	floor vault
FR	from
GEN	general site
HAR	hearth
HAT	hatchway

HI or IH	instrument height
HORIZ	horizontal
HT	height
INT	interior
ISO	isolated find
L	length
LEVL	level
MATL	material
MEB	mealing bin
MIXD	mixed/disturbed context
N	north
NIC	niche
NO	number
NOSC	not screened
NST	nonstructure
ORIG	original
OTH	other
PAT	pass-through
PLR	pillar
PNS	pit
POS	posthole
POT	pit, other
PREL	preliminary
PSL	pit, slab-lined
QUA	quadrant
REF	reference
RT	right
S	south
$S^1/_2$	screened $^1/_2$ inch mesh
$S^1/_4$	screened $^1/_4$ inch mesh
$S^1/_8$	screened $^1/_8$ inch mesh
SECT	section
SEG	segment
SHVL	shovel
SMTL	small tools, e.g. paintbrush, dental pick
SPSS	special samples
SRSO	survey surface collection
STLV	stratum-level
STR	structure
STRA	stratum
SURF	surface
TRA	transect
TRPK	trowel and pick

TRSH	trowel and shovel
TRWL	trowel
TUN	tunnel
UNKN	unknown
VERT	vertical
VSH	ventilator shaft
VTN	ventilator tunnel
W	west
WI	width
WOT	wall

GEOLOGIC SYMBOLS

This is an example of codes used for geologic materials discovered during archaeological fieldwork.

Genetic classes

A	Alluvial
C	Colluvial
E	Eolian
F	Fill, artificial
G	Glacial
L	Lacustrine
M	Marine
R	Residual
S	Slide
V	Volcanic

Lithologic symbols

b	boulders
c	clay
d	diatomaceous material
e	erratic blocks
g	gravel
k	cobbles
m	silt
o	organic material
p	peat
r	rock rubble

s	sand
t	trash or debris

Qualifying genetic symbols

Alluvial: fan (f), terrace (te), floodplain (fp), pediment (p), debris flow (df), delta (de)

Colluvial: slope wash (sw), rock avalanche (ra), talus (ta), creep deposits (cr)

Eolian: dune morphology (d), loess (l)

Fill: engineered (e), uncompacted (u)

Glacial: undifferentiated till (t), lodgment till (lt), ablation till (at), esker (es), morainal ridge (m), Kame (k), outwash (o), ice contact (i)

Lacustrine and marine: beach (b), undifferentiated estuarine (et), swamp (sp), delta (de), marsh (ma), tidal channel (tc), undifferentiated offshore (o)

Residual: full soil profile (sp), B horizon (bh), C horizon (ch), saprolite (sa), undifferentiated weathering products (wp)

Slide: rotational (ro), translational (tr), earthflow (fl), fall (fa), slump or soil slip (sl)

Volcanic: airfall (af), pyroclastic flow (pf), surge (s), undifferentiated pyroclastic (py), lahar (l), water-deposited pyroclastic (pw), pyroclastic cone (pc)

Physical modifier symbols

c	cemented
e	expansive
h	hydrocompactible

Engineering geologic symbols for rocks

Sedimentary

CG	conglomerate
CH	chert
CK	chalk
CS	claystone
DO	dolomite
DT	diatomite
LS	limestone
SH	shale
SS	sandstone
ST	siltstone

Igneous

AN	andesite
BA	basalt
DI	diorite
FE	felsite
GA	gabbro
GR	granite
IG	undifferentiated
RH	rhyolite
SY	syenite
TU	tuff
VO	volcanic

Metamorphic

AR	argillite
GN	gneiss
GS	greenstone
HO	hornfels
MA	marble
ME	undifferentiated
PH	phyllite
QT	quartzite
SC	schist
SE	serpentinite
SL	slate

Artificial rock

CC	Portland cement/concrete
AC	asphaltic concrete
PA	undifferentiated pavement

--- **GLASS ARTIFACT CODES** ---

This is an example of a coding system for glass artifacts.

DGL	decorated glass
GBD	glass bead
GBF	glass bottle fragment
GCO	glass container
GLB	glass bottle > 50% complete
GLF	miscellaneous glass fragment

GLM	glass marble
GTU	drinking glass/tumbler
MGL	mirror glass
WGL	historic window glass

GROUND-STONE ARTIFACT CODES

This is an example of a coding system for ground-stone artifacts.

ABR	abrader
ANV	anvil stone
AXE	ax
BAM	bar amulet
BAN	bannerstone
BIR	birdstone
BOA	boatstone
CEL	celt
CHS	chisel
FCR	fire-cracked rock
FOS	fossil
GKN	ground-stone knife
GOP	gorget/pendant
GOR	gorget
GOU	gouge
GSF	ground-stone fragment
GSP	ground-stone point
HAM	hammerstone
HAN	hammer/anvil stone
MAN	mano
MAU	maul
MET	metate
MIC	mica fragment
MMG	miscellaneous modified ground stone
MOR	mortar
MUL	muller
NCD	non-chert detritus
NET	netsinker
PES	pestle
PIC	pick
QUA	quartz crystal
ROK	unmodified rock

RST	rubbing stone
SBE	stone bead
SDG	seed grinder
SEF	stone effigy
SGD	stone gaming disk
SPE	stone pendant
SPI	stone pipe
WHT	whetstone

ORGANIC ARTIFACT CODES

This is an example of a coding system for types of organic artifacts.

CAR	carbonized artifact
CHA	charcoal
CLH	cloth
CPL	carbonized plant remains
CPT	coprolite
CSA	carbon sample
HWA	historic wooden artifact
LEA	leather
LYE	lye
MOM	miscellaneous organic material
PWD	preserved wood
SSA	soil sample

PACKAGING COMPOSITION CODES

This is an example of a coding system for the composition of packaging artifacts.

A	paper
B	steel/tin
C	aluminum
D	plastic
E	glass
F	aerosol
G	wood
H	ceramic

J	leather
K	rubber
L	copper/brass
M	textile
N	other

SHELL ARTIFACT CODES

This is an example of a coding system for shell artifacts.

CLA	clam shell
MCL	modified clam shell
MMS	miscellaneous modified shell
SHB	shell bead
SHF	shell fragment
SHP	shell pendant

STONE CODES

This is an example of a coding system for types of stone.

A	sandstone
B	basalt
C	chert
D	diorite
E	silicate
F	flint
G	shale
H	breccia
J	jadeite
K	chalcedony
M	maachite
N	sedimentary rock
O	obsidian
P	jasper
Q	quartzite
R	rock crystal
S	slate
T	steatite

APPENDIX: ABBREVIATIONS AND CODES

V	igneous volcanic rock
X	mylonite

--- **SURVEYING ABBREVIATIONS** ---

These are abbreviations for some standard surveying terms.

BM	bench mark
BS	backsight
C	center
CAD	computer-aided drafting
CADD	computer-aided drafting & design
CB	crub
CL	center line
DOT	Department of Transportation
DSCON	discontinuity
DTM	digital terrain model
EDM	electronic distance meter
EFB	electronic field book
FS	foresight
GPS	Global Positioning System
HI	height of instrument
MRM	mile reference marker
NA	nail
NAD	North American datum
NAVD	North American Vertical datum
NGS	National Geodetic Survey
PC	point of curvature
PI	point of intersection
POST	point on semi-tangent
POT	point on tangent
PT	point of tangency
ROW	right of way
RTK	real-time kinematic
SB	stone-bound
SDR	survey data recorder
SPK	spike
STK	stake
TBM	temporary bench mark
TEL	telephone pole
TIN	triangulated irregular network

TK	tack
TP	turning point
USC&GS	United States Coast and Geodetic Survey
USGS	United States Geological Survey

TOOTH ARTIFACT CODES

This is an example of a coding system for artifacts involving teeth.

MCN	modified canine
MIN	modified incisor
MTA	miscellaneous tooth artifact
MTF	modified tooth fragment
TBE	tooth bead
TPE	tooth pendant